Mobile Methods

In the twenty-first century, more than ever, everything and everybody seems to be on the move. Global flows of people, goods, food, money, information, services and media images are forming an intensely mobile background to everyday life. Social scientists, too, are on the move, seeking new analytical purchase on these important aspects of the social world by trying to move with, and to be moved by, the fleeting, distributed, multiple, non-causal, sensory, emotional and kinaesthetic.

Mobile Methods addresses the challenges and opportunities of researching mobile phenomena. Drawing on extensive interdisciplinary discussion, the book brings together a collection of cutting-edge methodological innovations and original research reports to examine some important implications of the mobilities turn for the processes of 'research', and the realm of the empirical. Through analyses that address questions such as 'how are social relationships and social institutions made in and through mobility?', and 'how do people experience mobility in twenty-first-century world cities?', the authors mobilise sociological analysis, bringing new insights and opening up new opportunities for engagement with contemporary challenges.

This book is a key text for undergraduate and postgraduate students of disciplines including Anthropology, Cultural Studies, Design, Geography, Social Policy, Sociology and Research Methods.

Monika Büscher is Senior Lecturer in Sociology at Lancaster University. She is a member of the Centre for Mobilities Research and Co-director of the Mobilities Lab – an interdisciplinary research laboratory. Her recent books include *Configuring User–Designer Relations: Interdisciplinary Perspectives* (Springer 2009), *Ethnographies of Diagnostic Work* (Palgrave 2009) and *Design Research: Synergies from Interdisciplinary Perspectives* (Routledge 2010).

John Urry is Distinguished Professor of Sociology at Lancaster University, where he is also Director of the Centre for Mobilities Research. His recent books include *Sociology Beyond Societies* (Routledge 2000), *Mobile Technologies of the City* (Routledge 2006), *Mobilities* (Polity 2007), *Aeromobilities* (Routledge 2009) and *Mobile Lives* (Routledge 2010).

Katian Witchger is a PhD student in Humanities at the Center for Interdisciplinary Studies on Society and Culture, Concordia University, Montreal. Her current research interests include digital objects, sound recording, online music, intellectual property law and the Internet.

Mobile Methods

Edited by Monika Büscher,
John Urry and Katian Witchger

Routledge
Taylor & Francis Group

LONDON AND NEW YORK

First published 2011
by Routledge
2 Park Square, Milton Park, Abingdon, Oxon OX14 4RN

Simultaneously published in the USA and Canada
by Routledge
270 Madison Avenue, New York, NY 10016

Routledge is an imprint of the Taylor & Francis Group, an informa business

Typeset in Times by Wearset, Boldon, Tyne and Wear
Printed and bound in Great Britain by CPI Anthony Rowe, Chippenham, Wiltshire

British Library Cataloguing in Publication Data
A catalogue record for this book is available from the British Library

Library of Congress Cataloging-in-Publication Data
Mobile Methods / edited by Monika Büscher, John Urry and Katian
Witchger.
p.cm.
1. Social sciences – Research. 2. Social change. 3. Movement
(Philosophy) I. Büscher, Monika, 1964– II. Urry, John, III. Witchger,
Katian.
H62.M537 2010
330.72′2–dc22

2010002252

ISBN13: 978-0-415-49241-6 (hbk)
ISBN13: 978-0-415-49242-3 (pbk)
ISBN13: 978-0-203-87990-0 (ebk)

Contents

Illustrations

Contributors

Rein Ahas is Professor of Human Geography at the University of Tartu Institute of Geography, Estonia. His main research interests include mobility studies and mobile positioning, urban studies and planning, particularly the impacts of suburbanisation and urban sprawl, seasonality of human activities, tourism geography, geography of social networks and climate change. He studies mobility as a lifestyle and a main problem of human civilisation in the twenty-first century. Together with Ülar Mark he has developed social positioning methods to study social flows in time and space by analysing the location coordinates of mobile phones and the social identifiers of the people carrying them.

Monika Büscher is Senior Lecturer in Sociology, Lancaster University. She is a member of the Centre for Mobilities Research and Co-director of the mobilities.lab – an interdisciplinary research laboratory. Her ethnographic studies include investigations of mobile professional work practice in art and design, healthcare, software development, event management and emergency response. Through close collaboration with professionals and designers her work contributes to innovation in these fields of work. This often requires experimental realisation of (partial) futures, enabling 'ethnographies of change'.

Paul Coulton is Senior Lecturer at the Department for Communications Systems, Lancaster University. His principal interest in mobile technologies is to push the boundaries of innovation to create uniquely mobile experiences. He is founder of the Mobile Radicals group and his Forum Nokia blogs seeks to excite and challenge developers to think 'outside the box'.

Harry Ferguson is Professor of Social Work at the School of Sociology and Social Policy, Nottingham University. His teaching and research interests lie in the areas of child abuse/protection, domestic violence, gender/family relations, in particular social interventions into fatherhood, men's lives and masculinities, and the social science of social work. At the heart of his research (which has been funded by government and non-government agencies and the EU) is a focus on evaluating social work and social care interventions to increase understandings of how these practices 'work' and their outcomes for service users. He draws on a range of sociological concepts (such as risk society, reflexivity, intimacy, individualisation, life politics, mobilities) to inform empirical research with the aim of developing theoretical understandings of the nature of social work.

Jennie Germann Molz is Assistant Professor of Sociology at the College of the Holy Cross in Worcester, Massachusetts. Her research focuses on the intersections between mobile technologies, tourism mobilities and social life. She has published articles and book chapters on the topics of tourism, technology, globalisation and belonging and recently co-edited (with Sarah Gibson) *Mobilizing Hospitality: The Ethics of Social Relations in a Mobile World* (Ashgate 2007). Her current research focuses on the way leisure travellers incorporate new social media, including blogs and social networking sites, into their journeys.

Julia Gillen is Senior Lecturer in Digital Literacies in the Literacy Research Centre, Lancaster University and a member of the Centre for Mobilities Research, also at Lancaster University. She studies relationships between literacies, learning and technologies, taking ethnographic and other interpretive methods to studies of informal and formal learning and material culture more generally. Her current publications include J. Gillen and C.A. Cameron (eds) (in print) *An International Perspective on Early Childhood Research: A Day in the Life* (Palgrave Macmillan) and A. Peachey, J. Gillen, D. Livingstone and S. Robbins (eds) (in print) *Researching Learning in Virtual Worlds* (Springer).

Michael Haldrup is Associate Professor in Human Geography at Roskilde University, Denmark. He has a special interest in theories of space, practice and performance and his research includes studies of mobility, tourism and place. He has written extensively on such issues and has co-authored *Performing Tourist Places* (Ashgate 2004) (with J.O. Bærenholdt, J. Larsen and J. Urry) and *Tourism, Performance and the Everyday* (Routledge 2009) (with J. Larsen).

Nigel Hall is Emeritus Professor at Manchester Metropolitan University. He has written numerous books and articles on literacy and childhood, but more recently is researching into different aspects of the history of literacy, including writing and the early postcard.

Drew Hemment is Associate Director of Lancaster University's Imagination@Lancaster research lab, director and founder of the *Futuresonic* festival, established 1995, and director of *Futureverything*, a non-profit creative studio. He is a founder member of the Loca art group, developed during an AHRC Research Fellowship at Salford University, and of PLAN, the Pervasive and Locative Arts Network (EPSRC). Other projects include Urban Play and the Social Technologies Summit. He is curator of numerous exhibitions on media art, mobile culture and locative media, and was involved in early UK electronic dance culture as DJ and event organiser. He completed a PhD at Lancaster University in 1999, and an MA (Distinction) at the University of Warwick, when he was a participant in the *Virtual Futures* events.

Paola Jirón is Assistant Professor at the Institute of Housing at the Faculty of Architecture and Urbanism, University of Chile. She has carried out extensive research, teaching and consultancy work in the areas of housing, gender in human settlements, urban quality of life and urban mobility practices in developing countries. Her research interests include theoretical and methodological approaches to the experience of space, as well as finding ways of relating this type of research to urban planning practice. Her website is: www.santiagosemueve.com.

Eric Laurier is Senior Research Fellow at the University of Edinburgh. He is principal investigator on 'Assembling the Line: Amateur & Professional Work, Skills and Practice in Digital Video Editing', funded by the ESRC, working together with Barry Brown and Ignaz Strebel. Although officially completed, he continues to work on the ESRC-funded 'Habitable Cars: The Organisation of Collective Private Transport' with Barry Brown and Hayden Lorimer. Alongside this he organises the Scottish Ethnomethodology, Discourse, Interaction & Technology group (SEDIT) with Beatrix Futak-Campbell and various activities of the Human Geography Research Group at the School of Geosciences, Edinburgh. Previously he was the PI on 'The Cappuccino Community: Cafes and Civic Life in the Contemporary City', carried out with Chris Philo, and before that held an Urban Studies Research Fellowship which allowed him to pursue research on community practices in the city.

Christian Licoppe is Professor of Sociology of Information and Communication Technologies at ENST, Paris Telecom. His research interests include sociological studies on the uses of information and communication technologies in professional contexts, mobile gaming, comparative studies of mediated interactions, consumption at a distance, co-present and distributed courts of law, call centre work (banking and telecom sectors) and case studies on innovation and user-centred design.

Glenn Lyons is Professor of Transport and Society and Director of the Centre for Transport and Society (CTS) at the University of the West of England, Bristol. He has a long-standing interest and involvement in research that considers the interactions between information and communications technology and transport. His aim and that of CTS is to improve and promote understanding of the inherent links between lifestyles and personal travel in the context of continuing social and technological change.

Preben Holst Mogensen is Associate Professor at the Computer Science Department, University of Aarhus, and CEO, partner and co-founder of 43D

ApS. He has been coordinating, managing and participating in several EU projects since 1990, most recently as co-coordinator in the EU Integrated Project PalCom: A New Perspective on Ambient Computing. His research interests concern tools and techniques for active user involvement in system development (participatory/cooperative design), pervasive computing, cooperative analysis, prototyping, CSCW and object-oriented approaches to system development.

Lorenza Mondada is Professor at the Department of Linguistics, University of Lyon2, France and director of the ICAR research lab (CNRS, University of Lyon). Her research focuses on language in social interaction in a variety of settings, from conversation to interactions in professional and institutional contexts; she is particularly interested in the sequential organisation of multimodal resources in interaction (language, but also gesture, body postures, gaze, etc.) and in the timed coordination of interactional practices. Her publications include several monographs, a large number of edited and co-edited volumes (recently, a special issue of ROLSI on assessments, with Anna Lindström, 2009) and of journal articles on turn-taking and sequence organisation, the analysis of video recordings, grammar and interaction, multilingual professional interactions and talk at work.

Julien Morel is a researcher in the Department of Economic and Social Sciences of TELECOM ParisTech. In the tradition of conversation analysis and ethnomethodology, he works on natural organisation of face-to-face and mediated human interactions.

John Urry is Distinguished Professor and Director of the Centre for Mobilities Research, Lancaster University. He is noted for his work in the sociology of tourism and mobility, and has written about many aspects of modern society, including the transition away from 'organised capitalism', the relationship between society and space and complexity theory. He is a Founding Academician of the UK Academy of the Social Sciences. He is one of the founding editors of the journal *Mobilities*. He is the editor of the International Library of Sociology.

Laura Watts is a Senior Research Associate at the Department of Sociology, Lancaster University. She is concerned with the role of landscape and place in the production of high-tech and mobile futures. Her doctorate, in the field of Science Studies, was on the futures and archaeologies of the mobile telecoms industry around London, and she is currently weaving this together with an ethnography of high-tech futures in the islands of Orkney, Scotland. Publications and podcasts of her work can be found on her website: www.sand14.com.

Katian Witchger is a PhD student in Humanities at the Center for Interdisciplinary Studies on Society and Culture at Concordia University in Montreal, Quebec. Her current research interests include digital objects, sound recording, online music, intellectual property law and the Internet. She is currently working on an ethnographic study on gestural games with the Technoculture Arts and Games Lab at HEXAGRAM: Institute for Research-Creation in Media Arts and Technologies in Montreal.

Foreword

When social science methodologies are neither arcane nor overly technical they become hard to write out and equally challenging to write about. By contrast a methodology book in statistics is filled with step-by-step instructions that you will need to complete your correlative of descriptive task. They are sandwiched between accompanying warnings of the common errors that will lead to artefacts or bias in the results. As regularly refreshed software packages have proliferated, the methodology books have expanded in size and shortened in cycle. They are also quite unreadable unless you really are learning to do a T-test in statistics (or set aperture priority on your camera). While the keen student looking for instructions may be disappointed by this collection, the general reader will be relieved to learn that this is an immensely readable and varied collection; there is much here to stimulate them. They will come upon a number of simple methodologies in the social sciences that are nevertheless as long-standing, strong and essential as a knife and a chopping block are in the kitchen. These are the trusty Hagerstrand time–space diagram, the ever-ready participant diaries and the surety of shadowing. In what follows, their blade is turned to fresh material and techniques of precision, economy and craft can be learnt from the marks left on each chapter.

And yet, mobility, as also becomes apparent in this collection, is evolving and changing. While the familiar sawblades of ethnography or social history edge through the grain of mobility and open it up one way, because it is a shifting topic it allows the social sciences to re-jig, re-figure and re-calibrate their means of recording and describing the world. Except that the recording and description devices, the technologies of writing, photographing and videographing, are part of that self-same evolution out of which these inquiries rise. In other words, research topic and research resource are confounded, and profitably so. To research the geographies of mobile phone use, the locative possibilities provided by the handsets and the network are an ideal way to do so. To investigate online travel it makes good sense to couchsurf through new networks of tourist knowledge. These are just a hint of the new possibilities of producing accounts of recently emerged mobilities.

There is for me a delight in seeing a body of methods that does not stitch together. It should not, because, as hinted above, mobility is not one thing. It is a collection of social matters that have been left out of more sedentary studies. It is several shifts of perspective on the eternal questions of concern that have occupied the social sciences (and other sciences besides) since their outset, such as the nature of time, space and, indeed, timespace. Mobility is also its equipment: phones, laptops, luggage, timetables, aeroplanes, bicycles and credit cards. For the researcher keen to become mobile themselves, here is the guidebook to pack as either PDF or paper in the bottom of your shoulder bag.

Eric Laurier

1 Introduction
Mobile methods[1]

Monika Büscher, John Urry and Katian Witchger

'Hold still, don't move.'

William Gibson, *Neuromancer* (1984: 31)

Comings and goings

Law and Urry argue that existing methods of research in and around the social sciences deal poorly

> with the fleeting – that which is here today and gone tomorrow, only to re-appear again the day after tomorrow. They deal poorly with the distributed – that is to be found here and there but not in between – or that which slips and slides between one place and another. They deal poorly with the multiple – that which takes different shapes in different places. They deal poorly with the non-causal, the chaotic, the complex. And such methods have diffi-culty dealing with the sensory – that which is subject to vision, sound, taste, smell; with the emotional – time–space compressed outbursts of anger, pain, rage, pleasure, desire, or the spiritual; and the kinaesthetic – the pleasures and pains which follow the movement and displacement of people, objects, information and ideas.
>
> (2004: 403–4)

The temptation is to hold down and dissect these phenomena to study them – but this would destroy them. In this book we address some problems and opportun-ities of doing research which respond to these challenges by trying to move with, and to be moved by, the fleeting, distributed, multiple, non-causal, sensory, emo-tional and kinaesthetic. It is especially through engaging with what we and others term the mobilities turn that purchase can be gained on these important aspects of the social world.

The book seeks to enable and to reinforce new forms of social science inquiry, explanation and engagement. It not only remedies the academic neglect of various movements, of people, objects, information and ideas. It also gathers new empirical sensitivities, analytical orientations and methods to examine social phenomena that are especially important in the contemporary world with many living 'mobile lives' or at least being affected by the mobile lives of others (Elliott and Urry 2010). This chapter reviews various 'mobile methods' for studying (im)mobilities which the authors of the subsequent chapters design, develop and deploy. We discuss some of the new entities that these methods come to enact and explore important implications for the relationships between the empirical world, theory, critique and engagement. But we end with a cautionary tale: that the development here of productive methods has an urgency in that there are other social forces also developing powerful mobile computer-based methods and these may win out in part because of their interconnections with forms and forces of monitoring and surveillance.

Through investigations of movement, blocked movement, potential movement and immobility, dwelling and place-making, social scientists are showing how various kinds of 'moves' make social and material realities. Attention to the fluid, fleeting, yet powerful performativity of various everyday (im)mobilities transforms conceptions of social science inquiry, explanation and critique. We take it that there is no research and no social science without theory, but at the same time we argue that the mobilities turn folds analysis into the empirical in ways that open up different ways of understanding the relationship between theory, observation and engagement. It engenders new kinds of researchable entities, a new or rediscovered realm of the empirical and new avenues for critique.

Especially significant in the development of this new paradigm were the varied writings of Simmel developed in the heyday of the railway journey and the letter and postcard (see Gillen and Hall, in Chapter 2 of this volume, on the huge growth in postal services in late-nineteenth-century Britain). Simmel, especially, analyses the fragmentation and diversity of modern life and shows how motion, the diversity of stimuli and the visual appropriation of place are centrally important features of new modern urban experience. Moreover, because of the effect of money, with its colourlessness and indifference, and its twin, the modern city, a new precision becomes necessary in social life. Agreements and arrangements need to demonstrate unambiguousness in timing and location. Life in the mobile onrushing city presupposes punctuality and this is reflected in the 'universal diffusion of pocket watches' (Simmel 1997: 177). The watch a century ago was as symbolic of the 'modern' as the ubiquitous mobile phone is today (see some contemporary uses of mobile phones in Chapters 8–11 below). Simmel argues that the 'relationships and affairs of the typical metropolitan usually are so varied and complex that without the strictest punctuality in promises and services the whole structure would break down into an inextricable chaos' (Simmel 1997: 177; Urry 2007: ch. 2).

Some of Simmel's ideas were developed within the Chicago School which in the first half of the twentieth century provided a range of post-Simmelian mobility studies especially concerned with the itinerant (mobile) lives of hoboes, gangs, prostitutes and migrants, with what would now be characterised as the 'underclass' (see, for example, Park 1970). However, this development was cut short in its tracks as many structural or static theories took over, including structural functionalism, positivist analysis of 'variables', structural Marxism and so on. Meanwhile, the study of mobilities was turned into the professional examination of 'transport' and to a lesser extent of 'tourism', which were taken to be specific domains to be researched far away from the provocative promptings of Simmel's essays on metropolitan life.

But over the past decade or so, influential new initiatives such as those examined in this book have begun to reappropriate Simmel's work, directly or more indirectly. This has developed through research within various domains, symbolic interactionism, cultural studies, science and technology studies, ethnomethodology, material culture, cultural geography, (participatory) design and others, as reflected in various books and journals, including *Mobilities*. This work is developing what may become a distinct mobilities *paradigm*. We delineate some of the premises, promises and risks of these developments. But we do not try to reconcile the conflicts between the theoretical orientations we see contributing to such a paradigm. Some differences are irreconcilable and there are incompatibilities that challenge as well as shape mobilities research. Nevertheless, there is a powerful transformative and 'therapeutic' potential for social science in the interferences generated where these studies meet and gather emergent empirical sensitivities, analytical orientations, methods and instruments to examine crucial social and material phenomena.

This analysis of mobilities and especially of multiple and intersecting mobility systems, where each is in an adaptive and evolving relationship with each other, is an example of 'post-human' analysis (Hayles 1999). However, arguing that there is a substantive shift from the human to the post-human presupposes that there was a previous era where the world was 'human' and principally constituted through disembodied and dematerialised cognition. This Enlightenment view presumes what Ingold terms a primacy of head over heels, mind over body, humans separate from and productive of society and culture, and a neglect of the mobile practices of walking (2004). A mobilities turn is part of the critique of such a humanism that posits a disembodied *cogito* and especially human subjects able to think and act independently of their material worlds (Latour 1993). This book is based around the claim that the powers of 'humans' are co-constituted with/by various material agencies of clothing, tools, objects, paths, footwear, buildings, machines, paper and so on. And thus we have never been simply 'human', nor simply 'social'.

Following Marx we might indeed claim that there are not only the relations of life but also the forces of life, encountering, clashing with, realising, enlisting or suppressing the creative power of the material world. Life and matter come to matter and are made meaningful as people, objects, information and ideas move and are (im)mobilised (see Barad 2007). People, objects, information and ideas may be:

- held in place (prisoner, clamped car, poster, rhetoric figure);
- fixed in place (agoraphobic, building, a sense of place);

- temporarily stationary (visitor, car in garage, graffiti, a presentation);
- portable (baby, laptop, souvenir);
- part of a mobile body (foetus, iPod, ID card, designer label);
- prosthetic (disability assistant, contact lenses, name badge, gender);
- constitutive of a mobility system (Highway Code, timetable, speed);
- consisting of code (cyborg, BlackBerry, digital document, computer virus).

This classification brings out huge variations in how relations and forces of life are encountered, realised, enlisted or suppressed, but in all cases humans are nothing without many different objects and meanings organised into systems. The systems come first and serve to augment the otherwise very limited powers of individual human subjects. Those subjects are brought together and serve to develop extraordinary powers only because of the systems they build and which implicate them, and especially because of those systems that move them, or objects, ideas and information.

In the following, we explicate the mobilities paradigm and then connect it with a review of emergent 'mobile methods' for studying (im)mobilities that make social and material realities. We discuss important implications of the mobilities paradigm for research and delineate new ways of understanding the relationship between theory, observation and engagement. We contextualise the various pieces of research presented in the chapters in this book, where the authors make various efforts to 'run' with the mobilities paradigm. They do so in order to bring to light previously hidden elements of the social world. And in so running they come to experience various novel kinds of phenomena and seek to allow themselves and their readers to be moved by them.

The mobilities paradigm

Overall we can say that the mobilities paradigm is not just substantively different in remedying the academic neglect of various movements, of people, objects, information and ideas (see Sheller and Urry 2006; Urry 2007). It is also transformative of social science, generating an alternative theoretical and methodological landscape. It enables the 'social world' to be theorised as a wide array of economic, social and political practices, infrastructures and ideologies that all involve, entail or curtail various kinds of movement of people, or ideas, or information or objects. And this paradigm brings to the fore and enacts theories, methods and exemplars of research that so far have been mostly out of sight.

The term 'mobilities' refers not just to movement but to this broader project of establishing a 'movement-driven' social science in which movement, potential movement and blocked movement, as well as voluntary/temporary immobilities, practices of dwelling and 'nomadic' place-making are all viewed as constitutive of economic, social and political relations.

Such a paradigm is crucial, because historically the social sciences have mostly analysed ongoing geographically propinquitous communities based on more or less face-to-face social interactions with those present. Much social science presumes a 'metaphysics of presence', proposing that it is the immediate presence of others that is the 'real' basis of social existence. This metaphysics generates analyses that focus upon patterns of more or less direct co-present social interactions.

But many connections with people and social groupings are not propinquitous, and this is of course more now than a century or so ago, at least in parts of the world. There is a substantial empirical realm of 'imagined presence' achieved through objects, people, information and images travelling, carrying connections across, and into, multiple other social spaces from time to time (Chayko 2002). Social life involves continual processes of shifting between being present with others (at work or at home, as part of leisure and so on) and being distant. And even when there is physical absence there may be imagined presence depending upon multiple connections. All social life, of work, family, education and politics, presumes relationships of intermittent presence and absence depending in part upon multiple technologies of travel *and* communications that move objects, people, ideas, images across varying distances. And this has been a marked feature of the contemporary world characterised by many people living 'mobile lives' (Elliott and Urry 2010). Presence is thus intermittent, achieved, performed and always interdependent with other processes of connection and communication.

Indeed we can say that there are five interdependent 'mobilities' that produce social life organised across distance and which form (and re-form) its contours:

- The *corporeal travel* of people for work, leisure, family life, pleasure, migration and escape, organised in terms of contrasting time–space modalities (from daily commuting to once-in-a-lifetime exile).
- The *physical movement* of objects to producers, consumers and retailers, the sending and receiving of presents and souvenirs, as well as the assembly and (re)configuration of people, objects and spaces as part of dwelling and place-making.
- The *imaginative travel* effected through talk, but also the images of places and peoples appearing on and moving across multiple print and visual media.
- *Virtual travel* often in real time that enables presence and action at a distance, transcending geographical and social distance (attending conferences 'in' Second Life or forming a smartmob).
- *Communicative travel* through person-to-person contact via embodied conduct, messages, texts, postcards, letters, telegraph, telephone, fax and mobile.

Although research may focus upon one of these separate mobilities and its underlying infrastructures, the mobilities paradigm especially emphasises the complex interdependencies between these different mobilities. In so doing it examines the many voluntary or enforced, temporary or long-term, enjoyable or troublesome moments of immobility they entail, that may make and contingently maintain social connections across varied and multiple distances (Urry 2007). Moreover, it makes the 'moves' that make these (im)mobilities constitutive of economic, social and political relations interesting for study, highlighting how discourses that may prioritise one or other such mobility (such as the belief that business has to be done 'face-to-face') simplify – rather than explain – such relations.

Mobilities are embodied, involving fragile, aged, gendered, racialised bodies. Such bodies encounter other bodies, objects and the physical world multi-sensuously. Travel involves corporeal movement and consequential forms of pleasure and pain. Such bodies perform themselves in between direct sensation of the 'other' and various sensescapes. Bodies are not empirically fixed and given but involve performances to fold notions of movement, nature, taste and desire into and through the body. Bodies sense and make sense of the world as they move bodily in and through it, creating discursively mediated sensescapes that signify social taste and distinction, ideology and meaning. This embodied nature of movement is brought out in Jirón's account of moving around Santiago, Chile (Chapter 3), in Ferguson's analysis of the movement of social workers, especially by car, who are examining potential child abuse within homes distant from their 'office' (Chapter 5), and Watts' and Lyons' account of how train travel is corporeally performed (Chapter 7).

The body thus senses as it moves, through kinaesthetic skill, merging sensory experience that informs one what the body is doing in space through the sensations of movement registered in joints, muscles, tendons and so on with intention and bodily memory (Merleau-Ponty 1962; Dant 2004). This combines with touch, sight, hearing, smell and other sensory impressions to perform the body's motion, as well as intense emotions, including pleasurable car driving (Sheller 2004), passive waiting (Bissell 2007) and road-rage irritation (Lupton 1999).

Various objects and mundane technologies sensuously extend human capacities into and across the world. Various assemblages of humans, objects, technologies and scripts contingently produce durable and stable movement. They reflexively shape sensory experiences as 'technologies' provide various ways of framing and forming impressions. These range from the views afforded by the windows of a railway carriage, the car windscreen, the aeroplane or the camera/ camcorder viewfinder (Urry 2007); the 'extreme' thrill of riding a surfboard (Dant and Wheaton 2008); the new intimacies enabled through the Global Positioning System (GPS) and mobile video phone screens (Licoppe 2009; Morel and Licoppe, Chapter 10 of this volume); or different senses of travel time created by rail passengers not only with laptops but also books, sweets and music (Watts and Lyons, Chapter 7). Such hybrid assemblages roam countrysides and cities, making and remaking landscapes and townscapes as they circulate around the world.

On occasions and for specific periods, face-to-face connections are made through often extensive movement, and this was also true in the past. People travel to meet face-to-face and these moments of co-presence need explanation. Among the processes that generate face-to-face meetingness, five are particularly powerful (Urry 2003). These are formal – legal, economic and familial – obligations to attend official meetings; social obligations to meet and to converse, often involving strong expectations of presence and attention of the participants; practical obligations to be co-present with others to sign contracts, to work on or with objects, written or visual texts; experiential obligations to be in and feel a place 'directly' through movement and touch; and emotional obligations to experience a 'live' event that happens at a specific moment and place. These obligations can be very powerful and generate what Durkheim termed 'effervescence' (1915). Chayko describes this 'powerful force or "rush of energy" that people sometimes feel within them in circumstances of togetherness' (2002: 69–70). Such empirical feelings of intense affect generate a compulsion to travel, often at specific times along particular routes. This is examined by Haldrup in relationship to family groups performing as a unit while on holiday (Chapter 4), and by Büscher *et al.* with regard to memorable events such as festivals where through new software the public develop a more concrete sense of how their movements are mapped, tracked and interrogated (Chapter 8).

Mobile methods

So in this book we examine an array of methods that in different ways capture, track, simulate, mimic, parallel and 'go along with' the kinds of moving systems and experiences that seem to characterise the contemporary world. Researchers will benefit if they capture, track, simulate, mimic and shadow the many and interdependent forms of intermittent movement of people, images, information and objects (Sheller and Urry 2006). This kind of research has not been much developed previously to the current century, although Marcus' 'multi-sited ethnography' approaches this when he refers to 'chains, paths, threads, conjunctions, or juxtapositions' (1995: 105).

Further, as a consequence of allowing themselves to move with and to be moved by subjects, researchers can become tuned into the social organisation of 'moves'. Investigations of how people, objects, information and ideas move and are mobilised in interaction with others reveal how actions – like moves in a game – are oriented towards and reflexively shape orders of social, economic and political relations (Wittgenstein 1953; Garfinkel 1967). By immersing themselves in the fleeting, multi-sensory, distributed, mobile and multiple, yet local, practical and ordered making of social and material realities, researchers come to understand movement not as only governed by rules but as methodically generative. Germann Molz thus argues against the strong division between moving and knowing; they are and have been highly interdependent as in the case of eighteenth-century Grand Tourists (Chapter 6). This makes it less interesting to find and define 'underlying' rules or structures but challenging to describe the methods that people use to achieve and coordinate the making of an always contingent ordering (including material agencies, software design and use, as examined in Büscher *et al.*, Chapter 8)

We now outline a dozen mobile methods and briefly indicate how the subsequent chapters exemplify these.

First, there is 'observing' people's movement: their strolling, driving, leaning, running, climbing, lying, photographing and so on, a method found in Simmel and in Goffman's many works which are seminal here. Marcus refers to this as 'following the people' (1995). It involves directly observing mobile bodies either through overt methods such as 'shadowing' others, or covert methods that are in effect a kind of sociological 'stalking'. Jirón uses the former method of shadowing her informants who struggle to negotiate the fearsomely complex routeways of Santiago in Chile. She comes to be known by her research subjects as 'the shadow' (Chapter 3). Watts and Lyons used both methods in order to examine the complex materialities involved in performing often complex journeys in part by train (Chapter 7).

There is also observing the movement of objects, such as the picture postcards that became so widespread in the late nineteenth century in Britain (Gillen and Hall, Chapter 2). Methods need to follow objects, to 'follow the thing' (Marcus 1995). In particular, objects move as part of world trade; objects move in order to be combined into other objects (such as the components of a computer that travel the equivalent of a journey to the moon); some objects travel and lose their value (cheap souvenirs) while others enhance their value through movement (an 'old master'; Lury 1997); and as objects travel, their cultural significance can grow as they accrete material and symbolic elements. Lash and Lury describe this as involving a cultural biography of objects (2006). Also, the geographical flows of messages and of people can be tracked through the use of GPS and other technologies involved in contemporary communications (Licoppe 2004). Social-positioning methods increasingly enable the digital mapping *and* measuring of people's space–time movement through streets, buildings and neighbourhoods (Ahas, Chapter 11; Rickets *et al.* 2008).

Especially significant in observation is to see how people bring about face-to-face relationships with other people, places and events. Mobility involves occasioned, intermittent face-to-face conversations and meetings within certain places at certain moments, encounters that seem obligatory to some or all of the participants, such as on a family holiday as observed by Haldrup (Chapter 4). Such observations may be enhanced through observations that are filmed still or through video (Morel and Licoppe, Chapter 10). The importance of *face* is enormously complex and problematic, for example when social workers travel to the homes of potential child abusers and have only fragments of time to observe the faces of potential perpetrators through a door perhaps only a few inches wide. The poor have to be treated as immobile and available for inspection by the social worker who always arrives (and sometimes leaves rapidly) by car (Ferguson, Chapter 5).

Second, there are several ways of 'participating' in patterns of movement while simultaneously conducting research. This can involve what Morris terms the method of 'walking with' that he deployed in research with farmers in Peru and the Yorkshire Dales (2004). Such 'walking with' people involves sustained engagement within their worldview (Ingold 2004; Ingold and Vergunst 2008) and reveals the emplacement of professional judgements (Büscher 2006), emotional attachments, activity patterns and life-style possibilities. Kusenbach describes and elaborates the 'walk along' as an ethnographic research tool that enables the development of a 'street ethnography' (2003). Through such 'co-present immersion' the researcher moves within modes of movement and employs a range of observation and recording techniques. Jirón as 'the shadow' especially deploys such 'co-present immersion' (Chapter 3). Laurier uses this method when researching office working 'on the motorway' while doing a 'ride-along' (2004; Kusenbach 2003: 464, on the 'ride-along'), or more generally investigating the organisation of car travel (Laurier *et al*. 2008), while Watts and Lyons explore pleasures of train travel (Chapter 7). The 'walk-along' or 'ride-along' can also involve 'participation-while-interviewing', as Haldrup uses in his research on mobile tourists in Denmark (Chapter 4). Here the researcher first participates in patterns of movement, and subsequently interviews people individually or in focus groups, as to how diverse mobilities constitute their patterning of everyday life while on holiday.

Third, using mobile video ethnography. It requires mobility in the form of 'anticipatory following' (Garfinkel 1967: 147), because to capture people as they move and interact with others on film, the researcher needs to anticipate their moves and must position the camera's viewfinder in place as, or ideally before, actions unfold. Exploring the work of visual anthropologist Rouch, Macbeth shows how the continuous shot can reflect an anticipatory-responsive, analytical-participant aspect of participant observation as an 'inquiry from within the social order' (Macbeth 1999: 163; Mohn 2002; Büscher 2005). Such inquiry from within can inform explorations of futures through collaborative analysis and innovation projects, where the portability of video data produced by researchers on the move enables ethnographically informed participatory design (see Büscher *et al*., Chapter 8). Analysis and design grounded in rich audio-visual records of lived practice can provide inspiration for 'appreciative interventions' (Karasti 2001). Büscher *et al*. explore multi-disciplinary collaborative innovations using mobile ethnography in ways that blur the boundaries that divide design and use (Chapter 8; Suchman 2007; see also Adey 2010).

Fourth, time–space diaries. Here respondents record what they are doing and where, how they move during each period and the modes of movement (Kenyon 2006). Such a diary enables researchers to plot, for example, how the household, and indeed different household members, move through time–space and perform activities intermittently on the move, such as the participants moving around Santiago (Chapter 3). The diary can be textual, pictorial or digital or some combination. Haldrup deploys time–space diaries in his research on tourists moving around Jutland (Chapter 4; see Bærenholdt *et al*. 2004: ch. 4). The use of mobile voicemail diaries (Palen and Salzman 2002) or wearable automatic time-lapse cameras (Harper *et al*. 2008) enables subjects not to interrupt their (mobile) activities to reflect upon and note down where they have been. This information is recorded through audio-visual diary entries on the move. Moreover, 'automatic diaries' such as Harper *et al*.'s SenseCam can provide insights that are 'at once different to the experiences recollected by participants and yet [bring] a sense of wonder, depth and felt-life that [is] strangely enriching' (Harper *et al.* 2008). Like video, diaries also lend themselves to collaborative analysis with research subjects, who reveal a picture of daily lives and movement that would be difficult to construct through unaided reflection. In a reflexive move the researcher's own trajectories of travel and affordances may also be interrogated through diary research in order to examine how they are generated on the move and how they move along with those being researched (Watts and Lyons, Chapter 7).

Fifth, there are varied methods that explore virtual mobility through texting, websites, multi-user discussion groups, blogs, emails and listservs, as well as older moving messages such as those conveyed on picture postcards (Gillen and Hall, Chapter 2). Germann Molz tracks the interplay between travellers' websites and blogs and the corporeal travel of round-the-world-travellers (2006; Chapter 6 below). This research involves web-surfing, in-person and email interviewing, and interaction in interactive sites and discussion groups, in effect moving with travellers to their blogs, videos, email, meetings and so on and examining their strategies of coordination and repair especially when things go badly wrong. Mondada examines this issue of breakdown through examining the complex, Internet-supported conversations between a car-breakdown call centre, a mobile mechanic and a stranded broken-down motorist. One issue that becomes crucial is joining up 'fragmented geographies' through talk and maps on the Internet to determine exactly where the broken-down car and driver actually are (Mondada, Chapter 9). Overall, the communication and movements in virtual spaces of research subjects are often not easily available to the researcher. Record and replay of digital activities in combination with analysis of ethnographic experiences are one way of tracking the multi-sited, collective or collaborative action of distributed mobile participants (Crabtree *et al.* 2006).

Sixth, there are art and design interventions concerned with imagining mobile alternatives and futures and experimenting with them. This involves playful appropriation of prototypes of mobile technologies, for example, mobile content-generation technologies (Coulton *et al.* 2006), location-tracking and context-sensitive technologies (Mann *et al.* 2003; Hemment *et al.* 2006; Ciolfi and Bannon 2007), location-based gaming (Benford *et al.* 2004; Licoppe 2009) and live 3D visualisations of movement for event management (Büscher *et al.* 2008). A key challenge here is how prototypes themselves move. In Chapter 8, Büscher *et al.* use a variety of mobile methods, from 'radical' design interventions to ethnographically informed participatory design, to effect playfully various kinds of social intervention. These methods are mobile, not just in making researchers move with mobile subjects, but also metaphorically in researchers being moved by people to the opportunities and implications for design and future innovation. Watts and Lyons somewhat analogously develop a 'travel remedy kit' in order to engage with and be moved by subjects envisioning different affordances for their journey, to rethink their journey through a different material assemblage (Chapter 7).

Seventh, mobile positioning methods can provide insight into the movements of large mobile populations, such as commuters or tourists (Ahas, Chapter 11;

Ahas and Ülar 2005). Mobile phones are used so widely that capability of capturing their positions – either actively by looking at live positions or passively by working with historical databases – provides opportunities for unprecedented studies of everyday spatial behaviour and everyday life. In addition, there are opportunities for phone-based digital questionnaire surveys. New methods of data gathering and visualisation and the large numbers of potential respondents make it possible to obtain invaluable information about people's everyday movements. Finding solutions to ethical challenges around surveillance is difficult. But research based on mobile positioning data is a rapidly developing field in geographical and urban studies, and many research institutions and information technology companies are now involved in data gathering and experiments based on mobile tracking. Rhythms, large and very large-scale patterns of movements and networks can become visible and inform urban planning decisions. Ahas (Chapter 11) provides an overview and practical advice.

Eighth, capturing 'atmosphere'. Much movement involves experiencing or anticipating in one's imagination or avoiding the 'atmosphere' of a particular place or kind of place. Ferguson details the intimidating nature of homes in which child abuse may be taking place and the visiting social workers' strategies to cope with this. He describes entering such homes as often a 'deeply sensual experience' (2006: 10; Ferguson, Chapter 5). Other research includes that by Watts and Lyons on how to make train environments less 'boring' through the addition of various objects that can afford a different atmosphere to the travel experience (Chapter 7). Creating the nature of a place's atmosphere and its appeal or repulsion to imaginative travel will generally necessitate multiple qualitative methods including especially literary, artistic and imaginative research (Bærenholdt *et al*. 2004; Haldrup, Chapter 4). Tolia-Kelly examines especially through art the sense of foreboding experienced by Asian visitors within the 'paradise' of the English Lake District (2007).

Ninth, researching the active development and performance of 'memory'. Memories can 'haunt' people, places and meetings. Recovering them necessitates methods that qualitatively investigate how postcards, photographs, letters, images, souvenirs and objects are used within especially family and friendship groups (Gillen and Hall, Chapter 2; Larsen 2005, 2008). This can involve researching the pictures and objects that people carry around with them and which are then used to reassemble memories, practices and even landscapes in their varied sites of dwelling. However, as much of this is familial or private there is a major research challenge to get inside such private worlds and to excavate 'family secrets', through often complex and difficult conversations, especially about people who are no longer alive or have moved away (Kuhn 1995). Germann Molz examines the ways that visual reminders of people and place are extensively circulated on social networking sites (Chapter 6).

Tenth, 'real' places are not necessarily fixed and can be mobile. Implicated within complex networks (as researched in Bærenholdt *et al*. 2004), places are dynamic, 'places of movement' according to Hetherington (1997). They are not fixed within one location but move around as geographies are stretched, contracted and folded through the opening or closure of airports, news of conflict or environmental devastation, the award of favourable ratings in newspaper travel pages or online blogs, or the algorithmic logic of search engines (Germann Molz, Chapter 6). Places move within networks of human and non-human agents as brought about by Haldrup's account of the changing choreographies of visitors (Chapter 4). Such hybrid systems that contingently produce distinct places need examination through methods that plot, document, monitor and juxtapose places on the go or places that are no longer on the go (see Urry 2002; Sheller and Urry 2004, for various 'moving places').

Eleventh, the examination of conversations which are in many ways the stuff of life and central to how and why people are moving about (Boden and Molotch 1994; Hutchby 2001). These define the situation at hand, the relationship of the speakers and project the future of the interaction in question (Schegloff 1972). Formulating places takes on specific forms, for example, when giving directions (Psathas 1991), when talking on a mobile phone (Laurier 2001; Weilenmann 2003) and when there is a demand to assemble fragmented and mobile geographies. Formulating places and situations has a particularly urgent and complex character as part of work in emergency calls (Mondada, Chapter 9; Fele 2007) and in making sense of incident reports en route (Landgren 2005). Mondada shows how accurate awareness of the situation and physical location has to be produced from often incomplete accounts provided by interlocutors in situations of stress (Chapter 9). The formulations produced are critical for guiding speedy and accurate movement of help and resources. Conversation/interaction analysis and investigations of how people augment verbal descriptions with visual, cartographic, textual as well as technological information such as GPS coordinates can inform understanding of how situation awareness is produced and folded into the mobilisation of resources and the development of mobility strategies (Büscher *et al.* 2008).

Twelfth, it is possible to research various kinds of activities and places en route where certain sorts of movement are slowed down, refocused or redirected. Ling and Yttri (2002), for example, describe the practical micro-coordination and expressive 'hyper-coordination' that is necessary to the fluidity of networked teenage mobilities. It also has become possible to examine how multiple tracks of people pass through various 'transfer points', places of in-between-ness. 'Populations' passing though such transfer points are often monitored by various agencies charged with policing that territory; and simultaneously can be researched as they are temporarily immobilised. This occurs within lounges, waiting rooms, cafés, motels, amusement arcades, parks, hotels, harbours (Büscher *et al.*, Chapter 8), stations and carriages (Watts and Lyons, Chapter 7) and airports (Cwerner *et al.* 2009). The social scientist can use those moments of slowed-down movement in order to assemble their analysis of, or surveillance of, moving populations as Germann Molz discusses in Chapter 6. Particular focus can be on what have been termed 'interspaces' – places created on the move, in-between events, in-between origins and destinations (Hulme and Truch 2005). Material objects, too, move through such transfer points and they, too, may be tracked (and researched) as they move through such nodes. However, these transfer places are often heavily surveilled by private or public agencies so there may be many limits placed on the possibility of doing social science research that is informed by engagement and social innovation.

Conclusion

When researchers follow Simmel's call for dissolving dogmatic rigidity into the living and moving processes to 'mobilize' their studies, they do empirical inquiry, theory and critique differently. In this book we examine a multitude of new or rediscovered researchable entities including:

- fluxes and flows, passivity, dwelling, place-making;
- moves and ethnomethods of creating and seeing scenic intelligibility;
- the importance and effervescence of co-presence;
- the relation of (imagined) presences, absences, deferrals;
- practically achieved phenomena of trust, emotion, appreciation;
- the emplacement of professional judgement, affect and sense-making;
- boundaries between multiple presents and futures, users and designers, critique and engagement;
- patterns of movement recalled or automatically recorded;
- sensory experiences;
- practices of seeing, imagining, remembering, formulating places;
- the cultural biographies of objects;
- interactional adaptations and adoptions of new mobile technologies;
- interspaces;
- places on the move.

Mobility-oriented social science highlights the importance of investigating how worlds (and sense) are made in and through movement. By doing so on the move, mobility researchers provide fresh analytical leverage to important opportunities and challenges including many of the leading global issues, such as world food and water shortages, global terrorism, climate change, new genomics, the 'virtual' and so on. Thus studies of movement, blocked movement, potential movement and immobility, dwelling and place-making not only illuminate important phenomena but provide compelling new modes of knowing. Inquiries on the move – such as the shadowing, stalking, walk-alongs, ride-alongs, participatory interventions and biographies we describe – enable questions about sensory experience, embodiment, emplacement, about what changes and what stays the same, and about the configuration and reconfiguration of assemblies of objects, spaces, people, ideas and information.

And inquiries on the move can become 'inquiries from within'. To 'follow the people', analysts rely on developing skills to understand 'indigenous' mobile methods, employed by those whose mobile activities they study to organise their movement. For example, to understand how people navigate within and orient to the scenic intelligibility of interactions in public as well as virtual spaces, analysts must learn to recognise and register what guides people's moves. For many forms of research – interviewing while walking, virtual and video ethnography – the researchers' skill needs to be acute enough to enable them to anticipate their subjects' next moves. Analysts being 'on the move' in this sense create a kind of 'double transparency' that allows them to study and describe mobility in the making, while simultaneously drawing the methods used in their production to their own and their audience's attention (Lynch 1993).

Moreover, this work is public, drawing inspiration from Burawoy's call for public sociologies that 'enrich public debate about moral and political issues by infusing them with sociological theory and research' (2005: 1603). But the mobilities turn is about more than feeding scholarly discourse into debate. Mobile research and, for that matter, innovation requires 'engagement' and commitment to 'placing relations among science, technology, and public interests at the centre of the research program' (Sismondo 2007: 21). This makes research and innovation 'hybrid' in the sense that analysis, design and everyday practice become so intermingled as to be inseparable, making them 'mutually instructively descriptive' for scientists, engineers, designers, artists and practitioners (Garfinkel 2002: 101), shown by Büscher *et al.* (Chapter 8).

Thus the mobilities paradigm enables a step change in critical social theory. It makes clear that cultural studies, globalisation studies, anthropology, the sociology of knowledge, science and technology studies are not enough to 'explain' complex, chaotic yet ordered social and material realities. It is not just about how people make knowledge of the world, but how they physically and socially make the world through the ways they move and mobilise people, objects, information and ideas. Through critical engagement in and through mobilities studies, researchers are making a difference to the ways in which (im)mobilities are conceived of, in research, design and areas of public policy.

But not all is rosy here. As various contributors bring out, engagement is difficult and there are powerful social forces involved in the monitoring and surveillance of populations who are on the move and forming and reforming new kinds of social grouping. Fluid socialities are increasingly recordable (Thrift 2007) and calculable. Qualculation involves the ability to compile huge amounts of data and to design increasingly powerful algorithms to sort, correlate, categorise and rank this mobile data (see Germann Molz, Chapter 6) – combining objective calculation with qualitative judgement in actuarial predictions. It is said that these developments in computation and calculation are bringing about a new world order, somewhat captured in the 2008 BBC drama *The Last Enemy*.

These forces, huge corporations, fashionable consultancies and fearful states are likely to dominate future mobilities research, which opens up questions of whether social science should join in, get left behind or try to find ways to critique and engage constructively. It may be that we cannot join in because of the confidential and commercial nature of much of the information collected about moving subjects. So there is a danger of being left behind in the slow lane of research, somewhat mirroring Savage and Burrow's concerns about the future of social science research more generally (2007). They argue that social transactional data now routinely collected, processed and analysed by many private and public institutions makes the sample survey and the in-depth interview increasingly outdated research methods, unlikely to provide a robust social science. Savage and Burrow argue for a 'politics of method' and we too will end with a similar call to arms.

Given the hugely troublesome character of mobile lives and their role in transforming environments and people and in making a major contribution to the warming of the planet and the running down of oil supplies, societies need good social science research now. We hope that we have made some contribution to developing this in this book, but the twenty-first century may provide an inhospitable environment for much of the work outlined here. This work involves efforts to deal methodologically with the fleeting, the distributed, the multiple, the non-causal, the sensory, the emotional and the kinaesthetic. These are qualities difficult to reduce to algorithms but there is little doubt that powerful corporations and fearful states will seek to develop what we might call a *qualculating mobile method* at odds with much of what we have argued for here. Once social science gets its hands on an important topic for research it can rest assured that other forces are already there reordering the world to other interests. There are indeed struggles over method.

Note

1 See Büscher and Urry (2009) for an early version of this chapter.

Bibliography

Adey, P. (2010) *Mobility*, London: Routledge.
Ahas, Rein and Ülar, Mark (2005) 'Location Based Services: New Challenges for Planning and Public Administration', *Futures* 37: 547–61.
Barad, Karen (2007) *Meeting the Universe Halfway: Quantum Physics and the Entanglement of Matter and Meaning*, Durham, NC: Duke University Press.
Bærenholdt, Jørgen Ole, Haldrup, Michael, Larsen, Jonas and Urry, John (2004) *Performing Tourist Places*, Aldershot: Ashgate.
Benford, Steve, Flintham, Martin, Drozd, Adam, Anastasi, Rob, Rowland, Duncan, Tandavanitj, Nick, Adams, Matt, Row-Farr, Ju, Oldroyd, Amanda and Sutton, Jon (2004) 'Uncle Roy All Around You: Implicating the City in a Location-Based Performance', in *Proceedings of ACE '04*, Singapore, 3–5 June 2004.
Bissell, David (2007) 'Animating Suspension: Waiting for Mobilities', *Mobilities* 2(2): 277–98.
Boden, Dede and Molotch, Harvey (1994) 'The Compulsion of Proximity', in Roger Friedland and Dede Boden (eds) *NowHere: Space, Time and Modernity*, Berkeley: University of California Press.
Brown, Barry and Laurier, Eric (2005) 'Maps & Journeying: An Ethnomethodological Approach', *Cartographica* 4(3): 17–33.
Burawoy, Michael (2005) '2004 American Sociological Association Presidential Address: For Public Sociology', *British Journal of Sociology* 56(2): 259–94.

Büscher, Monika (2005) 'Social Life under the Microscope?', *Sociological Research Online* 10(1). Online: www.socresonline.org.uk/10/1/buscher.html (accessed 20 November 2009).

—— (2006) 'Vision in Motion', *Environment and Planning A* 38(2): 281–99.

Büscher, Monika and Urry, John (2009) 'Mobile Methods and the Empirical', *European Journal of Social Theory* 12(1): 99–116.

Büscher, Monika, Kristensen, Margit and Mogensen, Preben (2008) 'When and How (Not) to Trust IT? Supporting Virtual Emergency Teamwork', in Frank Fiedrich and Bartel Van de Walle (eds) *Proceedings of the 5th International ISCRAM Conference*, Washington, DC, May 2008.

Chayko, Mary (2002) *Connecting: How We Form Social Bonds and Communities in the Internet Age*, New York: State University of New York Press.

Ciolfi, Luigina and Bannon, Liam (2007) 'Designing Hybrid Places: Merging Interaction Design, Ubiquitous Technologies and Geographies of the Museum Space', *Co-Design* 3(3): 159–80.

Coulton, Paul, Rashid, Omar and Bamford, Will (2006) 'Experiencing "Touch" in Mobile Mixed Reality Games', *Proceedings of the Fourth Annual International Conference in Computer Game Design and Technology*, Liverpool, 15–16 November 2006, pp. 68–75.

Crabtree, Andy, French, Andrew, Greenhalgh, Chris, Benford, Steve, Cheverst, Keith, Fitton, Dan, Rouncefield, Mark and Graham, Connor (2006) 'Developing Digital Records: Early Experiences of Record and Replay', *Computer Supported Cooperative Work* 15(4): 281–319.

Cwerner, Saolo, Kesselring, Sven and Urry, John (eds) (2009) *Aeromobilities*, London: Routledge.

Dant, Tim (2004) 'The Driver-Car', *Theory, Culture & Society* 21(4/5): 61–79.

Dant, Tim and Wheaton, Belinda (2008) 'Windsurfing: An Extreme Form of Material and Embodied Interaction?', *Anthropology Today* 23(6): 8–12.

Durkheim, Émile (1915 [1912]) *The Elementary Forms of the Religious Life*, Chicago: Free Press.

Elliott, Anthony and Urry, John (2010) *Mobile Lives*, London: Routledge.

Fele, Giolo (2007) ' "Where Did It Happen?" Deciding Where an Emergency Is Located', paper presented at the Tenth International Pragmatics Conference, Gothenborg, 8–13 July.

Ferguson, Harry (2006) 'Liquid Social Work: Welfare Interventions as Mobile Practices', *British Journal of Social Work* 38(3): 561–79.

Garfinkel, Harold (1967) *Studies in Ethnomethodology*, London: Polity.

—— (2002) *Ethnomethodology's Programme. Working out Durkheim's Aphorism*, New York: Rowman & Littlefield.

Germann Molz, Jenny (2006) 'Watch Us Wander: Mobile Surveillance and the Surveillance of Mobility', *Environment and Planning A* 38(2): 377–93.

Gibson, William (1984) *Neuromancer*, New York: Penguin.

Harper, Richard, Randall, Dave, Smyth, Nicky, Evans, Carwyn, Heledd, Lisa and Moore, R. (2008) 'The Past Is a Different Place: They Do Things Differently There', in *Proceedings of DIS (Designing Interactive Systems)*, ACM Press.

Hayles, N. Katherine (1999) *How We Became Post Human: Virtual Bodies in Cybernetics, Literature, and Informatics*, Chicago: University of Chicago Press.

Hemment, Drew, Evans, John, Humphries, Theo and Raento, Mika (2006) 'Locative Media and Pervasive Surveillance: The Loca Project', in Joan Gibbons and Kaye

Winwood (eds) *Hothouse Papers: Perspectives and Paradigms in Media Arts*. A VIVID publication in association with Article Press, Birmingham. Online: www.drewhemment.com (accessed 6 April 2008).

Hetherington, Kevin (1997) 'In Place of Geometry: The Materiality of Place', in Kevin Hetherington and Rolland Munro (eds) *Ideas of Difference*, Oxford: Blackwell.

Hulme, Michael and Truch, Anna (2005) 'The Role of Interspace in Sustaining Identity', in P. Glotz, S. Berscht and C. Locke (eds) *Thumb Culture: The Meaning of Mobile Phones for Society*, New Brunswick, NJ: Transaction.

Hutchby, Ian (2001) *Conversation and Technology: From the Telephone to the Internet*, Cambridge: Polity Press.

Ingold, Tim (2004) 'Culture on the Ground: The World Perceived through the Feet', *Journal of Material Culture* 9(3): 315–40.

Ingold, T. and Vergunst, J. (2008) *Ways of Walking: Ethnography and Practice on Foot*, Aldershot: Ashgate.

Karasti, Helena (2001) 'Bridging Work Practice and System Design: Integrating Systemic Analysis, Appreciative Intervention and Practitioner Participation', *Computer Supported Cooperative Work* (10)2: 211–46.

Kenyon, Susan (2006) 'Reshaping Patterns of Mobility and Exclusion? The Impact of Virtual Mobility upon Accessibility, Mobility and Social Exclusion', in Mimi Sheller and John Urry (eds) *Mobile Technologies of the City*, London: Routledge.

Kuhn, Anette (1995) *Family Secrets: Acts of Memory and Imagination*, London: Verso.

Kusenbach, Margarethe (2003) 'Street Phenomenology: The Go-along as Ethnographic Research Tool', *Ethnography* 4(3): 455–85.

Landgren, Jonas (2005) 'Supporting Fire Crew Sensemaking Enroute to Incidents', *International Journal of Emergency Management* 2(3): 176–88.

Larsen, Jonas (2005) 'Families Seen Photographing: The Performativity of Family Photography in Tourism', *Space and Culture* 8: 416–34.

—— (2008) 'Practices and Flows of Digital Photography: An Ethnographic Framework', *Mobilities* 3: 140–60.

Lash, Scott and Lury, Celia (2006) *Global Cultural Industries: The Mediation of Things*, Cambridge: Polity.

Last Enemy, The (2008) BBC drama, www.bbc.co.uk/drama/lastenemy (accessed 4 April 2008).

Latour, Bruno (1993) *We Have Never Been Modern*, New York: Harvester Wheatsheaf.

Laurier, Eric (2001) 'Why People Say Where They Are during Mobile Phone Calls', *Environment and Planning D: Society and Space* 19(4): 485–504.

—— (2004) 'Doing Office Work on the Motorway', *Theory, Culture & Society* 21: 261–77.

Laurier, E., Lorimer, H., Brown, B., Jones, O., Juhli, O., Noble, A., Perry, M., Pica, D., Sormani, P., Strebel, I., Swan, L., Taylor, A.S., Watts, L. and Weilenmann, A. (2008) 'Driving and "Passengering": Notes on the Ordinary Organization of Car Travel', *Mobilities* 3: 1–23.

Law, John and Urry, John (2004) 'Enacting the Social', *Economy and Society* 33(3): 390–410.

Licoppe, Christian (2004) ' "Connected" Presence: The Emergence of a New Repertoire for Managing Social Relationships in a Changing Communication Technoscape', *Environment and Planning D: Society and Space* 22: 135–56.

—— (2009) 'Recognizing Mutual "Proximity" at a Distance: Weaving Together Mobility, Sociality and Technology', *Journal of Pragmatics* 41(10): 1924–37.

Ling, R. and Yttri, B. (2002) 'Nobody Sits at Home and Waits for the Telephone to Ring: Micro and Hyper-Coordination through the Use of the Mobile Phone', in J. Katz and M. Aakhus (eds) *Perpetual Contact: Mobile Communication, Private Talk, Public Performance*, Cambridge: Cambridge University Press.

Lupton, D. (1999) ' "Road Rage" and Cyborg Bodies', *Body and Society* 5(1): 57–72.

Lury, Celia (1997) 'The Objects of Travel', in Chris Rojek and John Urry (eds) *Touring Cultures: Transformations of Travel and Theory*, London: Routledge.

Lynch, Michael (1993) *Scientific Practice and Ordinary Action*, Cambridge: Cambridge University Press.

Macbeth, Douglas (1999) 'Glances, Trances, and their Relevance for a Visual Sociology', in P.L. Jalbert (ed.) *Media Studies: Ethnomethodological Approaches*, Lanham, MD: University Press of America.

Mann, Steve, Nolan, Jason and Wellman, Barry (2003) 'Sousveillance: Inventing and Using Wearable Computing Devices for Data Collection in Surveillance Environments', *Surveillance & Society* 1(3): 331–55.

Marcus, George (1995) 'Ethnography in/of the World System: The Emergence of Multi-Sited Ethnography', *Annual Review of Anthropology* 24: 95–117.

Merleau-Ponty, M. (1962) *Phenomenology of Perception: An Introduction*, London: Routledge & Kegan Paul.

Mohn, E. (2002) 'Filming Culture', in *Spielarten des Dokumentierens nach der Repräsentationskrise*, Stuttgart: Lucius und Lucius.

Morris, Jake (2004) *Locals and Experts: The New Conservation Paradigm in the MANU Biosphere Reserve, Peru and the Yorkshire Dales National Park, England*, PhD thesis, Lancaster University, UK.

Palen, Leysia and Salzman, Marilyn (2002) 'Voice-Mail Diary Studies for Naturalistic Data Capture under Mobile Conditions', in *Proceedings of the Computer Supported Cooperative Work Conference*, ACM Press.

Park, Robert E. (1970 [1925]) 'The Mind of the Hobo: Reflections upon the Relation between Mentality and Locomotion', in Robert E. Park, Ernest W. Burgess and R. McKenzie (eds) *The City*, Chicago: University of Chicago Press.

Psathas, George (1991) 'Direction-Giving in Interaction', in Dede Boden and Don Zimmerman (eds) *Talk & Social Structure*, Cambridge: Polity Press.

Ricketts Hein, J. and Jones, P. (2008) 'Mobile Methodologies: Theory, Technology and Practice', *Geography Compass* 2(5): 1266–85.

Savage, M. and Burrow, R. (2007) 'The Coming Crisis of Empirical Sociology', *Sociology* 4(5): 885–99.

Schegloff, Emanuel (1972) 'Notes on a Conversational Practice: Formulating Place', in David Sudnow (ed.) *Studies in Social Interaction*, New York: Macmillan/Free Press.

Sheller, Mimi (2004) 'Automotive Emotions: Feeling the Car', *Theory, Culture & Society* 21: 221–4.

Sheller, Mimi and Urry, John (eds) (2004) *Tourism Mobilities: Places to Play, Places in Play*, London and New York: Routledge.

Sheller, Mimi and Urry, John (2006) 'The New Mobilities Paradigm', *Environment and Planning A* 38(2): 207–26.

Simmel, George (1997) *Simmel on Culture*, ed. D. Frisby and M. Featherstone, London: SAGE.

Sismondo, Sergio (2007) 'Science and Technology Studies and an Engaged Program', in Edward J. Hackett, Olga Amsterdamska, Michael Lynch and Judy Wajcman (eds) *The Handbook of Science and Technology Studies*, Cambridge, MA: MIT Press.

Suchman, Lucy (2007) *Human–Machine Reconfigurations: Plans and Situated Action*, 2nd edn, Cambridge: Cambridge University Press.

Thrift, Nigel (2007) *Non-Representational Theory: Space, Politics, Affect*, London: Routledge.

Tolia-Kelly, Divya (2007) 'Fear in Paradise: The Affective Registers of the English Lake District Landscape Re-visited', *The Senses & Society* 2(3): 329–51.

Urry, John (2002) *The Tourist Gaze*, 2nd edn, London: SAGE.

—— (2003) 'Social Networks, Travel and Talk', *British Journal of Sociology* 54(2): 155–75.

—— (2007) *Mobilities*, Cambridge: Polity Press.

Weilenmann, Alexandra (2003) ' "I Can't Talk Now, I'm in a Fitting Room": Availability and Location in Mobile Phone Conversations', *Environment and Planning A* 35(9): 1589–605.

Wittgenstein, Ludwig (1998 [1953]) *Philosophical Investigations*, trans. G.E.M. Anscombe, London: Blackwell.

2 Any mermaids?

Early postcard mobilities

Julia Gillen and Nigel Hall

We shall argue that the early-twentieth-century postcard can be seen as an astonishing instantiation of an era of revolutionary change in mobilities and that the study of them can contribute to enriching understandings of a mobilities paradigm. The postcard phenomenon we focus on burst into being in an extremely dynamic period of cultural change. During the second half of the Victorian era and the succeeding Edwardian period the population of Britain was beginning to move around in large numbers as never before, with new patterns of trade, leisure and fast-paced changes in transport; the railway system was at its zenith (Pooley *et al.* 2005). Existing notions of space and time were 'annihilated' according to prominent commentators (Schivelbusch 1978: 31). At this point of rapid technological change came what we can term a 'new communications landscape' (Kress 1998) with parallels to the contemporary digital revolution, as we shall show. Yet, as Urry (2007: 157) has argued: 'the study of travel and transport within the academy has been largely conducted separately from the analysis of communications, as though these were different and unrelated systems'. This chapter contributes to the development of mobile methods through exploring the truly remarkable phenomenon of the early postcard. We contrast interactions around postcard mobilities in the present day as well as their original heyday and in so doing offer a new exemplar of mobile methods.

The focus of our interest is the period from 1870, when the first British postcard was issued by the Post Office on 1 October, to the end of the Edwardian period in 1910. The introduction of the postcard created what How (2003) termed a new epistolary space, for, in comparison with letters, postcards were perceived as less formal, shorter and cheaper, and therefore in some way as having the potential to alter how people could deal with the networks of relationships in the world. Especially significant is the period after 1902 when the plummeting price of paper, innovations in colour-printing technology and most of all a new accessibility to rapid communications at extremely low cost created a remarkable 'tipping point' (Gladwell 2000). As with the tipping point in 1990 identified by Urry (2007), instantiated with the sudden growth in use of the fax machine in offices, so in 1902 the combination of material conditions and a new ruling of the Post Office created the right condition to facilitate an explosion in use of the postcard. A cultural shift in everyday communications practices ensued; our investigations of the Postmaster General's reports lead us to calculate that almost six billion of these cards were sent in the UK in the Edwardian age (the equivalent of 200 cards per person). With up to ten deliveries a day in major cities, rapid responsivity was enabled in a simple, exceedingly cheap way that simply did not exist for written communications in the era between the First World War and the introduction of emails and SMS messages, save for the telegraph, a medium that demanded very short communications and which was very expensive.

We shall start by introducing our methods of investigation by exploring the contrasting circulation patterns between cards today and in their heyday at the beginning of the twentieth century. Second, we examine the massive take-up of the card and how it may exemplify a revolutionary moment in communications, and we shall outline the material, technical and social factors that led to its emergence. Third, we shall suggest three aspects of the phenomenon that have some resonance in the light of today's 'digital revolution'. Finally, we consider how tracking the early postcard through space and time generates insights as to the interrelationships between communications media, transport communications and new social networks.

The changing circulation patterns of the early postcard

There are fundamental changes in the mobilities of the early picture postcard when contrasting how they circulated in the late Victorian and Edwardian era, as communications that were often perceived as collectable, with how the same cards move around today, as objects collected by hobbyists. In their original era, some might simply have been purchased by people to add to their own collections; most were sent through the then massive apparatus of the Post Office (working from statistics provided by Cecil (1969), we have calculated that 74 per cent of civil service workers in the UK in 1914 worked for the Post Office). Apart from its huge network of post offices, pillar boxes were ubiquitous, and cards as well as letters could be posted in other places too, for example on some trains.

The central activity through which surviving historical postcards circulate today is trading at postcard fairs, and so this is our first layer of involvement as we study the changing mobilities of postcards. Subsidiary to fairs as temporary locations for cards are other places where cards can be found, bought and sold such as house clearances, junk or antique shops, the Internet and auction houses. For most people involved in those secondary trading places, however, they are involved in passing them on, essentially, because they come across cards and understand that they have some value to others. The fairs are a more concentrated focus of activity, where collectors and dealers meet (see Figure 2.1). Although we occasionally buy cards in secondary trading places, it is postcard fairs that are key to our activities as collectors and as researchers, adopting an ethnographic perspective. As collectors, the second author began in the UK and

USA by collecting a distinctive subgenre: 'Why haven't you written?' cards. We engaged in multimodal analysis examining the relationship of the designed combination of printed words and images on the picture side with the messages handwritten by senders on the other (Hall and Gillen 2007). We progressed to a different collection as we shall describe below. Attending fairs as collectors gives us an excellent gateway to acting as researchers. For the purposes of this chapter, we attended a national postcard fair in Nottingham, recording interviews with dealers, collectors, the fair organiser and publisher of collectors' books and periodicals, and we took photographs. We triangulated insights gained there with conversations at regional postcard fairs, including the major Stockport and Chester fairs. To understand the postcard-related practices of the Victorian and Edwardian eras we consulted many secondary sources, including periodicals written for postcard collectors in the British Library, the Postmaster General's annual reports for the era and historical newspaper databases.

At the beginning of the twentieth century, collecting cards was an extremely popular pastime; most-valued examples were often placed in albums. Today, an album will generally be gutted by a dealer or collector, who will sort cards according to the subject of the image. Apart from our work and very few other exceptions, the historical postcard has only been valued in the contemporary era for one of its sides: the picture side. The other, the written message side, has been almost totally disregarded and even deliberately obliterated. Cards which

Figure 2.1 Photograph: Postcard Fair, Nottingham, 1 November 2008 (source: Julia Gillen).

survive are categorised, dealt in and valued according to the images – which are exponentially more varied than the contemporary postcard, limited as it is to tourism and art with few other exceptions. It is not just the content of the image that is significant; other characteristics can be of interest, for example, relating to the materiality of its production, such as if silk has been used, or according to the specific identity of the publisher, with some being more prized for their distinctiveness than others.

The rationale behind our collection of postcards is different, as our interests in vernacular literacies leads us to a distinctive perspective and thus a unique collection (Gillen and Hall, forthcoming). We have been collecting cards for their sender's written comments, acquiring cheaply priced cards posted in the Edwardian era (1901–10) and which have more than 20 words in the written message. We have 1,500 cards in this collection, plus a much smaller collection of earlier cards. When we acquire these cards we do not select according to the picture side, thus the picture sides are relatively random and diverse. They are often topographic (i.e. landscapes and views of towns, cities or single buildings), but many other subjects feature.

In contrast, most collectors search for postcards according to pictorial themes. These, too, are often topographic. For example, typical collections focus upon a particular town, but any theme is possible. 'Any mermaids?' was one enquiry overheard by us at the Postcard Fair in Nottingham on 1 November 2008. 'Not just at the moment', came the calm response of the stallholder, after rapidly mentally reviewing his stock of probably a few thousand old postcards.

Frequently, as the collecting hobby develops, collectors become dealers, fluidly moving between each side of the desks. One man we interviewed explained his trajectory as follows:

> I've been collecting over twenty years – it's a hobby gone mad. People start collecting and progress to dealing and eventually to this shambles! I sell postcards to everyone, you try to satisfy every wish, most are topographic, others collect cooking, football, cinema and so on. I'm interested in glamour and children rather than our own little village; our cards reflect our interests. Some collect by publisher, or, if you're a military person, you collect your own regiment or the Boer war – whatever interests you. There's no end … you think you've heard everything and then someone comes up to you and asks for pawnbrokers … it's a lovely hobby and has given me a great deal of pleasure; I've met a lot of people over the years.

In order to sell cards a dealer needs to organise them individually (that is, remove them from their albums if that was how they were bought and file them in searchable categories). Categorising the cards presents a constant but fascinating challenge. Another dealer explained: 'It's difficult to categorise the cards. You categorise a card according to where you think it will sell better. Advertising, children's clothes … they're popular; there's a lot in "garage", it's more likely to sell there than in the county.' Colour coding can help:

You have one colour for a major category – these are all shipping cards – red for general shipping. Then you split them up, green categories: Cunard, P & O, miscellaneous lines, lifeboats, things to do with shipping ... so you can find what you want.

A photograph of part of the box referred to is shown in Figure 2.2. When asked then if this dealer specialised in shipping he was quick to deny it, saying this was simply 'part of my general stock'.

When collectors die, their cards are often sold in auction, picked up directly or indirectly by dealers. Collections are split and the cards recommence their circulation.

It is then by combining a multiplicity of methods in an ethnography of material culture (Vannini 2009) that we are able to elucidate the complex choreographies of these cards and how these contrast in the present time to their original era. Their trajectories are much more complex than a potential initial assumption of 'buy, write, send, receive' might encapsulate. We turn now to the reasons why the material affordances of the card prompted its emergence and phenomenal popularity, notwithstanding its lack of privacy in comparison to the letter as a communications technology.

Figure 2.2 Photograph: Categorising postcards (source: Julia Gillen).

An extraordinarily popular innovation

Material properties of the postcard as mobile object

From its introduction the postcard was a highly regulated object; in the UK the shape and size were determined by the Post Office. Unlike an email or text message, a postcard is a very physical object. The light weight of the card enabled it to be sold at one halfpenny rather than the penny cost of sending a letter. The relative stiffness of the card from which they were made meant that for the Post Office they were easy to sort and move and strong enough to survive a great deal of handling. However, as *The Times* pointed out, 'The substitution of Post cards, thin, light, and uniform in size, for ordinary letters greatly aids the work of packing and carriage, but not that of delivery' (*The Times*, 8 October 1870) and the extra work 'created a large amount of dissatisfaction' among the letter carriers (*The Times*, 5 October 1870). At the same time, the highly portable cards were stiff enough to be written on across a knee or even in the hand and its very constrained space actually made it very attractive for carrying short written communications. On its first day over half a million were sold, and during its first year 75 million postcards were bought, even though at that time they were only available from post offices.

In 1894 pictorial postcards were introduced to the UK, giving the opportunity of combining a very short message in the margin of a picture. With an increasing choice of images as printers spotted the opportunities, there was an immediate explosion in communication, as a newly almost universally literate population grasped the opportunity for quick, informal and attractive written messages. Users were quick to combine use of the postcard image as a gift, with the appropriation of the small space for a message for their own purposes not necessarily directly connected to the topic of the image at all; see Figure 2.3 as an example.

In January 1902 the Post Office gave in to popular demand and permitted the use of postcards on which one side was wholly taken up by an image, and the other side was half address and half message. Vernacular literacy is 'essentially ... not regulated by the formal rules and procedures of dominant social institutions and ... [has its] origins in everyday life' (Barton and Hamilton 1998), and with the postcard, people were given the opportunity to create messages that were not going to be constrained by the relatively formal letter-writing etiquette, or the rules prescribed by formal education and manuals. Combining these texts with images – some of which were originated through personal transaction with a photographer/printer, or customised in some way, for example, through annotation – gave a fabulous opportunity for creativity in multimodal design that at such a low price and efficiency has probably not been equalled until the twenty-first century. In this light, we will now examine three aspects of the postcard phenomenon that have resonance in the light of today's digital revolution: the speed of postcard communications, the relationship between image and message and the passionate social reactions engendered.

Caerlaverock Castle.   RELIABLE [logo] SERIES.

Hope to see you this evening. love. nessie

Figure 2.3 Postcard: Sent in Lockerbie, 28 September 1903.

'Wont be down today': the speed of postcard communications

As exemplified by Figure 2.3, our collection furnishes ample internal evidence that writers of early postcards could rely upon the rapidity of communications. That card was sent and received within the vicinity of a single town. However, many of our cards referring to events later that same day were sent over longer distances. In 1906 'Hetty' wrote that she was going to travel later that day by train from Birmingham to Worcester to visit her addressee. Four years later somebody filled the message space of a card reporting on the aftermath of the previous day's visit:

> My Dear M
> I did not
> get home last night
> until after 10 oc. I
> had 3 punctures in
> back tyre but mended
> them myself. Your loving friend
> JS

Perhaps as an afterthought, another few more words were then squeezed upside down into the only space available, at the very top of the card:

> very sorry wont be down today. very wet.

The service was so impressively efficient that it could be used in connection with decisions regarding that day's meals. One dealer we interviewed recalled seeing orders for that day's meat delivery despatched by postcard, and our cards feature interpersonal messages with short-term instructions or suggestions such as the following:

> … if
> George is not coming
> today our George will
> come and fitch the
> peelinges and bring
> you a bit of pork
> so don't get any meat

This is an early form of the kind of micro-coordination noted by Ling and Yttri (2002), with a view to the mobile telephone: greater personal mobility, enhanced by considerable use of transportation, especially in urban contexts, and combined with the need to maintain intimate relationships, led to the use of the mobile phone in closely synchronising social arrangements, often by SMS. In its day, the postcard enabled the equivalent – not readily possible by other written means in the periods between these eras.

Relationship between the written message and the image

Since our collecting is also governed by cost considerations, there must be caution applied to any definitive sense of correlation between the images in our collection and those available in the postcard's heyday overall. Nevertheless, it is clear from contemporary and historical sources of evidence that topographic cards have had enduring appeal; three-quarters of our sample are of views or pictures of single buildings. During the postcard's heyday it seems that every city, town and even village was represented through a range of cards. Often the connection between the image and the message is difficult or impossible for us to make – we can never know what significance an image might actually have had to the addressee. Certainly the images of topographic cards are sometimes explicitly mentioned in the writers' messages and even where they are not, the postmark may indicate that they are contributing to conveying information as to the sender's location and how he/she wants to communicate its qualities. Urry (2007: 259) sees the growth of the postcard as contributing to 'new technologies of the gaze' as tourism and photography fused together and shaped perceptions of landscapes and views. Written communications and the selected image together provide an interesting fusion, unique in each synthesis. Without being able to trace how communications are received, it is impossible to straightforwardly trace how social bonds may actually have been stretched into and across places as these cards are sent from one location to another, each potentially of some interest to the two human parties of the interaction. We may, however, gain some fragmentary understandings of how the writers appear to try to construct or appeal to such bonds as they apparently infuse denotation and description of place with some affective colouring.

While on holiday near Birmingham in 1905, Tom has written to someone who was also on holiday, in Bristol; his postcard makes use of his knowledge of the landscape as shown on the picture side. The image is a professional illustration of a local tract of ancient woodland, captioned, when Tom bought the card, 'Gumslade, Sutton Park'. He has added to the informativeness of the printed description, putting an opening bracket before 'Sutton' and adding some information, so that the annotated caption now reads: 'Gumslade (Sutton Park so some 8 or 9 miles in circumference).' He then locates his host within the neighbouring landscape in an approving description:

> ... This house is very pleasingly
> situated on a hill, with a view for miles
> round of pretty wooded country. Has about
> half an acre of garden – ground, a field at
> the back & quite a poultry farm for
> Will has 45 Chicks, so that his garden
> & poultry keep him outside most of the day.
> I am glad to see he looks capital...

Will's 'garden & poultry' seem to be evolving into part of a countryside that is newly amenable to visual regard, instancing 'the shift from land to landscape ... [that] marks a particular way of being in the world, as places are performed through comparison, contrasts and collections' (Urry 2007: 269). Through taking the trouble to communicate multimodally his view, sending it on in a preserved fashion to someone who evidently thought it worth keeping, we have a sense of how, sometimes, with this new tourist sensitivity, transient holiday pictures are not transient at all but 'have an enduring after-life ... a vital part of life-stories and spaces of everyday life' (Bærenholdt et al. 2004: 122). We also mention at this point that our collection contains many cards sent to people on holiday (e.g. in boarding houses in seaside resorts); in their heyday postcards were not solely to be sent from vacations to those back at home or in the office but were part of a constantly maintained dialogue – similar to how the mobile phone operates, especially in the European Union since EU regulatory powers curtailed maximum prices for voice calls and SMS texts.

Occasionally, the image is commented on in a more or less didactic fashion, as when C. Hudson sends a photograph of the tomb of St Withberga, explaining she is the daughter of a king (Anna, of the Anglo Saxons) whose tomb they previously had visited together. A writer to a Mr Maxwell in Manchester sends a colour illustration of a broad London panorama (Figure 2.4). On the message side he explores the spatial potential of the card through writing extremely tiny characters while remaining entirely legible. He includes greetings and a little personal news and then copious explanation of the buildings and monuments

Figure 2.4 Postcard: Charing Cross, London, sent 7 July 1906.

illustrated (Figure 2.5). So, whether or not the actual experience of travelling to the capital was accessible to Louis Maxwell, the instructive multimodal communication of the features of such key sites might be felt to reproduce 'the cultural sense of a national imagined presence' (Urry 2007: 262).

Selecting images already published was not the only option available to users. It was also easy to commission a photograph and have it turned into a postcard for one's own use. Although portraits were understandably common, and we have some such examples with explanatory messages, this could also be done with topographic views. So in 1905 J.H.C. had a local photographer in Morecambe take a photograph of a street so oriented that he could point out by writing small numbers onto windows some rooms available to rent which he then described on the message side. The building in question is viewed from a favourable angle, to include trees, and J.H.C. takes the opportunity to extol not just the advantages of the lodging, but some appealing aspects of local facilities too, even suggesting the possibility of taking a steamer trip from Morecambe to Ireland. He provides details of the costs, how to contact the landlady and even reveals he has made some preliminary inquiries. Of course, we cannot know if the preservation of the card to the present day owes anything to the persuasiveness of his multimodal message to Miss Croom.

Overtly romantic opportunities were designed and made use of accordingly. One card shows a couple in an embrace, captioned 'A Blissful Moment'. An unsigned but presumably easily identifiable sender posted it to a Miss Ivy Blake soon after seeing her:

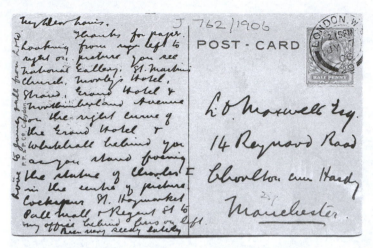

Figure 2.5 Postcard: Charing Cross, message side.

> That is all I want
> if its only one. you
> was Looking sweet
> yesterday when I
> met you. I should
> like to take you
> out for a Blissful
> <u>Moment</u>

Just to make his intention even more plain, he has annotated the picture side by adding 'with you' to the caption.

Collecting cards of celebrities was a common interest both of Edwardians and of some postcard collectors today. Owing to our financial constraints, we do not tend to access such cards but have found that by coincidence our collection does feature a number of portraits of bishops. Messages written on celebrity cards can focus specifically on the image, often offering it as a gift intended to extend the addressee's collection. Sometimes this agenda of gifting the card as valued image is combined with other purposes. In a card which packs a staggering 166 words covering a diverse range of topics including a death, illness, a party and a complaint about money, Harold comments to Edith on the photographic image he has sent of the Archbishop of Canterbury: 'Do you like this it will keep the Archbishop of York company. Will you send me some celebrities in return. I have got Mr Chamberlain. Should like some musicians…' Another card, featuring again a highly posed image of the Bishop of Southwell, provides illustration to the account of his arrival as witnessed by the sender. Of course, the image on any picture postcard could lend itself to explicit reference on the message side, if so desired, and a great variety were so employed; often the effect is to enrich the synthesised interpretation of both.

Passionate reactions to the early picture postcard

Through examining *The Times* newspaper, other generally available publications and samples of the vast media directed to postcard collectors and uses, we have identified diverse, often passionate reactions to the introduction and subsequent explosion in popularity of the early postcard. Here we single out some currents of opinion that were clearly influential in their time and that are also of interest as resonating with some contemporary reactions to today's 'digital revolution'.

There was considerable recognition from early days as to the benefits of this means of communication; *The Times* ran a generally approving review of the history of the postcard on 1 November 1899. Later, possibly the most forward-looking paean to the postcard was written by a London journalist in 1907:

> When the archaeologists of the thirtieth century begin to excavate the ruins of London, they will fasten upon the Picture Postcards as the best guide to the spirit of the Edwardian era ... Like all great inventions, the Picture Postcard has wrought a silent revolution in our habits.
>
> (Douglas 1907, cited by Staff 1979: 76)

Such 'revolutions' are not universally approved. The infiltration into written language of email, text, and other recent forms of electronic and digital communication have been accompanied by many criticisms about how such technologies are ruining the English language. Such critiques are nothing new, for the same kinds of comments occurred when the postcard first appeared and for a long time after. There were a number of grounds for complaint but perhaps the most interesting involved implicit or explicit comparisons between letter-writing and postcard-writing.

Indeed, in its 1899 review, *The Times* commented, 'some people, too, urged that the use of a post-card was little short of an insult to the recipient, inasmuch as, if the communication were not worth a penny, it was not worth sending at all' (*The Times*, 1 November 1899), while James Douglas, quoted above, also acknowledged: 'There are still some ancient purists who regarded postcards as vulgar, fit only for tradesmen,' for, 'The picture postcard carries rudeness to the fullest extremity' (cited by Staff 1979: 81). Even in 1908 it was possible for a character in a story to say, 'I have always been brought up to think it rather rude to send postcards, unless they are picture ones for people to put in their albums' (Williamson and Williamson 1908). George Sims (1900) admitted that they 'are utterly destructive of style, and give absolutely no play to the emotions'. One assessment of the letter–postcard relationship related to the decline of a friendship, when 'Letters in turn gave place to mere notes and postcards, scribbled in violent haste, at wider intervals' (Richardson 1910), and one character in another book, when asked to correspond using postcards, exclaimed: 'How can I tell from postcards what you are thinking and feeling?' (Douglas 1907).

However forthright some of these comments may be, the popularity of post-cards even among the first users must give some weight to the conclusion of *The Times*' review of 1899: 'The fact that post-cards have become a most useful adjunct of social and commercial intercourse must far outweigh any disadvantage which the old-world letter-writer ascribes to its use' (*The Times*, 1 November 1899). Of course the cheapness of the postcard relative to the letter was partly in respect of its regular, small size and weight and partly owing to the simplicity of its format. This, however, made it potentially liable to lack of privacy, perhaps with respect to other people in the addressee's household and certainly to the postman. Indeed, we can mention in passing that, unsurprisingly in a situation where the post was delivered potentially many times a day, the deliverer became a familiar figure, as is evidenced by such factors as the relatively common inclu-sion of an image of the postman in certain subgenres and indeed cards written to home-area postmen by holiday-makers while away. Encountering this threat to privacy, early postcard users employed a range of creative strategies. Some employed means that made the cards at least difficult to read easily, for example superimposing words or lines, changing the orientation of the writing several times on a card or using extremely tiny writing. More developed means of dis-guising one's message include the use of rebus, mirror-writing or codes.

Enthusiasm for codes was readily commercialised; in 1908 a Captain Bernard compiled a book titled, *The Postcard Code: A Novel and Private Method of Communicating by Postcard*. In his introduction he claims:

> No longer need collectors keep or remove post cards from their albums, for it would be almost impossible for their friends to remember any particular numbers that pertain to the tender messages that are usually found at the bottom of a pretty card ... No longer will the servant or the Village Postman be able to read your private messages, no longer will the mistress know of the tender phrases sent by the maid's followers, no longer will parents scowl, or the sister's brother tease her, for when in possession of this book, by simply placing a few figures on a post card, a private message can be sent to any part of the United Kingdom for a halfpenny.

Bernard's book features 136 pages of numbers with the expanded messages they represent; these indeed are revelatory of some social preoccupations of the time, for example a whole section relating to 'rinking' (that is, ice-skating). 'Courting couples' are given many suggestions for compressing their messages, for example, '35a' being suggested to represent: 'My own dearest darling. It seems ages since I last saw you, and I am counting even the minutes until we meet again.' As a review in the *Cornish Telegraph* quoted in the back of the book claimed, 'Tender messages can be sent with impunity.'

Despite all the codes and ciphers, it seems that most people did not worry, just as few really worry about their emails and texts today; after all, most of these messages then and now demand little privacy, for as *The Postcard Collector* commented in 1903:

> And as for privacy, who expects it in these days. If he has secrets to hide from the light of day, by all means let him use a sheet paper, enclose it in an envelope, seal it with red wax, put on a penny stamp and be happy.
>
> (*The Postcard Collector* 1903: 324)

However, there were some genuine reasons for concern. Sending postcards was for a time regarded in legal terms as a public act, resulting in controversies analogous to disputes that arose over the introduction of the World Wide Web, when the transgressions of national boundaries created problems for governments' attempts to ban the distribution of undesirable information, or for individuals trying to have injunctions enforced. There are references to postcards being found as either 'defamatory' or 'libellous' in legal cases reported in *The Times* in the early years of the twentieth century; perhaps the most surprising example to modern sensibilities is the following:

> Melita Macready, a music teacher, was charged with defamatory libel, having sent the principal of the Guildhall School of Music a postcard saying, 'You old rogue, villain and liar. You old coward. Why don't you fight?' Melita Macready was committed for trial.
>
> (*The Times*, 20 May 1905: 16)

Discussion

Analysis of the early postcard mobilities provides intriguing illumination of both the physical movements and written communications in a society which enjoyed its own communications revolutions. As Urry (2007) asserts, new forms of social networking co-evolve with extensive changes to transport and communication systems. The postal system was so efficient that no comparison can be made for the speed, efficiency and cheapness of written communications in the period between the First World War and the era of contemporary digital communications, especially email and SMS text messaging. For the first time in history it was common for ordinary people to contact one another by writing in rapid processes of micro-coordination. So the writer of the following card advises the addressee not, then, to travel on the following day; what is very clear is an enmeshing of travel arrangements and the possibilities for negotiating these through the rapid exchange of written communications:

> Dear Lily,
> Your letter to hand tonight
> Don't trouble to come tomorrow.
> I will come on Sunday perhaps
> after dinner, but can't say. Glad

Mother arrived home safe on
Tuesday. I was going to write
to say you had no need to
come tomorrow. before I got
your letter. Yours [?]

So the early postcard is fascinating as a hitherto largely overlooked mobile object and communications technology that illustrates the interweavings of personal mobilities and creativity in the uptake and shaping of a new communications technology in the furtherance of multiple everyday purposes. It was the creation and the subject of intense regulation, posing challenges for public authorities in its popularity and perceived challenges to officially sanctioned ways of doing things including styles of written communication. Its particular affordances in terms of combination of image with word are rich, and may well have contributed to reimaginings of shared cultural resources, including the tourist landscape. In this way and as interpersonal communications, postcards can be seen as both carriers and instantiations of social and cultural change – globalization in current terms (Thurlow *et al.* 2010). As Thurlow *et al.* argue in connection with, specifically, tourist postcards, deploying the lenses of the mobilities paradigm enables us to examine the qualities of the postcard not only as carriers of messages but also as objects of material culture. We are studying the early postcard not just as illuminating the social practices of the Edwardians but also in their remarkably intricate circulation patterns of today.

Bibliography

Barton, D. and Hamilton, M. (1998) *Local Literacies: Reading and Writing in One Community*, London: Routledge.

Bærenholdt, O., Haldrup, M., Larsen, J. and Urry, J. (2004) *Performing Tourist Places*, Aldershot: Ashgate.

Bernard, Captain (*c.*1908) *The Postcard Code: A Novel and Private Method of Communicating by Postcard*, London: British Library: 012331.de2301233.

Cecil, R. (1969) *Life in Edwardian England*, London: B.T. Batsford.

Douglas, A. (1907) *Franklin Kane*, London: T. Nelson and Sons.

Gillen, J. and Hall, N. (forthcoming) 'Edwardian Postcards and Ordinary Writing', in D. Barton and U. Papen (eds) *The Anthropology of Writing*, London: Continuum.

Gladwell, M. (2000) *The Tipping Point: How Little Things Can Make a Big Difference*, Boston: Little, Brown and Company.

Hall, N. and Gillen, J. (2007) 'Purchasing Pre-Packed Words: Complaint and Reproach in Early British Postcards', in M. Lyons (ed.) *Ordinary Writing, Personal Narratives: Writing Practices in the 19th and Early 20th Century*, Berne: Peter Lang, pp. 101–17.

How, J. (2003) *Epistolary Spaces: English Letter-Writing from the Foundation of the Post Office to Richardson's 'Clarissa'*, Aldershot: Ashgate.

Kress, G. (1998) 'Visual and Verbal Modes of Representation in Electronically Mediated Communication: The Potentials of New Forms of Texts', in I. Snyder (ed.) *Page to Screen: Taking Literacy into the Electronic Era*, London: Routledge.

Ling, R. and Yttri, B. (2002) ' "Nobody Sits at Home and Waits for the Telephone to Ring": Micro and Hyper-Coordination Through the Use of the Mobile Phone', in J. Katz and M. Aakhus (eds) *Perpetual Contact: Mobile Communication, Private Talk, Public Performance*, Cambridge: Cambridge University Press.

Pooley, C., Turnbull, J. and Adams, M. (2005) *A Mobile Century? Changes in Everyday Mobility in Britain in the Twentieth Century*, Aldershot: Ashgate.

Richardson, H. (1910) *The Getting of Wisdom*, London: William Heinemann.

Schivelbusch, W. (1978) 'Railroad Space and Railroad Time', *New German Critique* 14 (Spring): 31–40.

Sims, G. (1900) *The Picture Post Card*, August 22.

Staff, F. (1979) *The Picture Postcard and Its Origins*, London: Lutterworth Press.

Thurlow, C., Jaworski, A. and Ylänne, V. (2010) ' "New" Mobilities, Transient Identities: Holiday Postcards', in C. Thurlow and A. Jaworski (eds) *Tourism Discourse*, Basingstoke: Palgrave Macmillan.

Urry, J. (2007) *Mobilities*, Cambridge: Polity.

Vannini, P. (ed.) (2009) *Material Culture and Technology in Everyday Life: Ethnographic Approaches*, New York: Peter Lang.

Williamson, C. and Williamson, A. (1908) *The Chauffeur and the Chaperon*, New York: The McClure Company.

3   On becoming 'la sombra/the shadow'

Paola Jirón

German philosopher Martin Heidegger wrote about the use of phenomenology to understand the experience of being in the world (Heidegger 1999). According to Seamon (2000: 161), this implies that it 'is impossible to ask whether person makes world or world makes person because both exist always together and can only be correctly interpreted in terms of the holistic relationship, being-in-world'. This experience is always already situated in a world and in ways of being.

This chapter proposes a hybrid and interdisciplinary methodology to understand the experience of mobility in the city of Santiago de Chile from a phenomenological point of view. This approach accepts that the totality of experience can never be fully apprehended by the researcher, and she will never fully understand how the experience of being in mobility takes place, as this will always be partial, incomplete, in process, becoming. As Bruner explains, 'we can never know completely another's experience, even though we have many clues and make inferences all the time' (1986: 5). How do we address this limitation? Geertz (1986) suggests listening to what, in words, images and actions, people say about their lives. This chapter suggests embarking on a reflexive and inter-subjective process from not knowing anything about the multiple and hybrid experiences of mobility to becoming increasingly closer to them, by getting very close, but never fully being, as, in Heidegger's sense, this being is always someone else's. This reflexive and intersubjective process entails reassessing methods as experiences become unveiled, accepting one's position and experience as part of understanding the other's and situating the experience in a broader context.

Getting closer to experiences requires moving with people both physically and in interaction (in dialogue and embodied interaction), and one way that this chapter suggests doing this is to accompany urban travellers by shadowing their practices. Shadowing involves 'following selected people in their everyday occupations for a time' (Czarniawska 2007: 17). For this, an ethnographic approach is presented as the most adequate, given the possibility of immersing oneself deep in the observation of a practice by being there and providing an in-depth description of it through fieldwork. Thus 'becoming the shadow' of mobility practices, as a reflexive endeavour, involves not only acknowledging routines, but also entering into practices, into dialogue and interaction in a constant engagement with the people whose lives they constitute. Throughout, the researcher's position and the methods of inquiry need to be adapted reflexively.

A deeper understanding of multiple and hybrid mobility experiences is important, because mobility is such a pervasive feature and is constitutive of contemporary living and urban space. By looking closely at experiences, the ideas of fixity, permanence and duality present in most urban analysis are questioned and mobile experiences emerge as fluid, multi-scalar processes in their situated complexity. This way of analysing mobility practices is part of the mobility turn that is enabling considerable theoretical, methodological and practical advances in the social sciences and their role in shaping contemporary societies.

The mobile methods presented here attempt to capture the ways in which mobility is experienced in cities today; this involves adapting, combining and modifying traditional research methods. It also means that, as important as knowing how much, at what time or in what mode people travel, research on mobility needs to examine the experiences of mobility practices, that is, the way people enact, experience and give meaning to mobilities in the way they prepare, embody and construct them on a daily basis. This requires innovative methods of inquiry, analysis, representation and negotiation, which necessitate flexible and dynamic methods as opposed to strict adherence to predefined tools. The proposed mobile methods are always in construction, always becoming.

Moving with people – in the case of the research at hand, urban dwellers in Santiago de Chile – in this way allows the researcher to witness and share everyday mobility experiences and practices (Kusenbach 2003; Ingold and Vergunst 2008). To explain the methodology adopted, this chapter is divided into three sections, starting with a description of the various ways in which mobile methods have evolved. It then explains the ethnographic shadowing approach adopted for this research. It concludes with a description of one case study on how mobility practices in Santiago de Chile were studied by using narratives, time–space mapping and photography.

Towards mobile methods

Mobility has been studied extensively from a transport point of view, mainly from the disciplines of transport engineering, economics, geography, planning, business and regional sciences (Johnston 1981; Small 2001), which are mostly interested in understanding travelling patterns through origin and destination of daily trips. In contrast, the 'mobility turn' in social sciences has revealed that most transport research assumes space and people's use of space as fixed and contained within areas. This critique unveils a need to move towards methods that are able to better capture the way mobility practices take place and how these exert a major influence on urban environments, including transport networks. This section provides a brief overview of some of the methods sociologists, anthropologists and geographers have used to apprehend mobility over time.

In the attempt to capture the experience of living in the city in and through the range of mobilities city life demands and is constituted of, qualitative methods have been applied in numerous ways by researchers. An early example of this is the work of George Simmel who aimed at understanding the sociology of the city in the nineteenth century by observing people, particularly in public areas in Berlin, including public transport (Simmel 1969; Frisby and Featherstone 1997). Moreover, by understanding the city as text, Walter Benjamin aimed to analyse the way modernity presented itself in the city from the character of the *flâneur* that strolls, in a seemingly aloof manner, the arcades of Paris, yet observes the crowds from afar. Benjamin analyses this through nineteenth-century literature, particularly that of Charles Baudelaire (Benjamin 1973, 2002).

More recently, French artist Sophie Calle controversially exposed urban experiences by following strangers and photographing them in Paris and Venice (Calle 1998). In the Latin American context, anthropologist Nestor García Canclini explored urban imaginaries by using historical and current photography and film of people travelling in Mexico City and presenting these for discussion to contemporary urban travellers (García Canclini *et al.* 1996; García Canclini 1997).

Closer to the aim of the research at hand, Michel de Certeau proposed walking the city as an elementary form of experiencing it, as for him it is on the streets that ordinary city life is made (de Certeau 1986). Although de Certeau's pedestrian speech acts are urban acts integral to the city, other forms of daily mobility are also significant in understanding urban living experiences. Along these lines, Augé's ethnology of the Parisian Métro provides detailed discussion of what travelling is like: the remembrances it evokes, the traces experienced and encounters it leaves behind, the cultural meaning that stations, connections, trains provide people (Augé 2002). Maspero contributes to this line of inquiry, but explores the diverse places and the production of their different senses of place surrounding the flow by travelling on the Roissy Express in Paris and getting off at each station to observe and participate in the spaces around it (Maspero 1994).

In human geography, time geography has made a major contribution to mobility studies by seeing 'time and space as universally and inseparably wedded to one another' (Pred 1996: 646; see also Haldrup, Chapter 4). Time geography suggests that the study of aggregate populations masks the true nature of human patterns of movement and highlights the importance of understanding disaggregated spatial behaviours (Hägerstrand 1970), arguing that time, while objectively the same everywhere, is not experienced, valued, used or available in the same way to all, as time is also spaced (Jarvis *et al.* 2001).

To illustrate how a person simultaneously navigates his or her way through the spatio-temporal environment, time–space mapping was developed. This notation device was used to demonstrate how human spatial activity is often governed by limitations and not by independent decisions of spatially or temporally autonomous individuals.

Time–space mapping has been criticised as being 'too physical, mechanistic and an exponent of social engineering' (Lenntorp 1999: 156), as it places too much emphasis on individuals as objects. Giddens (1985) considers the approach as theoretically naive in treating individuals as coming into being independently of their daily social settings, giving little attention to the essential transformative character of all human actions. Similarly for Harvey (1989), time geography and time–space mapping are a useful description of how the daily life of individuals unfolds in space and time, yet it reveals nothing about

> how 'stations' and 'domains' are produced, or why the 'friction of distance' varies in the way it palpably does. It also leaves aside the question of how and why certain social projects and their characteristic 'coupling constraints' become hegemonic, and makes no attempt to understand why certain social relations dominate others, or how meaning gets assigned to places, spaces, history and time.
>
> (Harvey 1989: 212)

Feminist critique of time geography highlights another shortcoming of time–space mapping. As discussed by Rose, 'time geography insists on a singular space; the space through which it traces people's paths claims to be universal. In other words, time geography assumes that its space is exhaustive' (Rose 1993: 19). These criticisms illustrate how time–space mapping neglects to question the transparency of space. As a tool it could be greatly enhanced if combined with other approaches that uncover the power relations, the meanings, embodiments and consequences of experience *in situ*.

Over the past few years, a sort of revival of time–space mapping has emerged, not least because it provides a much-sought-after sense of concreteness; it represents space and time not as simple social containers but as actual constraints on human action; it provides a geographical ethics in terms of the wise use of time and space; it offers a language to explain time and space, most importantly in terms of visual representations in maps and diagrams (Thrift 2005). It is currently being used in transport planning by mapping origin and destination surveys (Newsome *et al.* 1998) or in spatial mapping using Geographical Information Systems or virtual interaction (Miller 2005). Also, as a way of reflecting the way human activities affect the natural environment (Peuquet 1994), time–space mapping is being incorporated as a notation device. Moreover, it has been used in gender studies (Kwan 2002) and migration analysis (Southall and White 2005), all of which adopt a quantitative approach to human behaviour.

Critically, by aggregating mobility patterns, these studies dismiss the richness of experience and provide limited discussion on the power relations, meanings, embodiments and effects that are enacted in and through mobility practices. Approaching urban daily mobility using only time–space mapping is insufficient to capture the experience of urban living and more qualitative tools are needed to be able to highlight these issues. In mobility analysis, time geography can highlight people's allocation of time in geographic space, the importance of quotidian routines, urban performances and geographies of rhythms and the constraints present in society that inhibit urban dwellers from accessing the city in an even manner.

A more sophisticated example of this is Alan Latham's work, which uses time–space mapping in a participative manner through a diary–photograph/diary–interview method, where people are asked to write diaries and photograph their daily experiences, the interesting and/or significant places and events of their week. These are then notated in a version of time–space maps to explain the travels along with photographic material (Latham 2003, 2004). Through this participatory approach, Latham minimises the researcher's input into what and how things are recorded (Bijoux and Myers 2006), providing rich data gathered by the participants who are in control of what is captured.

However, the difficulties with Latham's type of research relate to the reliability of participants' dedication. Their commitment becomes crucial in the success of the method, running the risk of being overly demanding on interviewees' disposition and willingness to participate, particularly when daily mobility experiences are filled with temporal and spatial limitations, thus risking the possibility of obtaining accurate, detailed or any information at all. This technique has proven to be quite useful with youth participants who appear eager to try them, as was the case with Dodman (2003).

For the research at hand, focused on the everyday mobilities of urban travellers in Santiago, the diary–photograph/diary–interview technique seemed inadequate because of the difficulty in having participants accept this extra work. However, Latham's approximation of mobility practices provides a useful way to capture the experiences and rhythms of mobility (see Haldrup, Chapter 4). As suggested by others using Latham's technique (Zimmerman and Wieder 1977; Dodman 2003; Meth 2003; Bijoux and Myers 2006), time–space maps could be complemented with interviews, focus groups, mental maps, among other methods. In order to get closer to travellers' experiences by becoming their shadow, this research considered an ethnographic approach as valuable.

Ethnography involves a researcher:

> participating, overtly or covertly, in people's daily lives, for an extended period of time, watching what happens, listening to what is being said, asking questions, in fact, collecting whatever data is available to throw light on the issues that are the focus of the research.
>
> (Hammersley and Atkinson 1995: 21)

Ethnographic fieldwork is 'carried out by immersing oneself in a collective way of life for the purpose of gathering first hand knowledge' (Shaffir and Stebbins 1991: 5). An essential part of ethnography involves carrying out fieldwork as a way of 'being there' (Geertz 1988). Ethnographic research is characterised by a proliferation of styles and texts, and has reached into diverse areas of human experience, including medicine, education, journalism and urban studies (Atkinson *et al*. 1999; Hannerz 2003). In the latter, it has provided more effective methodological means to apprehend urban practices and experiences than traditional research methods (see Wacquant 2007). Moreover, 'the flexibility of the ethnographic research approach, combined with the availability of new technologies for the storage, retrieval, and presentation of data, allows for the emergence of new directions to better understand how social behaviour is shaped and organised' (Shaffir 1999: 685).

A useful way to look at mobility practices from an ethnographic point of view is multi-sited ethnography, which has been developed as a way to follow 'the thread of cultural processes' (Marcus 1995: 97). Multi-sited ethnography involves research that is not 'confined within one single place. The sites are connected with one another in such ways that the relationships between them are as important for this formulation [of a topic] as the relationships within them' (Hannerz 2003: 205). It is the linkages allowing for these connections that are relevant; these make multi-site studies 'different from a mere comparative study of localities' (Hannerz 2003: 205), even if comparisons are also made. Among the many types of multi-sited ethnography, studies include observations of migration, social movements, cyberspace or the global cultural economy. Multi-sited ethnography can be classified according to the different ways in which the object of study is followed: following the people, the thing, the metaphor, the plot, the story or allegory, the life or biography, the conflict, or it can also be strategically situated (Marcus 1995). Multi-site ethnography builds on the ethnographic tradition of studying cultures and their situated practices, but it seeks to enable a broadening of the investigation to study of movement, interactions on the move, connections and, as in this case, mobility experiences.

For the research in Santiago, a mobile multi-sited ethnographic approach was chosen as the most appropriate way to describe mobility experiences. It allows for flexibility and possibility of exploring, through thick description, the daily routines of mobile urban dwellers, offering a 'deep' and 'multi-faceted' description. Depth is crucial to understanding and explaining experience and I was particularly interested in the way different groups experience and enact urban mobilities. This approach allowed me to understand the hows, whys and whats (Shaffir 1999) of a specific urban practice, by allowing me to immerse myself in the way different people perform mobilities and produce knowledge about what the experience is like for them. Also, given that an ethnographic approach requires a considerable amount of time dedicated to fieldwork, it allows for reflexivity and the possibility of adapting methods as insights begin to manifest, and the researcher begins to understand experiences, becoming closer to them.

Although I was interested in observing travellers, I was not, unlike Augé, interested in observing strangers. In a very similar way to Latham's work, I wanted to know the meaning travellers gave to their experience, what had taken them to the journey and what happened to them during and afterwards, in a very similar way to Spinney (2007), who follows his participants on bicycles while filming them. In order to accompany the experience, I wanted to move with the people in my study, which was made possible by introducing a shadowing technique. Shadowing involves accompanying the participants individually on their daily routines, observing the way the participants organise and experience their journeys, sharing and collaboratively reflecting on their experience on the move. This is done either by discussing issues during the shadowing period or afterwards. The journey may be filmed or photographed during the shadowing process. This technique enabled me to capture important aspects of the experiences of urban daily mobility in Santiago, as will be detailed in the next section.

Becoming the shadow

It was important for me, as a researcher, to experience at least part of what travellers experienced, as one of my participants mentioned about the implementation of Transantiago, a new public transport system in the city of Santiago in 2007: 'if planners ever got on a bus like we do, they would understand why their proposals will never work' (Bernardo). To understand the complexity of changing transport modes, of climbing on and off buses, of body pressing against body, getting lost, feeling scared or disoriented, being fondled, robbed or amused, one needs to experience it. The lack of such understanding all too often leads architects, engineers and planners to ignore these complexities in transport innovation. I wanted to accompany travellers in order to understand what they did and how they did it and the traces left behind in their bodies and mental and emotional lives. I also wanted to discuss with them while they were travelling, see what they saw, understand why their gaze lingered or chose to ignore, and what they made of it afterwards. Also, understanding social–spatial experiences as embodied, multi-sensory and emotional (Bijoux and Myers 2006), I wanted to know what they touched, heard, smelled or tasted in the experience. Thus, I wanted to talk about the way the experiences were embodied. I also used photography to record mobility practices and to elicit reflection about them afterwards. The process of capturing the experience by becoming a shadow was a constant construction, shaped by constant reflexive inquiry into how and why which methods of mobile inquiry worked or not.

The overall structure of the methodology involved case selection, a period of access, a shadowing period and then returning to discuss the experience. When selecting the cases, I was primarily interested in analysing mobility practices of different income groups, since most studies which touch on urban inequality generally tend to focus on the poor, the excluded, though not on the relation they have with other social groups. As a way of making these associations, I compared travelling experiences of individuals living in different income neighbourhoods but located relatively close to each other. In this research, the cases were defined as urban travellers living in three different income neighbourhoods in a specific area of the borough of La Florida in Santiago (for detail on the case study, see Jirón 2007, 2008).

After explaining in detail what the research entailed, a process of exploring the field took place. Although my informants had agreed to participate, I began getting closer to their experience by carrying out extended interviews with each one. Here we began to discuss their personal history, background, choice of current place of residence, how they came to live in their current neighbourhood as well as detailed description of their regular daily trajectories using maps and 24-hour time budgets to trace these and talk about them. As relations with each participant became more relaxed, longer informal discussions began to take place on more specific issues of their everyday life and mobility experiences in the city. Through these discussions I slowly became closer to their experiences and prepared the way for shadowing their mobility practices.

It was after this period of getting to know each other that we agreed that I would accompany them on their journey as a mobile shadow. I shadowed each participant on a regular weekday, from the time they left their house until their day was over. This involved arriving at their house, according to our prior arrangement, often before they left in the morning, observing how they prepared to leave the house, then going through the day with them, how they managed riding on an overcrowded bus at rush hour or driving around the city all day, the boredom of shopping or the fear of coming home late at night, among many other activities. Finally, it involved coming back home at night (or leave at night and come back in the morning in the case of security guards). Although I had a broad idea of their journeys from previous discussions, the actual journeys were very different from what I would have expected, particularly in terms of the time precision and coordination in executing them. This required me to always be on time, as I could not delay their routines, and I had to be flexible, in case their plans changed or something unexpected happened.

I adapted to their situation, and although most participants were quite organised in terms of knowing ahead of time their daily activities, the details of how they were pursued were often unexpected. Sometimes participants would cancel at the last minute; other times I would stay with them until very late. They also asked me to help them and I never refused; consequently, I ended up packing shirts for delivery, choosing tomatoes, corn and beans in the street market, carrying elderly women's shopping, tucking children into bed, selecting gifts for clients or filling out forms in the hospital, among other things. Through this form of participant observation, 'being there' in their daily routines became possible.

The time–space dimension of the practice was incorporated through time–space maps, for which time and location were recorded to be later geo-referenced in the maps. The maps were used in a qualitative manner to provide a clear expression of the spatial use of the city. These were complemented with narratives, to describe the experiences people had during their daily journeys, particularly in terms of the strategies used for mobility and the consequences these have on their daily lives.

Details of the journeys were recorded as well as photographed by the participants or myself. As a visual method, photography was used as a way of reporting the journey and to carry out photographic interviews (Rose 2001) or photo-elicitation. As a visual reporting tool, the journeys were photographed to accompany the narratives and time–space maps, to 'follow' the journey and see specific aspects of the trajectory (see Figures 3.1–3.6). Photographs provide a closer approximation to the journey than the time–space maps on their own would depict. In this sense, the maps and photographs attempt to create a 'moving picture' of what is being described in the narrative. This moving picture provides a better idea of the spatial approximation of the traveller through the city, while at the same time it allows for rich and immediate perception of the spaces travelled by, as well the spaces travelled in (the car, the bus, the tram, the metro). Each element on its own would not provide as rich a picture of the journey as when observed together. This does not attempt to provide an exhaustive or comprehensive account of the journey, but to expose several interconnected dimensions of travelling.

In post-fieldwork photo-elicitation during individual and group interviews, photography was used to evoke discussion on specific topics. Here the photograph loses its claim of objectivity and presents the subjectivity of those who see the image differently from the researcher (Harper 2004). The participants often provided description of situations that would be very difficult to become aware of by simply observing the situation. After shadowing them and returning to talk about the journey, I would present the photos that would lead them to talk about experiences, motivations, practicalities, thoughts and emotions. This was particularly useful to identify processes of place-making. Both types of visual methods are recognised as not being neutral, as suggested by Rose (2003), and produce difference, as through their selection of captured moments and views certain people or elements remain invisible or hidden. Although I played a major role in the production of the images, I tried to be participative in letting my interviewees take photographs and reflect on them in discussion. As a result, part of their spatial experience was revealed, and they were able to explicate in depth their own interpretations, thoughts and reflections.

During the trips I also took notes, and some issues were discussed as they occurred, while others were saved for later discussion, depending on the convenience of the situation, the people around us or the topic of discussion. Although travelling with someone constantly and continuously during a full day had the potential of difficulty, all my experiences were quite positive regardless of participants being tired or stressed. Soon they started calling me 'la sombra' (the shadow) and that is what I became. Shadowing their moves became the closest way to understanding their experience. I was clearly unable to grasp it fully, but I came as close as I could. Their explanations and interpretations were crucial to this process.

This process of understanding the experiences of mobility involved going back to talk to each participant about the journeys, asking specific questions about the experience and discussing the photographs and maps with them. This provided a chance for deeper discussions on issues that had either been said or observed. It was also a way of being reflexive, after taking some distance, of returning to discuss with them the things that struck me. At this point, there were often issues that the participants brought up and wanted to discuss with me, reflections of their own lives that had come out of the research process.

The amount of data collected was considerable. Analysis was carried out by systematising the information as quickly as possible: most interviews were transcribed or notes about them were written as soon as the interview was over; photographs were downloaded and organised right after the interview; maps were elaborated within a few weeks of having carried out the journeys. This expediency was important to be able to discuss issues with participants by showing the time–space maps and photographs, which made it easier to elicit discussion on issues of travelling experience. The following section provides an example of how this information was put together to understand mobility experiences in Santiago de Chile.

Getting by with a little help from my friends: Laura's journey

Contemporary work patterns are increasingly mobile, requiring some to move around, while others' multi-job lifestyle obliges them to move from one work location to another. Flexible jobs also involve working nightshifts or seeking extra work to compensate for low-paying jobs or to pay off debts, as is the case for Laura. Her flexible and multiple work patterns are woven together with other activities that include household chores and social and family relations.

Laura is 45 years old, separated and lives in Jardín Alto with her 19-year-old daughter Catalina who just started university. For the past 16 years Laura has been working as a health professional at the Municipal Health Corporation and as a nurse at a public surgery two or three nights a week for extra income. Most of her activities are carried out within the borough she lives in, she hardly moves further away into the city. Laura's extensive network of friends and colleagues help her get by, especially through rides from friends, colleagues and even Municipal ambulances, hence she seldom pays for transportation. These details of her experience of mobility practices and her multiple connections are difficult to capture through traditional transportation analysis, where multiple connections and uses of mobility opportunities are generally missed. With the use of a variety of tools, as presented here, the richness of Laura's journeys, co-presence in mobility and innovative ways of moving are unveiled.

She gets up at around 07:00 and quickly cleans the house and prepares her things for work. She leaves the house at 08:00; five minutes earlier her friend had rung her to tell her she was leaving.

She walks for less than five minutes to Rojas Magallanes, the main street (see Station 1 in Figures 3.1 and 3.2) and waits at the corner until her friend Julieta picks her up at 08:10. Julieta has two children who go to a private school nearby. They drive through the back streets to avoid traffic. While Julieta walks the children to the entrance, Laura puts on her make-up in the car (see Station 2 in Figures 3.1 and 3.3). She tells me that she prefers using this time to do it instead of earlier in the morning when she can have breakfast and watch the news. On the way to work they drive through rough neighbourhoods which they call 'barrios peludos' (Chilean slang for difficult neighbourhoods), they say they have to be careful, keep the windows and doors shut, and hide their handbags to avoid being robbed, as has happened before. Laura doesn't really look at the

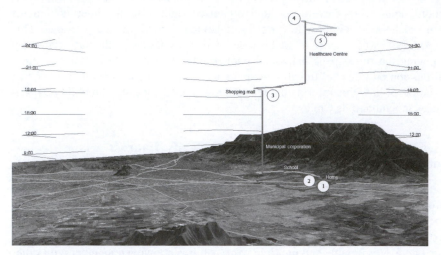

Figure 3.1 Map of Laura's journey.

Figure 3.2 Laura walks to street corner.

Figure 3.3 Laura waits for a friend.

cityscape outside; she tells me later how important this time with her friend is to her, as once in the office, they can't talk about intimate details. They talk all the way and arrive at work at 08:40. Although she can arrive later, it is important for her to arrive before 09:00 today, so she can leave by 17:30.

She mentions that on the days when she doesn't have a shift, she sometimes goes to the mall to pay bills after work, or for drinks or shopping with her girl-friends; many live close to her, so she gets lifts back home. Today, however, she leaves the office at 17:30, gets a lift from a friend to the shopping mall, then walks a few metres to the 'colectivo' stand, quickly finds hers and it leaves by 17:45. They head towards Los Quillayes, a large social-housing estate known for security problems, but she knows it well as she used to live there a few years ago (see Station 3 in Figures 3.1 and 3.4). She arrives at 17:55, changes into her nurse outfit and works non-stop until midnight, when Dr Santos, who lives in one of the gated communities close to her house, gives her and another nurse a lift home at 00:10 (see Station 4 in Figures 3.1 and 3.5). They mention how at this time of night the streets are dangerous, which is why they don't stop at the traffic lights, to avoid thieves, but they are also on the lookout for car races on the main streets. It has been a very long day and she gets home by 00:25 (see Station 5 in Figures 3.1 and 3.6). Tomorrow she has to get up early for an out-of-town session with her regular job.

Figure 3.4 Laura on 'colectivo' (shared fixed-route taxis).

Figure 3.5 End of shift: waiting for lift home.

Figure 3.6 Dr Santos drops Laura off at home.

Although her monthly income is approximately CLP$1,200,000 (approximately £1,200) at the Corporation, classifying her among the top 20 per cent of income earners in the country, she still needs the extra CLP$200,000 (approximately £200) she makes at the surgery to cover her debts. She enjoys being a nurse, she says, but she finds it tiring as she goes to bed at 01:00 on the days she has shifts and gets up at 07:00 the next day. She relies on friends to perform her routines, making travelling convenient, comfortable and friendly, but she also saves money. Without the lifts she gets, she would end up using this extra money she needs to cover her debts, mortgage and her daughter's university, and to pay for transport when necessary. However, her accessibility is influenced by the financial, physical and temporal dimensions of her life. She lacks the financial means to buy her own car and drive or pay for daily transport. Her travels may be dangerous as she travels after midnight and also through very poor areas of the city. However, she manages her constraints through her social capital; her networks allow her to make use of lifts that will support her to move around, easing access to her various jobs.

Understanding the complexity of the journey and travelling decisions was possible because of the depth of the observation of Laura's daily activities and by being with her during her mobility practices. This required more than just interviewing or just following her, or just photographing. It was the whole process of becoming her shadow that allowed for this comprehension. As the relationship with her became closer and more relaxed, details began to be unveiled. However, because the process was reflexive and it involved spending long hours with her over a long period of time, it allowed for discussing these issues with her and her daughter and observing them and going back to expand explanation when necessary.

Conclusions

The attempt to capture mobility experiences is always an incomplete one, always in process, always becoming, and understanding it will always be partial. This means that in the process of understanding the experience, the actual methodology becomes unveiled as the experiences unveil. This understanding is situated, and it requires a reflexive process whereby the researcher is constantly questioning and returning to understanding his/her position as a researcher. This also means that the knowledge of practices is not only subjective but intersubjective, as the researcher's own experience is also part of understanding others'.

An essential part of ethnography involves the need for fieldwork as a way of 'being there'. One possibility of becoming closer to the experience is to follow the practice in the form of a shadow using a multi-sited ethnographic approach. Furthermore, part of becoming the shadow involved a reflexive, flexible, open and vigilant approach, so as to dynamically adapt to the unfolding fieldwork experience. Undertaking this type of fieldwork with the disposition to modify ideas, methods and timing as required greatly enhanced the possibility of becoming closer to the participants and their experience. Although other methods and tools could have been used, including video, the information gathered was rich and diverse enough for the purposes of describing the experience of urban daily mobility practices.

It is clear that, as with any methodological approach, the whole picture is never completely revealed, nor is this the intention. However, the moving picture through which mobility experiences can be observed requires a complex and adaptive methodology. This means tools that can capture the different knowledges regarding mobility experiences, in terms of production, interpretation and representation. In this case it included mobile multi-sited participant observation through shadowing travellers in their daily journeys, time–space mapping, participatory photography, interviewing and collaborative analysis.

Future research could include further investigation into more situated knowledge of mobility experiences, as well as combining these methods with aggregate travel patterns (see also Ahas, Chapter 11) and moving towards creating methodologies to generate greater participation from those involved in the research process. This would facilitate the dialogue between the experience of mobility and mobile spaces/places with more traditional urban and transport planning methods, in order to make effective contributions in the mobility field.

One challenge presented by this method is how to generate knowledge that effectively informs policy. There is an urgent need to produce information regarding these everyday experiences of urban living to be fed back into the urban and transport planning process. This does not eliminate the need for other methodological approaches, including those used in planning or transport, but an ethnographic approach, for instance, would certainly enrich them by providing different views, and this would probably generate different transport or urban-planning interventions. These views are not necessarily better or worse, but are just as relevant as traditional planning views; however, they are often missed. Thus, capturing another way in which urban life is experienced requires broadening the epistemological scope of research and policy and requires finding ways in which these can capture experiences and their meanings.

Time–space mapping, complemented with photography and ethnographic narratives, can be useful as a way of tracking mobility in order to understand the way people move about the city, comparing movement while using the same base information. It can also help to visualise movement as a way of dimensioning the extent of mobility (or immobility) within the city. It can help to compare different trajectories and the time and space used. But more importantly, it can be a complementary way of providing more depth to a description of a situation, especially if combined with ethnographic narratives of urban daily mobility. This methodological approach enhances contemporary urban research as it provides a whole range of possibilities for generating knowledge of urban living experiences that would otherwise be lost in the research process. Mobile methods must include the way life is woven together by mobility practices, the way this experience affects life as a whole and the way spatial practices become embedded in space and vice versa.

Bibliography

Atkinson, P., Coffey, A. and Delamont, S. (1999) 'Ethnography: Post, Past, and Present', *Journal of Contemporary Ethnography* 28(5): 460–71.

Augé, M. (2002) *El Viajero Subterráneo: Un etnólogo en el metro*, Barcelona: Gedisa Editorial.

Benjamin, W. (1973) *The Flâneur. Charles Baudelaire: A Lyric Poet in the Era of High Capitalism*, London: New Left Book, pp. 35–66.

Benjamin, W. (2002) *The Arcades Project*, ed. R. Tiedemann, London: Belknap Press.

Bijoux, D. and Myers, J. (2006) 'Interviews, Solicited Diaries and Photography: "New" Ways of Accessing Everyday Experiences of Place', *Graduate Journal of Asia–Pacific Studies* 4(1): 44–64.

Bruner, E. (1986) 'Experience and Its Expressions', in V. Turner and E. Bruner (eds) *The Anthropology of Experience*, Chicago: University of Illinois Press, pp. 3–30.

Calle, S. (1998) *A suivre (Livre IV)*, Arles: Actes Sud.

Czarniawska, B. (2007) *Shadowing, and Other Techniques for Doing Fieldwork in Modern Societies*, Copenhagen: Liber.

de Certeau, M. (1986) *The Practice of Everyday Life*, London: University of California Press.

Dodman, D.R. (2003) 'Shooting in the City: An Autophotographic Exploration of the Urban Environment in Kingston, Jamaica', *Area* 35(2): 293–304.

Frisby, D. and Featherstone, M. (eds) (1997) *Simmel on Culture: Selected Writings*, London: SAGE.

García Canclini, N. (1997) *Imaginarios Urbanos*, Buenos Aires: Editorial Universitaria de Buenos Aires.

García Canclini, N., Castellanos, A. and Mantecón, A.R. (1996) *La ciudad de los viajeros: Travesías e imaginarios urbanos, México, 1940–2000*, Mexico: Grijalbo.

Geertz, C. (1986) 'Making Experience, Authoring Selves', in V. Turner and E. Bruner (eds) *The Anthropology of Experience*, Chicago: University of Illinois Press, pp. 373–80.

—— (1988) 'Being There', in *Works and Lives: The Anthropologist as Author*, Stanford: Stanford University Press, pp. 1–24.

Giddens, A. (1985) 'Time, Space and Regionalisation', in D. Gregory and J. Urry (eds) *Social Relations and Spatial Structures*, London: Macmillan, pp. 265–94.

Hägerstrand, T. (1970) 'What about People in Regional Science?', *Papers in Regional Science* 24(1): 7–21.

Hammersley, M. and Atkinson, P. (1995) *Ethnography: Principles in Practice*, London: Routledge.

Hannerz, U. (2003) 'Being There ... and There ... and There! Reflections on Multisite Ethnography', *Ethnography* 4(2): 201–16.

Harper, D. (2004) 'Wednesday-Night Bowling: Reflections on Cultures of a Rural Working Class', in C. Knowles and P. Sweetman (eds) *Picturing the Social Landscape: Visual Methods and the Sociological Imagination*, London: Routledge, pp. 93–114.

Harvey, D. (1989) *The Condition of Postmodernity: An Enquiry into the Origins of Cultural Change*, Oxford: Blackwell.

Heidegger, M. (1999) *Tiempo y Ser*, trans. M. Garrido, J.L. Molinuevo and F. Duque, 4th edn, Madrid: Editorial Tecnos.

Ingold, T. and Vergunst, J. (2008) *Ways of Walking: Ethnography and Practice on Foot*, Aldershot: Ashgate.

Jarvis, H., Pratt, A.C. and Wu, P.C.-C. (2001) *The Secret Life of Cities: The Social Reproduction of Everyday Life*, New York: Pearson Education.

Jirón, P. (2007) 'Unravelling Invisible Inequalities in the City through Urban Daily Mobility: The case of Santiago de Chile', *Swiss Journal of Sociology* 33(1) (special issue on Space, Mobility and Inequality): 45–68.

—— (2008) *Mobility on the Move: Examining Urban Daily Mobility Practices in Santiago de Chile*, PhD thesis, Geography and Environment in Urban and Regional Planning, London School of Economics and Political Science.

Johnston, R.J. (1981) *The Dictionary of Human Geography*, Oxford: Blackwell Reference.

Kusenbach, M. (2003) 'Street Phenomenology: The Go-Along as Ethnographic Research Tool', *Ethnography* 4(3): 455–85.

Kwan, M.P. (2002) 'Introduction: Feminist Geography and GIS', *Gender, Place and Culture* 9(3): 261–2.

Latham, A. (2003) 'Research, Performance, and Doing Human Geography: Some Reflections on the Diary–Photograph, Diary–Interview Method', *Environment and Planning A* 35(11): 1993–2017.

—— (2004) 'Researching and Writing Everyday Accounts of the City: An Introduction to the Diary–Photo Diary–Interview Method', in C. Knowles and P. Sweetman (eds) *Picturing the Social Landscape: Visual Methods and the Sociological Imagination*, London: Routledge, pp. 117–31.

Lenntorp, B. (1999) 'Time-Geography: At the End of Its beginning', *Geojournal* 48: 155–8.

Marcus, G.E. (1995) 'Ethnography in/of the World System: The Emergence of Multi-Sited Ethnography', *Annual Review of Anthropology* 24: 95–117.

Maspero, F.O. (1994) *Roissy Express: A Journey through the Paris Suburbs*, London: Verso.

Meth, P. (2003) 'Entries and Omissions: Using Solicited Diaries in Geographical Research', *Area* 35(2): 195–205.

Miller, H. (2005) 'Place-based versus People-based Accessibility', in D. Levinson and K.J. Krizek (eds) *Access to Destinations*, London: Elsevier, pp. 63–89.

Newsome, T.H., Walcott, W.A. and Smith, P.D. (1998) 'Urban Activity Spaces: Illustrations and Application of a Conceptual Model for Integrating the Time Space Dimensions', *Transportation* 25(4): 357–77.

Peuquet, D.J. (1994) 'It's about Time: A Conceptual Framework for the Representation of Temporal Dynamics in Geographic Information Systems', *Annals: Association of American Geographers* 84(3): 441–61.

Pred, A. (1996) 'The Choreography of Existence: Comments on Hägerstand's Time Geography and Its Usefulness', in J. Agnew, D. Livingstone and A. Rodgers (eds) *Human Geography: An Essential Anthology*, Oxford: Blackwell, pp. 636–49.

Rose, G. (1993) *Feminism and Geography: The Limits of Geographical Knowledge*, Cambridge: Polity Press.

—— (2001) *Visual Methodologies: An Introduction to the Interpretation of Visual Materials*, London: SAGE.

—— (2003) 'On the Need to Ask How, Exactly, Is Geography "Visual"?', *Antipode* 32(2): 212–21.

Seamon, D. (2000) 'Phenomenology, Place, Environment and Architecture: A Review', in S. Wapner, J. Demick, T. Yamamoto and H. Minami (eds) *Theoretical Perspectives in Environment–Behavior Research*, New York: Plenum, pp. 157–78.

Shaffir, W. (1999) 'Doing Ethnography: Reflections on Finding Your Way', *Journal of Contemporary Ethnography* 28(6): 676–86.

Shaffir, W.B. and Stebbins, R.A. (1991) 'Introduction', in W.B. Shaffir and R.A. Stebbins (eds) *Experiencing Fieldwork: An Inside View of Qualitative Research*, London: SAGE, pp. 1–24.

Simmel, G. (1969) 'The Metropolis and Mental Life', in R. Sennett (ed.) *Classic Essays on Culture of Cities*, New York: Appleton-Century-Crofts, pp. 47–60.

Small, K.A. (2001) *Urban Transport Economics*, London: Routledge.

Southall, H. and White, B. (2005) 'Mapping the Life Course: Visualising Migrations, Transitions & Trajectories'. Online: www.agocg.ac.uk/reports/visual/casestud/southall/introduc.htm (accessed 20 November 2009).

Spinney, J. (2007) *Cycling the City: Movement, Meaning and Practice*, PhD thesis, Royal Holloway, University of London, Department of Geography, p. 419.

Thrift, N. (2005) 'Torsten Hägerstrand and Social Theory', *Progress in Human Geography* 29(3): 337–40.

Wacquant, L. (2007) *Urban Outcasts: A Comparative Sociology of Advanced Marginality*, Cambridge: Polity Press.

Zimmerman, D.H. and Wieder, D.L. (1977) 'The Diary: Diary–Interview Method', *Urban Life* 5(4): 479–99.

4 Choreographies of leisure mobilities

Michael Haldrup

Dancing spaces

> Rather than ditching the methodological skills that ... had [been] so pain-
> fully accumulated, we should work through how we can imbue traditional
> research methodologies with a sense of the creative, the practical, and being
> with practice-ness.... Pushed in the appropriate direction there is no reason
> why these methods cannot be made to dance a little.
>
> (Latham 2003: 2000)

The ongoing 'mobility turn' in contemporary social science has in significant
ways emphasized the need for developing a repertoire of 'mobile methods'
capable of capturing social life 'on the move' (Urry 2007: 38; Büscher and Urry
2009 and Chapter 1, this volume). As new forms of corporeal, physical, imaginative, virtual and communicative travel (re)configure social and material
worlds, researchers in social and cultural studies have to rethink how to engage
in, capture, notate, analyse and (re)present the spatio-temporal rhythms that choreograph leisure and everyday mobilities.

In line with Latham's argument quoted above, this chapter argues that 'the
mobility turn' may benefit from the rich and heterogeneous heritage of methods
and approaches for capturing mobilities in relation to commuting, everyday life,
migration and so forth already developed in anthropology, sociology and human
geography (see Haldrup and Larsen 2009: 37–57). While focusing on the embodied mobilities of 'touring families' on holiday I will reflect on the use of 'time–
space diaries' as a method and source for uncovering the particular
choreographies or 'modes' of movement involved in performing tourism. More
specifically, I will discuss the inspiration that can be drawn from 'time-
geography' as a methodological framework for capturing and representing the
spatio-temporal rhythms of the everyday and explore how traditional methods,
rather than being ditched, might be made to dance together.

The metaphors of 'dance' and 'rhythmicity' have traditionally been popular
for grasping the performative and expressive aspects of embodied performances.
For social philosopher Henri Lefebvre, the rhythmical performances of music
and dance provided emblematic performances that pointed to a new, transdisci-

plinary science of 'rhythm-analysis'. By approaching the unfolding life of the everyday through engagements with the lived, sensed and perceived rhythms that orchestrate mundane lives and mobilities, Lefebvre argues that the 'rhythm analyst'

> not only observe[s] human activities he also hears … (in the double sense of the word: noticing and understanding) the temporalities in which these activities unfold. On some occasions he rather resembles the physician (analyst) who examines functional disruptions in terms of malfunctions of rhythm, or of arrhythmia.
>
> (Lefebvre 2004: 88)

By contrasting the various differences, changes and disruptions to movement, manners and habits as they emerge in the alternate rhythms of the 'most every-day' and the 'most extra-everyday', rhythm-analysis attempts to grasp the embodied and precognitive 'polyrhythmicity' of bodies, cities and societies. The same attention to rhythm and movement was also dominant in human(ist) geographer David Seamon's (1979: 54–5) notion of the 'place ballet', which was used to capture how places were constituted by routinized temporal and spatial habits in time and space (driving to work, picking up children and so forth):

> Basic bodily movements fuse together into body ballet through training and practice. Simple hand, leg and trunk movements become attuned to a particular line of work or action and direct themselves spontaneously to meet the need at hand. Words like 'flow' and 'rhythm' indicate that body ballet is organic and integrated rather than stepwise and fragmentary.
>
> (Seamon 1979: 55)

For both Lefebvre and Seamon, the advantages of the metaphors of rhythm, flow and dancing are that they help us to appreciate the iterative and precognitive character of the everyday. In doing this, they anticipate the role the 'dance' metaphor has had in contemporary theorizing of mobility, embodiment and space. In his history of mobility in the Western world, Tim Cresswell examines 'dancing' as an emblematic form of embodied mobility that illustrates how

> mobilities are produced in relation to other mobilities within particular contexts of meaning-making that enable and constrain particular practices of mobility. It delineates the geographical coding of movement types as correct and appropriate on the one hand and dangerous and threatening on the other.
>
> (Cresswell 2006: 128)

The example of dancing serves to show how mobile practices are policed, codified and choreographed at the same time as they can be mobilized as means of expression, improvisation and creativity; and how particular acts of dancing may be typified as either appropriate and correct or degenerate, potentially transgressive and threatening. Thus, dancing reveals particular normative geographies produced through complex embodied and representational processes (2006: 142). In doing this, dancing illustrates the tensions between regulation/choreographies and expression/performativity inherent in the field of mobilities.

While Cresswell mainly focuses on the representational processes and struggles related to interpreting and encoding the particular moves and movements of dance in the twentieth century, Nigel Thrift (2007) goes a step further in mobilizing the dance metaphor as a more general way of modelling and imagining the entanglements of performance, rhythms and time–space. According to Thrift: 'dance can sensitize us to the bodily sensorium of a culture, to touch, force, tension, weight, shape, tempo, phrasing, intervalation, even coalescence, to the serial mimesis of not quite a copy through which we are reconstituted moment by moment' (Thrift 2007: 140). To Thrift, 'dancing' exhibits and sums up a main point in 'non-representational' approaches to embodied movement and practice. As an ideal type of which all other types of embodied performance may be modelled, it illustrates how 'the body is not just written upon. It writes as well' (2007: 141). The dance, with its entanglements of discipline and creativity, improvisation and coded performances, focuses on the process of becoming and is therefore an improvisational process of touch with no real end-point.

The metaphors of rhythm and dance also figured strongly in the discussions surrounding the methodological development of 'time-geography' and, in what follows, I discuss the potential for mobilizing time-geography in studies of mobility, embodiment and spaces (see also Jirón, Chapter 3). I will do this through three short readings of 'time–space' diaries written by holidaying second-home tourists in Denmark. The first section uses the system of representation inherited from time-geography that might be translated into tourism and mobility studies. Using the vocabulary of time-geography I show how different everyday-life 'projects' manifest themselves in spatio-temporal 'paths' that can be depicted within three-dimensional 'dioramas'. The second section reinterprets these 'dioramas' as products of the social and cultural construction of leisure landscapes. Finally, the third section discusses how we may conceive of the temporalities and spatialities of tourists' corporeal mobility in terms of embodied and technologized performances.

Methods 'on the move' I: writing spaces

In many ways 'time-geography' grew out of the same concern for tracing the spatialities, temporalities and mobile 'biographies' of things, institutions and people that are also central in the turn towards mobilities. Among contemporary social theorists and analysts, 'time-geography' mainly received attention through Giddens' use of the method as an illustration of the profound situatedness of human interaction within everyday time–space contexts (see, in particular, 1984: 110–16). However, the recent acknowledgement of mobility, rhythm and embodiment in social theory also makes it interesting to take a look at the methodological framework of time-geography and its potential for mapping out life 'on the move'.

The main interest of time-geography was to map out the capabilities for and constraints on people's mobility within everyday life. By tracing out how mundane, routinized tasks (or 'projects') performed in people's everyday life took the form of temporal and spatial trajectories (or 'paths') within their daily activity spaces, Hägerstrand was able to examine the rhythms of work, social obligations and responsibilities, family life and the great variation (and often unequal distribution) of these. More broadly, Hägerstrand and his students also engaged with the flows and mobilities of personal life-time biographies, techno-logical innovations and even ecotopes. Throughout these different themes, the central concern was to track where bodies and things move, and develop an abs-tract notating system similar to the musical score – the 'diorama' (Hägerstrand 1982, 1983, 1984, 1985).

Although early time-geography did not engage much in studies of tourism, largely viewing it as an occurrence taking place outside everyday practices (Hall 2008: 25), it is interesting that in the only article addressing tourism, Häger-strand emphasized that time-geography's contribution to tourist studies might be to trace the rhythms and mobilities that connect tourism and the everyday and the sensuous geographies through which landscapes were encountered and per-ceived: 'Where leisure activities are concerned one may assume that questions of experience in all sensory dimensions, rhythmicity, enforced side effects because of chosen goals would all be of interest' (Hägerstrand 1984: 17). Research reported in *Performing Tourist Places* (Bærenholdt *et al.* 2004) used time–space diaries to identify how different time-geographical choreographies or 'modes of movement' were performed by second-home tourists on the Danish North Sea coast. Two types of time–space diaries were used. The first consisted of detailed registrations of the daily space–time budgets of the families through-out one week. Each day was divided into one-hour blocks, and the families were asked to record their activities and locations in each period. These time–space diaries helped to identify activity times and spaces as well as repetitions and rup-tures among these throughout each week. The second consisted of more open travel diaries for 11 families allowing thick descriptions of each day (see Bæren-holdt *et al.* 2004: 125–38 and Haldrup 2004 for details on methods and sample).

The space–time budgets showed major differences among the touring famil-ies, suggesting two typical mobility patterns among them tentatively named 'inhabiting' and 'navigating' modes of movement (Figures 4.1 and 4.2). Drawing on the conceptual framework of time-geography, it was furthermore observed that the different paths depicted in the dioramas below also express different projects for families' tourist performances.

Figures 4.1 and 4.2 show a time-geographical notation of the space–time cho-reographies of two tourist families in Northern Jutland. The dioramas depict the temporality (vertical axis) of spatial mobility (horizontal axis) centred on the families' stations (the summerhouses) during three days and shows major differ-ences in the domains of the families. While the paths of the navigating family (Figure 4.2) took them to three different countries, visiting virtually all possible major natural and cultural–historical attractions, the mobility paths of the

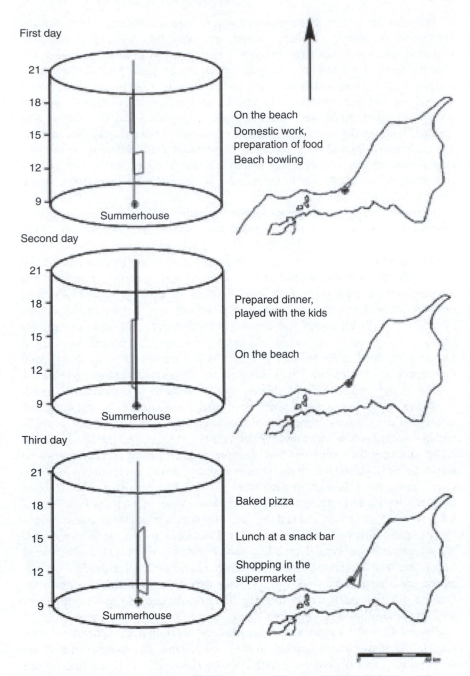

First day

21
18
15
12
9

Summerhouse

On the beach

Domestic work,
preparation of food

Beach bowling

Second day

21
18
15
12
9

Summerhouse

Prepared dinner,
played with the kids

On the beach

Third day

21
18
15
12
9

Summerhouse

Baked pizza

Lunch at a snack bar

Shopping in the
supermarket

Figure 4.1 Diorama of inhabiting families' time-geographical trajectories.

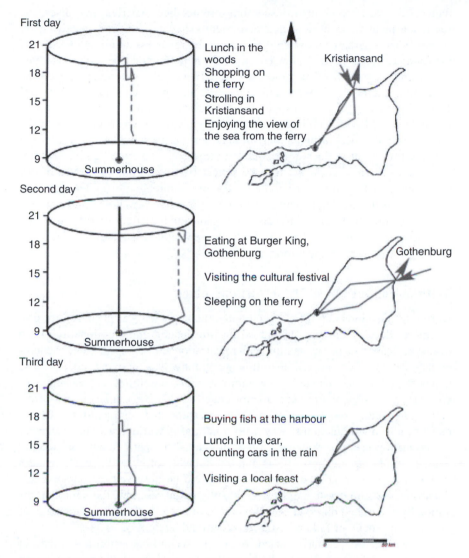

Figure 4.2 Diorama of navigating families' time-geographical trajectories.

inhabiting family (Figure 4.1) are hardly visible. Hence, the dioramas point out profound differences in the spatio-temporal mobilities performed by these families.

Löfgren (1999) suggests that the characters of Phileas Fogg and Robinson Crusoe metaphorically encapsulate two contradictory aspects of modern tourism. The first epitomizes the 'energetic and curious travellers who depart with the ambition to learn something, to widen their horizons'. The latter strive 'to create a utopian alternative to the humdrum of everyday life' (1999: 68). Whereas the flâneuristic Fogg represents a visual and disembodied experience of place, the Robinsonian quest is closely tied to the embodied use of, and practising of, space. What separates these two emblematic figures is essentially a question of the spatio-temporal rhythms they enact. To the hypermobile Fogg, space is transformed into a pattern of extraordinary attractions and sights emerging on the 'neutral' background of a web of meaning-less 'non-places' of movement (Augé 1995). Conversely, the Robinsonian tourist embarks on a project of creating a space for 'laid-back' mobilities, a deliberate slowing down of the pace of the normal everyday. Robinsonian tourism may be conceived not as an escape from home but for home, a quest for building a utopian 'home from home'. The dioramas depicted in Figures 4.1 and 4.2 reflect two such contradictory projects, expressions as they are of profoundly different choreographies. The tentative naming of the navigating and inhabiting modes of movement highlights manifestations of radically different projects of dwelling and travelling performed within the context of holidaying. This can be further elaborated if we turn to the more detailed diaries kept by the informants.

Methods 'on the move' II: performing place

During the development of time-geography, the approach was criticized for presenting a 'dead' geography devoid of the life, feeling and emotionality of the everyday. Due to its preoccupation with registration and representation, phenomenological observers argued that time-geography was drawing up a 'danse macabre', rather than capturing the improvisations, mobilities and meanings of the everyday. Hägerstrand later acknowledged the inherent antagonisms of his attempt to synthesize a humanist ambition to capture the complexities of everyday life in a non-reductionist way with a naturalist worldview. The system of representation used for drawing up the 'dioramas' of spatio–temporal mobility tended to hide the feelings, affects and emotionality of everyday performances rather than uncovering them, and in recollection he observed the paradox that the abstract notation system of time-geography might resemble the 'chilly observation by a detached observer, a hollow rattle of bones but no communication of the vibrating sound of full orchestra' (Hägerstrand 2006: xii).

In the 'time–space diaries' used to capture second-home tourists' mode of movement we observed that the diaries, rather than being unambiguous notes on time, position and activity (as requested by us in the written instruction), often included small memory notes on what to do the next day and reflections on the success and failure of those plans. There was much more to the accounts than simple reproduction of itineraries. Often the diaries ended up being a patchwork of children's drawings, mental maps and comments on disagreements within the family and so on (see Figure 4.3). In this way, the diaries enable us not only to trace the corporeal movement of people but also to examine the cultural categories and discourses through which their holiday experiences are filtered, reflected and made useful for future actions. This reading of the diaries refocuses the analysis on 'interpreted slices, glimpses and specimens of interaction that display

how cultural practices ... are experienced at a particular time and place by interacting individuals' (Denzin 1997: 247).

Thus, we may read the accounts in the pages of the 'time–space diaries' as
expressions of families' sense-making efforts; part of the work that people do to
establish realities, not mirror them or reporting them (Shotter 1993; Gergen
1994; Denzin 1997). From this perspective, the trajectories depicted in Figures
4.1 and 4.2 can be read as outcomes and effects of how families perform 'the
holiday'.

As Adler (1985, 1989a, 1989b) points out, deriving pleasure from movement
has always been a central part of performing tourism. Moreover, the particular
modes of movement are thoroughly inscribed with particular social and cultural
codes. Writing about the history of sightseeing, Adler observes that

> The traveller's body, as the literal vehicle of travel art, has been subject to
> historical construction and stylistic constraint. The very senses through
> which the traveller receives culturally valued experience have been moulded
> by differing degrees of cultivation and, indeed, discipline.
>
> (Adler 1989b: 8)

Following Adler, embodied mobility may be conceived of as a 'performed art'
with its own styles of relating to landscapes, sites and people encountered, perceived, experienced, made sense of and – in the end – enjoyed. Tourists' movements in space are not incidental but ways of encountering landscapes and places
through the deployment of various styles of movement. Tourists do not just
move through space; they navigate to find their way to a famous heritage sight,
the petrol station or a hamburger restaurant for a quick meal. They inhabit the
beach, the car and the cottage lawn and fill these places with social life and
meaning; they drift absentmindedly – open to the multi-sensual impressions
derived from the passing landscape – through the wood or along winding roads.
The two contrasting mobility patterns depicted in the dioramas (Figures 4.1 and
4.2) are manifestations of such particular styles or 'modes of movement'.

This can be further elaborated if we turn to the literature on the phenomenology of landscape, dwelling and practice which recently have problematized
the 'visual' reading of place and landscape (Wylie 2007: 153–4; Cresswell
2003). Ingold underlines the entanglements of people's paths and the performance of landscape and place, when he argues that '[t]here can be no places
without paths along which people arrive and depart; and no paths without places
that constitute their destinations and points of departure' (2000: 204). It is only
as people 'feel their way' through the world that it comes into being. Ingold
continues:

> Just as with musical performance, wayfinding has an essential temporal
> character ...: the path like the musical melody, unfolds over time rather than
> across space.... In music, a melodic phrase is not just a sequence of discrete
> tones; what counts is the rising or falling of pitch that gives shape to the

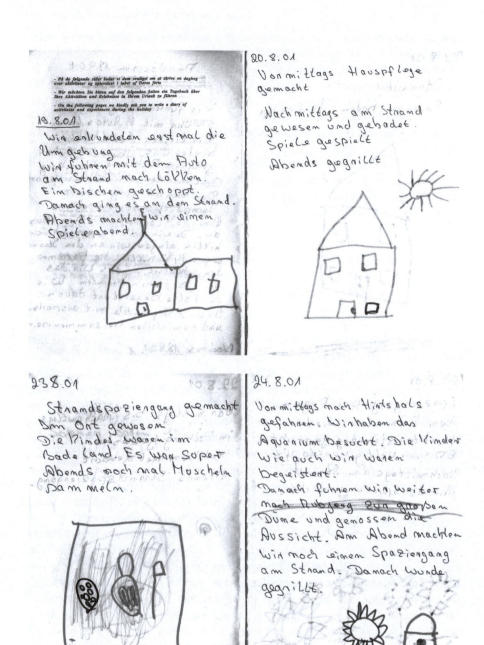

Figure 4.3 Pages from the time–space diary.

phrase as a whole. Likewise in wayfinding, the path is specified not as a sequence of point-indexical images, but as the coming-into-sight and passing-out-of-sight of variously contoured and textured surfaces.

(Ingold 2000: 238–9)

Places and paths are not reducible to points and trajectories in a generalized coordinate system, but produced through the embodied practice of particular modes of movement or 'wayfinding', each implying distinct temporalities and spatialities such as those of 'inhabiting' and 'navigating'. In the following I flesh out these contradictory 'logics' of inhabiting and navigating as they emerge in the diary pages of the respondents.

For the inhabiting family on holiday what matters is not seeing spectacular sights. Rather, it is the extraordinary ordinariness of personal social relations and the availability of spaces that afford such 'homely' relations and emotions to be performed that are central. 'To build is already to dwell', Heidegger has argued (2002: 348). This equation between building and dwelling also materialized in the diaries. One example are the frequent illustrations by children showing houses, trees and sun-drenched lawns (Figure 4.3), another is the account of how the social life in the holiday house is performed by taking possession of and inhabiting spaces and landscapes:

> Up for an early morning bath, at the beach all day, bathing, building castles in the sand, collecting mussel shells at the beach, the children tumbling around in the sand, had lunch on the beach. Walked to our house, decorated the house with shells and stones, played cards with the children.
>
> (German female, late 30s, travelling with spouse and son)

Building castles in the sand and collecting mussel shells and stones for decorating the holiday house are not only children's play, but a constructive effort to symbolically domesticate the stages of vacation; hence transforming the place of vacation into a home. 'My home is my sand castle', as Löfgren (1999: 231) sums up Robinsonian tourism. Tourist places are valued not for their immanent qualities, but for their ability to serve as landscapes in which the family can inscribe itself and its social roles. Such tourism practices construct hybrid landscapes of home and away:

> We arrived to [this place] where we have found out that we [had already been] 12–15 years ago too ... Here we found a lovely exclusive house, with small [private] dunes of its own just outside from where you can view the sea. The first road of course took us to the beach. Off with the shoes, and then off we went until we found a wonderful landscape of castles in the sand.
>
> (Dutch female, 50s, travelling with spouse, son and grandchild)

The joy of encountering exactly the house and the views anticipated is what triggers the mother to write this entry in the diary. The view of the house and the dunes immediately prescribe what should be done, and what path should be followed. The tracks of the family's taskscape are already laid out in the landscape in advance as 'the first outing took us to the beach', where the family comes across not an astonishing view, but a 'wonderful landscape of castles in the sand' – traces of already-anticipated holiday memories. For most tourists, the summer-house landscape of the Danish North Sea coast is well known as they have already holidayed here at some time in the past. It is a landscape invoking traces of emotions and associations to childhood memories, earlier vacations and so on.

In Figure 4.1 we see how the performance of inhabiting is inscribed in the diorama. Virtually all days are structured around a repetitive pattern with the holiday house as the hub. Time is spent together in the family, playing in the garden and preparing meals together, alternating with visits to the nearby beach or a crazy-golf course and, when necessary, a shopping trip for supplies to the nearest supermarket. The vacation is structured around activities in the immediate surroundings: the beach, the house and the lake. Each site constitutes the stage for a plurality of performances. Place is experienced as 'thick places' (Sack 1997): places to be inhabited and lived in. Hence, sequential clock time is dissolved into a flow of lived time. The spaces surrounding the holiday house of the family is primarily explored through long walks, jogging and biking in the woods or along the beach – laid-back mobilities that enable the visitor to become familiar with and domesticate the scene of holidaying. All activities unfold as part of the joint project of building a home for the imagined family. However, this project falls short if the place does not afford such 'home-making':

> In principle we like the house we have arrived at. Unfortunately, it's located directly on the main road to [a provincial town]. We are quite unhappy with these surroundings and I am quite surprised as I have been lucky to have enjoyed nice vacations in [other coastal regions in Denmark].
>
> We didn't find the track to the beach. Then we took the car. But we were rather frightened of all the cars we found there! What an odd thing to do!!! After having seen the beach we went back to our house and tried to make ourselves at home, moved the beds, found out that the key doesn't fit the kitchen door. Must call the agency tomorrow.
>
> (German male, 40s, travelling with spouse and son)

What makes up the disappointment of this family is first and foremost the unsuitability of the place to become a home. As the material spaces of the house and the beach turn into a hostile environment, the place loses its attraction. What we see here are the limits of the project of inhabiting: the symbolic significance of sites, landscapes and places inhabited are embedded in the particular narratives of the individual families and couples, their beings and doings, their project of home-making. If the place resists and does not allow for the construction of this imagined home, the project of 'inhabiting' falls short and the place loses its meaning.

While the performance of inhabitation of places draws its meaning through an annihilation of time through space, the picture changes when we consider how sightseeing trips are organized and planned, and rupture the laid-back mobilities discussed above. This rupture is not simply practical, but rather a shift between contrasting styles: different modalities. Rather than 'inhabiting' places, the practices related to sightseeing are defined through the point of arrival: the sites and spectacular places visited and (often) visually consumed. Thus, the point of a sightseeing trip is first and foremost about 'getting there', and the trick is to find one's way, that is, navigation through space. One family describes their first car trip around the region in the following way:

> Today the weather is not so that we necessarily have to stay on the beach. So this is a good opportunity for a sightseeing tour.
> After a shopping trip in Blokhus, we visited Blokhus-Candles where we had to fill up deposits with homemade candle-lights. Then we drove on the beach to Løkken ... and further we went – to Lønstrup. The visit to the lighthouse here and the cliffs around it is a 'must' for us. It is a good place for the children to run and climb the dunes, and Wolfgang documented the changes of the coastline since our last visit with photos and videocamera.
> (German male, late 30s, travelling with two daughters and son)

Navigating families appropriate the sites they encounter through a 'spectatorial gaze' (Urry 2002: 150) and often the trips are schematized (e.g. 'beaches', 'birds', 'collection of mussel shells', 'handicrafts'). Hence, they require serious planning and calculation of time. This even shapes the style of writing in the diaries, as the descriptions of the practice of navigating imply that the trip can be accounted for in points briefly summarizing the sites visited and the reasons for going there, as the following quotation indicates:

> We drove towards south-west: Slettestrand, Fjerritslev, Torup Strand and Bulbjerg [beaches and villages along the coast line]. If anything Slettestrand is boring. We inspected Han Herred Nature Center [Hands-on natural history museum], and found it very good and informative. Then we went further to Torup Strand, where we had the luck to see the arrival of fishing vessels, and how they were pulled upon the shore. Also here we bought fresh fish for our evening meal (fortunately we have a built-in refrigerator in our car). Finally we drove to the bird cliffs at Bulbjerg, which we inspected, from the upper side (among other things we spotted a gullery).
> (German male, late 30s, travelling with two daughters and son)

Plotting their route almost in the form of a travel guide, the diary of this family shows how they visit sites in order to 'inspect them', gain 'good and informative knowledge', 'spot' the local wildlife. Cars are not merely a means of transport and escape, but 'members of families' (Sheller 2004: 232–3), enabling gender and families to be performed, extending the capabilities of the family to track their way into unknown territory and encounter – to them – unknown or strange places. Through the car, the family may be transformed into an 'expedition group' finding their way, plotting the right course, navigating through space, classifying the sites encountered. To navigate means to depart from the well known and to set course towards points and places at which arrival is anticipated. It is as this objective is realized that the movement gains its meaning. Hence, navigation requires a rigorous organization of time and space, in which places to visit are planned in advance, possible routes considered, times of arrival scheduled. It involves a multiplicity of objects such as maps, clocks and guidebooks to provide images and knowledge against which the knowledge gained en route can be matched up. Movement is experienced on the map as well as through the landscape, and possible routes are being revised and reshaped when planned routes fail.

Places are appreciated for their immanent qualities as a source for edification. To see places is to learn from them, explore them and value them for what they are (or fail to be). Mobilities are tied to the significant and important points in space the path cuts through. The places visited are evaluated and explicitly judged according to how beautiful, boring or instructive they are. Navigation harbours a hypermobile urge. Movement is regarded as a practical problem of organizing time and space. Depending on the technological capabilities and planning skills of the family, the geographical trajectory can have a rather wide spatial horizon. Figure 4.2 maps the trajectory of a family with two teenage daughters navigating their way through their vacationscape. The trajectory also reflects that their explicit purpose is to go 'to explore the North', as they put it, and their choice of second-home residence is from the very start informed by these anticipations of exploring both Sweden and Norway. As such, the 'time-geography' depicted in Figure 4.2 can be seen as the outcome of an attempt to plan and schedule as many different place-encounters as possible. Eventually, their navigation collapses as they simply get lost on their way between two major sightseeing trips. The brief comments in the diary by one of the teenage daughters document this experience:

Day three:
10–11: Already in the car. On the way to Hjørring [provincial town]
11–12: Shopping in Hjørring (apparently there's some kind of party or festival there)
12–13: By car to Lønstrup – visiting the church [Mårup], having lunch in the rain
13–14: By car to Rubjerg Knude [cliffs at the edge of the sea] nearby
14–15: Walking, sand all over the place
15–16: In the car – driving
16–17: Drinking tea in the car, counting German and Danish cars (506). Location? Somewhere far away (not Rubjerg Knude)
(German teenage girl travelling with friend, one younger brother and parents)

Like 'inhabiting', the performance of navigating can meet its limits and eventually break down when a place no longer affords the project of family-making.

Whereas the project of inhabiting fails when the place does not afford home, the project of navigating dissolves when directions fail and routes are lost. As the teenage girl's account exhibits, such breakdowns enable a revision of routes and the modalities of movement used to perform them. Rain, loss of direction or antagonisms within the family may erode the project of navigating but may also enable alternative sensuous entanglements with space to emerge.

Methods 'on the move' III: entanglements of tourist space

The contradictory rhythmicities of inhabiting and navigating described in the two preceding sections can be easily inscribed in dioramas such as those in Figures 4.1 and 4.2. However, both modes of 'movement' contain moments of a third 'mode of movement' – the pleasure of movement itself; the pleasure of drifting: glancing at passing landscapes, sensing the kinaesthetics of corporeal movement or heading out into the unknown. Vision is an important, yet not exclusive way of sensing places. The sounds, odours and tactility of places are also qualities that constitute particular 'senses of place'. Hence, the haptic (touch, balance, kinaesthetics) and olfactory (taste, smell) senses are contributing to the particular sensuous geographies of tourist places and landscapes. Furthermore, places and landscapes are not encountered 'naked' but through a range of 'prosthetic' objects and technologies.

Visual technologies such as cameras are used not only to represent places and attractions, but also to choreograph and stage practices of family members and fellow travellers (Haldrup and Larsen 2003). Mobile technologies such as bicycles and cars are crucial not only to 'get around', but also to feel and discover landscapes and places encountered. Hence technologies, such as the ones mentioned, are central to the ways we grasp the world and make sense of it. They are decisive for how places are (and indeed can be) encountered, sensed and perceived (Haldrup and Larsen 2006).

One of the ambitions of time-geography was to examine the 'interpenetration of technology, society and landscape' (Hägerstrand 1983: 250). Hägerstrand explicitly advocates an approach to tourism mobilities that centres on the multisensuous and embodied aspects of mobility as central to how we encounter and perceive landscapes, and acknowledges that 'the geographical landscape is not just the visual landscape. It also contains the localised olfactory and tactile variables' (Hägerstrand 1984: 17).

However, these sensuous aspects of the geographies of landscape and mobilities disappear in the visual representation of bodies moving through three-dimensional space. As Gren (2001) observes, the problem did not rest with the physicalist worldview (and its alleged reduction of human life to the movements of dead bodies) but rather that it was never physical enough. By translating individual paths into an abstract, Euclidean time–space, landscapes and objects problematically emerge as a fixed and neutral background for people's trajectories through time and space. '[I]f corporeality is taken to its own limits', Gren argues 'it also implies that we are in fact dealing with multiple corporealities' (2001:

212). In effect, the time-geographical method hides sensuous geographies perceived and performed by the moving bodies (Rodaway 1994). In contrast to this, such 'geographies of bodily movement' (Cresswell 2006: 56) and sensuous, corporeal and kinaesthetic experience of the rhythms of mobility are voiced in the pages of the 'time–space diaries' as moments of intense joy, annoyance and excitement.

Such sensuous geographies of mobility show up in the accounts in descriptions of momentary incidents of intense joy in movement itself; of sensing the wind and the rain touching the skin; of the resistance offered by the dunes walked through or the hills conquered by bicycle. This pleasure of drifting is present in accounts dominated by the logics both of inhabiting and navigating. Motorized mobilities also produce such moments of pleasure. 'The thrill of racing in the car along the beach', or 'enjoying the view and the wind from the deck of the ferry' are statements that essentially give evidence to the same kind of pleasures as to 'run along the coastline': particular sites may even presuppose particular modes of movement to be enjoyed properly, as in this short excerpt from an account of a visit to the beach:

> Slept until 12. Got out of bed. Tried to find our way to the beach on our bikes. The sun was shining. Muttering over the cars, trying to figure out how many there were.* Back to the house.
>   Driving down the beach in the car ourselves. (see!)*
>
> (German male, 30s, travelling with spouse)

At this particular site one of the main attractions is to cruise the sands of the flat and broad beach. As this excerpt shows, this dominant way of domesticating the beach may impose problems on visitors trying to perform on the beach in other ways, for example, on foot or on bicycle. To this couple, the beach is not experienced as a joyful site until they have 'learned' to encounter it through the car. Through the car, sights, sounds, smells and bumps are transmitted to the driver and are added to soundscapes (radio, music) and the comfort of the car seat and the heating/cooling system. In so doing, the car itself becomes a central artefact for experiencing places, landscapes and sights. Like this, the time–space diary, in its reflections on mobile performances and sensations, also opens up for grasping the hybrid performance of driving/passengering 'in which the identity of person and car kinaesthetically intertwine' (Thrift 2004: 4). As the technologized and hybrid performance of mobility transform the driver-car (Dant 2004) into a multi-sensuous 'experience-machine', otherwise unreachable sensations come within reach.

Conclusion

In this chapter I have attempted a threefold reading of the legacy of time-geography and how people's mundane leisure mobilities are expressed in and can be traced through the use of time–space diaries. This has been done not so as to recapture the methodological merits of an already canonized tradition in human geography but rather to show how the current turn towards mobilities in the social sciences may benefit from earlier experiences with and ambitions to capture the mobile nature of much human life. Engaging with the performative aspects of time–space diaries provides an interesting way of uncovering how

> places are … distinctively constituted by a multitude of rhythmic constellations and combinations … In any space, the rhythms of a multitude of social actors … constitute space through their rhythmic and arrhythmic practices. And enduring, predictable, recognisable fixtures provide a backdrop to … flows of people and energy, further stabilising a sense of place through their rhythmic and arrhythmic practices.
>
> (Edensor and Holloway 2008: 48)

From a 'mobilities perspective' time-geography is interesting as a tool for capturing and representing the spatio–temporal performances and rhythms of the everyday.

First, it offers a system of representation that underscores the temporal rhythms embedded in space. Second, it opens up an understanding of the 'stylistic' and choreographic aspect of performances: to understand mobilities as performed rather than (just) movement, transport, dislocation of things and bodies. Third, it provides a view of bodies and mobilities as technologized and material. Thus, time–space diaries, together with a variety of other methods such as participant observation 'on the move' and multi-site ethnographies of people and things in motion (Haldrup and Larsen 2009: 37–57; Jirón, Chapter 3), may provide a repertoire of mobile methods to explore 'geographies of rhythm' (Mels 2004), uncovering the overlapping rhythmicities of leisure and the everyday performed through mundane mobilities.

This chapter has used the rather 'conventional' and mundane example of car-based sightseeing by second-home tourists for discussing how we might remake time-geography rather than ditch its methodological heritage. But why stop by observing the mobilities of moving bodies? Corporeality, space and embodiment are performed through a variety of mobile objects and systems. The 'everyday ballets' of mundane everyday life are not only performed through series of relatively 'simple hand, leg and trunk movements' (Seamon 1979: 55). The 'dancing spaces' of contemporary 'mobile worlds' (Urry 2007) are populated by bodies whose mundane performances on the 'floor' are orchestrated by a polyphony of rhythms emerging from mobile objects, text messages, phone calls, images, other bodies in motion, and so on. Here, the time–space diary method provides an interesting approach that enables analysts to map out mobile worlds as well as explore the meanings attached to various mobilities and, in doing this, uncover how mundane and leisure mobilities are choreographed, sensed and made sense of.

Bibliography

Adler, J. (1985) 'Youth on the Road: Reflections on the History of Tramping', *Annals of Tourism Research* 12: 335–54.

—— (1989a) 'Travel as Performed Art', *American Journal of Sociology* 94: 1366–91.

—— (1989b) 'Origins of Sightseeing', *Annals of Tourism Research* 16: 7–29.

Augé, M. (1995) *Non-Places*, London: Verso.

Bærenholdt, J.O., Haldrup, M., Larsen, J. and Urry, J. (2004) *Performing Tourist Places*, Aldershot: Ashgate.

Büscher, M. and Urry, J. (2009) 'Mobile Methods and the Empirical', *European Journal of Social Theory* 12: 99–116.

Cresswell, T. (2003) 'Landscape and the Obliteration of Practice', in K. Anderson, M. Domosh, S. Pile and N. Thrift (eds) *Handbook of Cultural Geography*, London: SAGE, pp. 269–81.

Cresswell, T. (2006) *On the Move*, London: Routledge.

Dant, T. (2004) 'The Driver-Car', *Theory, Culture & Society* 21(4–5): 61–79.

Denzin, N. (1997) *Interpretive Ethnography*, London: SAGE.

Edensor, T. and Holloway, J. (2008) 'Rhythmanalyzing the Coach Tour', *Transactions of the Institute of British Geographers* 33: 483–508.

Gergen, K.J. (1994) *Realities and Relationships*, Cambridge, MA: Harvard University Press.

Giddens, A. (1984) *The Constitution of Society*, Cambridge: Polity Press.

Gren, M. (2001) 'Time-Geography Matters', in N. Thrift and J. May (eds) *Timespace: Geographies of Temporality*, London: Routledge, pp. 208–25.

Hägerstrand, T. (1982) 'Diorama, Path and Project', *Tidjskrift vor Economische en Soziale Geografie* 73: 323–39.

—— (1983) 'In Search for the Sources of Concepts', in A. Buttimer (ed.) *The Practice of Geography*, London: Longman, pp. 238–56.

—— (1984) 'Escapes from the Cage of Routines: Observations of Human Paths, Projects and Personal Scripts', in J.R. Long and R. Hecock (eds) *Leisure, Tourism and Social Change*, Edinburgh: Conference proceedings, pp. 7–18.

—— (1985) 'Time-Geography: Focus on the Corporeality of Man, Society and Individuals', in S. Aida (ed.) *The Science and Praxis of Complexity*, New York: United Nations University, pp. 193–216.

—— (2006) 'Introduction', in A. Buttimer and T. Mels (eds) *By Northern Lights*, Aldershot: Ashgate, pp. xi–xiv.

Haldrup, M. (2004) 'Laid Back Mobilities', *Tourism Geographies* 6(4): 434–54.

Haldrup, M. and Larsen, J. (2003) 'The Family Gaze', *Tourist Studies* 3: 23–46.

—— (2006) 'Material Cultures of Tourism', *Leisure Studies* 25(3): 275–89.

—— (2009) *Tourism, Performance and the Everyday*, London: Routledge.

Hall, C.M. (2008) 'Of Time and Space and Other Things: Laws of Tourism and the Geographies of Contemporary Mobilities', in P.M. Burns and M. Novelli (eds) *Tourism and Mobilities: Local-Global Connections*, Wallingford: CABI.

Heidegger, M. (2002) 'Building Dwelling Thinking', in *Basic Writings*, London: Routledge, pp. 347–63.

Ingold, T. (2000) *The Perception of the Environment: Essays in Livelihood, Dwelling and Skill*, London: Routledge.

Latham, A. (2003) 'Research, Performance and Doing Human Geography: Some Reflections on the Diary–Photograph, Diary–Interview Method', *Environment and Planning A* 35(11): 1993–2018.

Lefebvre, H. (2004) *Rhythmanalysis*, London: Continuum.
Löfgren, O. (1999) *On Holiday: A History of Vacationing*, Berkeley: University of California Press.
Mels, T. (2004) 'Lineages of a Geography of Rhythms', in T. Mels (ed.) *Reanimating Places: A Geography of Rhythms*, Aldershot: Ashgate, pp. 3–45.
Rodaway, P. (1994) *Sensous Geographies*, London: Routledge.
Sack, R.D. (1997) *Homo Geographicus*, Baltimore: Johns Hopkins University Press.
Seamon, D. (1979) *A Geography of the Lifeworld*, London: Croon Helm.
Sheller, M. (2004) 'Automotive Emotions', *Theory, Culture & Society* 21(4–5): 221–42.
Shotter, J. (1993) *Constructing Life through Language*, London: SAGE.
Thrift, N. (2004) 'Driving the City', *Theory, Culture & Society* 21(4–5): 41–59.
—— (2007) *Non-Representational Theory*, London: Routledge.
Urry, J. (2002) *The Tourist Gaze*, 2nd edn, London: SAGE.
—— (2007) *Mobilities*, Cambridge: Polity.
Wylie, J. (2007) *Landscape*, London: Routledge.

5   Mobilities of welfare

The case of social work

Harry Ferguson

The emergence of a social science of mobilities has begun to increase understandings of the centrality of movement to everyday life. This is perhaps most obvious with respect to large objects that occupy public space, such as the car and the aeroplane and institutions such as airports (Adey 2009). There is a need to open up all sites, places and social practices 'to the mobilities that are already coursing through them' (Sheller and Urry 2006: 209) and to examine how new systems of mobility, such as information technology, the mobile phone and so on are impacting on them. One such site that I focus on in this chapter is the welfare state. The ways in which most if not all welfare policies and practices are designed and delivered presupposes elements of movement and non-movement. The ambulance is perhaps the exemplary object that embodies the necessity of movement and speed to promoting the safety and well-being of citizens. The hospital to which ambulances bring patients is clearly a solid structure, a building, which contains people who are, by definition of being ill, required to lie still in their beds, to be immobile. Yet in other respects hospitals are full of movement, of bodies being transported on trolleys to operating theatres, different wards, even ultimately to morgues; of staff moving around with differing degrees of urgency, be it rushing to emergencies or attending with a calm 'bedside manner' to the needs of a patient; of medicines travelling from pharmacies to wards and into patients, and blood flowing in similar ways. Hospitals embody the complex relationships between static, fixed, solid structures (walls) and constant movement ('traffic') that flows into them and goes on within them, that is typical of welfare institutions.

Beyond the fixed structures of enclosed institutions like hospitals, other welfare services are even more profoundly shaped by movement because the service is delivered in the community or home of the service-user/patient. Community nurses, for instance, work from the organisational base of clinics and make daily rounds of home visiting for which they have to carry medicines and the tools of their trade with them in their cars. The pervasiveness of movement to these practices means that researching welfare through a mobilities paradigm can provide new understandings of what these practices are and new theoretical insights into the nature of movement and non-movement in everyday life.

I shall make this argument and explore the contribution that mobile research methods can make to welfare by focusing on social work. Social work is a mobile practice in how home visits are required to establish the safety and well-being of children and the needs of frail, unwell or vulnerable adults. This involves moving to and from the office and the service-user's dwelling, journeying, usually, in a car. When in the service-user's home, negotiation goes on about where the professional may sit or stand, their right to move around and inspect the home should the level of risk justify it, whether other people can be present, be they moving through the home or stationary, and what should be done about the distractions from images and information flowing in from the TV, radio, mobile phones and the Internet. The car which transported the worker there is not only a vehicle that enables professional and service-user to meet, but in which direct work with clients goes on when they are being transported and in which social work supervision goes on when managers accompany front-line staff on difficult visits. The organisational base of social work, be it the office, clinic or hospital is also a site of mobile practices, as service-users travel there for interviews, other professionals visit for meetings, and information flows into the organisation through the Internet, telephone and so on. Social work exemplifies how welfare practices involve an intimate engagement by the (mobile) body with time and space, as workers move in and out of public organisations and the private domain and lives of service-users, all of which requires an understanding of the complex relationship between mobilities and immobilities.

Yet the mobile nature of social work and welfare practices (such as health visiting and community nursing) has been overlooked in theoretical work, accounts of practice and policy analysis. The literature lacks context as to how and where practice is actually performed on the key sites of the organisation/ office, car and home (visit). As Hall and Slembrouck (2009) have recently argued, there has been a remarkable absence of empirical work that has sought to observe worker–service-user communication. The mobility of human bodies, information and objects such as cars are ignored and practices are framed in sedentary ways and treated as though they are static. A mobilities approach, on the other hand, seeks to capture the 'flow' and 'flux' of these practices in movement (Urry 2007).

If the mobile nature of social work and welfare practices are to be accounted for and theorised, it is crucial that research methods are developed that can describe and analyse their mobilities and immobilities and get to the heart of what these practices are and how and where they are performed, capturing what gets done and experienced through their movement and stasis. The aim of this chapter is to contribute to the development of mobile methods for researching welfare's (mobile) practices. It begins by considering the origins and nature of social work as a mobile practice. It then shows how research has, or more to the point has not, addressed the mobilities of welfare and goes on to outline some mobile methods for the study of social work and welfare practices.

The emergence and development of mobile social work

In order to make the case for the development of mobile methods in social work it is necessary to first demonstrate the mobile forms that these practices take. The nature of social work and welfare practices today are inconceivable without the culture of the car and other socio-technological developments, which have transformed capacities to reach vulnerable people and provide services.

At the outset of their work in the 1870s and 1880s, social workers, in child protection for instance, used their legs, horse-drawn carriages and transport on trains to reach children. There are many moving accounts in the case records of the time of workers literally running while carrying dying children to places of safety (Ferguson 2004: 30–3). Yet the practice was a relatively static affair in that the technology did not exist to get them around more quickly or more extensively to outlying areas. Social workers in the UK began using the bicycle in the late 1890s, and in 1900 it was noted that increases in child-cruelty cases were 'partly owing to the provision of a Cycle for the Inspector, who has thus been enabled to visit Rural Districts otherwise less accessible' (STAR 1900: 14). Despite this increased mobility, the reach of practice remained local and its tempo slow. The motorcycle was in general use in social work by the 1930s and dramatically increased not only the reach of practitioners but the speed with which they could get to see their clients. The car had been commercially available from early in the twentieth century, most famously from the US production line of Henry Ford. In the UK the systematic use of the car in social work is evident from the 1950s, and it was the transport development which really transformed practice. It gave practitioners a new flexibility and autonomy to move (at speed) when and as they pleased according to their own timetable as it separated social work from the train timetable or waiting for a horse-drawn cab (on this formulation, cf. Urry 2007: 112). From the outset the car afforded new opportunities to transport people and objects and to help people in very practical ways, such as helping poor families move home and providing furniture for them. In addition to increasing its coverage and speed, the car opened up new dimensions to human relations in social work. For instance, social workers discovered through experience that the car was a place where children made disclosures about things they did not discuss elsewhere, a point I shall return to below. Car use is now central to social work and the need to travel faster and more often has arisen in part from the emergence of new knowledge about risk, especially since the 1970s when physical child abuse and the prevention of death became the central preoccupation of social work and protecting children quickly took on even more urgent meanings (Ferguson 2004).

Alongside the expansion of the capacity of social work to be mobile and reach its clients quickly came a focus on the home as the key site where casework needed to go on. Up to the late nineteenth–early twentieth century the primary strategy for reforming offending parents was to send them to prisons while their children went into temporary care. From early in the twentieth century imprisonment of parents virtually ceased and 'supervisions' focused upon the family home became the core methodology of social work. This shift fits with that identified by Foucault as being central to the creation of modern practices like social work, which he refers to as 'the movement from one project to another, from a schema of exceptional discipline to one of a generalized surveillance' (Foucault 1977: 209; Healy 2000). However, the solid language of 'surveillance' and conceptions of power which Foucault and his followers use is inadequate for a mobile sociology of welfare practices, implying as it does rigid structure and control in the community in a manner that mirrors the control possible in prisons and other total institutions. A modern form of social work practice took shape here, which, far from the implied solid, sedentary and literally confined 'gaze' of the total institution, was essentially mobile in nature. The very core of social work was now constituted by home visits and what practitioners were able to achieve through them, while being *mobile*. Seeing service-users required leaving the office, making a journey and entering their communities and homes to gain snapshots of their lives for relatively brief periods. The form that late-modern social work takes must be understood in terms of a *flow* of mobile practices between public and private worlds, organisations and service-users, the office and the home, at the heart of which is the sensual body of the practitioner on the move (Ferguson 2008).

In recent decades the organisation of social work within the welfare state has become highly sophisticated and delivered through huge bureaucracies. Social workers have been severely criticised by the media, politicians and held to public account for failures to prevent children who were known to be at risk from dying from child abuse. As a result risk-aversion has entered the system and managerialism and proceduralisation have increased with the effect that practitioners have to spend more time at their desks and computers filling in standardised forms and accounting for what they do and less time with service-users than was historically the case (Broadhurst *et al.* 2009; Garrett 2004; Munro 2004; Parton 2006; Webb 2006). This changing organisational landscape has led scholars to focus on the immobile features of social work, with an emphasis on the sedentary practitioner seated at her desk. This perspective has produced important insights into how the pressures to follow government-imposed targets and bureaucratic processes leads to practitioners having to take shortcuts in the amount of time and thought they can give to casework and developing relationships with vulnerable service-users (Broadhurst *et al.* 2009). But social work's core requirement to go on the move to fulfil its aims remains fundamental, for without it the protection of vulnerable children and adults cannot occur. While some interviews take place in offices, clinics and hospitals, social workers have to base their assessments on observation of naturally occurring activities that fundamentally go on in the home, such as parent–child relationships, and the home is so often a central reason why social workers are involved at all, such as when there are concerns about child neglect due to poor 'home conditions', or in assessing frail elderly people's capacities to live at home safely. A key aim of the mobile sociology of welfare and the development of mobile methods is to provide ways for researchers to go with the flow and produce new understandings of what social workers do when they leave their desks; when they go on the move.

Mobilising research into social work

What then would a mobile social science of welfare practices consist of? How might it be done? What would its key concerns be? Urry defines the term 'mobilities' as referring to a 'broad project of establishing a "movement-driven" social science in which movement, potential movement and blocked movement are all conceptualized as constitutive of economic, social and political relations' (Urry 2007: 43). Applied to welfare practices the key research questions that follow from this include: When and how do professionals move? Where do they move? When should they move and when do they not move when they should and why? What is the relationship between movement and non-movement, mobility and immobility? When can it be said that practitioners have not moved enough, or moved in the wrong way, or even moved too much? As I shall show, some answers lie in how social work always involves *potential* movement, as mobility does not always happen when it should, when movement is blocked and fails to occur and professionals do not move towards service-users such as children to establish their well-being by properly seeing, touching, hearing and walking with them.

While there is now a significant research literature on social work, little attention is given in it to the mobile forms the work takes, and practitioners' (mobile) experience of doing the work. This I believe has its roots in the sedentarist metaphysics (Cresswell 2006: 26) and static conception of theory that dominates social policy and social work. But it is also due to the ethical and practical sensitivities of researchers needing to gain prior informed consent from service-users to research their lives and finding ways of getting close enough to social worker–service-user encounters to be able to see first hand and record what is happening, without negatively affecting what are invariably already challenging enough situations for workers and service-users to manage. To get round this, researchers have relied heavily on interview methods which provide retrospective accounts of what happened during interventions, while ethnographers have mostly gathered data by observing what goes on in the office. Forrester *et al.* (2008) observe that the use of retrospective interviews limits the ability of studies to comment on how social workers achieve what they say they do. For this reason, what social workers, parents and others claim happened is unlikely to be accurate (Forrester *et al.* 2008: 25). To try to overcome this they used vignettes of simulated situations as prompts to explore social work skills, asking social workers how they would respond. Forrester *et al.*'s focus was on talk, and the skills social workers use to respond to client's speech. This takes research beyond the limitations of asking social workers what they say they said when they were with service-users to exploring with them what they would say in particular situations. While this research produced important insights, as Forrester *et al.* observe, an important limitation of the vignette approach is that the simulations cannot be considered reliable data on what actually happens in practice (Forrester *et al.* 2008: 26). To access the latter I am arguing we need also to devise ways of expanding the repertoire of skills and conception of practice under analysis to include not only talk but consideration of action in the sense of whether and how social workers move, walk around and inspect homes, how they relate to adults and to children, whether (and where) they interview, touch or examine them to ensure they are safe.

This kind of inquiry into the mobile, lived experience of practice is the terrain of ethnography; however, even most ethnographic studies are focused solely on participant-observation of what goes on in the office and analysing the occupational culture and how social workers talk about their clients (Pithouse 1998; Scourfield 2003). Or this has been done in tandem with interviewing service-users about their experience of the service (Buckley 2003). In some exceptional studies researchers have left the office and accompanied social workers and health visitors in their work (Dingwall *et al.* 1983), or used their own experience, including of home visiting, as data (de Montingy 1995). These studies are not only dated, the core issue is that systematic attention has not been given to the core mobilities of welfare practices and social workers' experiences of doing the work, such as home visiting. This is no mere oversight that can be corrected for by bolting some attention to movement onto what is known about what goes on in the office. We need to go much further than that and nothing less than a fundamental reformulation of the social science of welfare is needed to account for how mobility shapes social practices (Urry 2007; Adey 2009).

The car is central to the mobilities of welfare practices, yet the range of meanings and practices that go on in it has also been virtually ignored in research. In a study of how social workers and counsellors experienced and managed fear in their work, Smith (2003) found that their cars had huge significance for them as a 'secure base' to return to following interviews with violent, aggressive, intimidating clients. While Smith did not set out to research the role and meaning of the car, so many of his respondents raised it that the power of automobility in welfare practice was inescapable. Jerry Floresch's (2002) research into the practices of social workers who work with people with mental-health problems is exceptional for how it places the car at the heart of the analysis. He calculates the huge amounts of driving American workers have to do, travelling to get to see their service-users and in transporting them to various appointments. The car was experienced both as a source of freedom and security for workers (both physically in separating them from danger and economically in terms of mileage allowances) and as a place of danger because of how it places worker and client so close together in an enclosed space. Workers spoke of their extreme discomfort with the smell of clients who had neglected themselves and with managing manoeuvres like having to try to avoid touching their knee when changing gears. But it was valued as space for casework, both in therapeutic dialogue that went on and in practical ways such as when workers got service-users to fill out forms while they drove them to appointments. The car was vital as a tool for assisting in the social inclusion of clients whose car-less-ness reflected their powerlessness and marginality (Floresch 2002).

For the most part, then, ethnographies of social work have provided partial accounts of what these social practices are by applying immobile office-based methods to its mobile practices, neglecting to go with the flow by studying it in the various sites beyond the office within which it goes on. This has also meant that the flows and flux of the relationships between the sites of the office–car–home visit have been under-recognised, -researched and -theorised.

Moving scenes from social work

Research into the mobilities of welfare needs itself to be mobile by conducting ethnographies that focus on observing the actual (mobile) practices involved. I shall outline in more detail the mobile methods involved. But first I want to consider the important role that library-based research and discourse analysis has to play here. Analysis of key public policy texts using a mobilities perspective is important in showing how policy, theory and knowledge have presented one-dimensional static interpretations of practices, which are misleading because of the absence of attention to the mobilities involved. A good example is inquiry reports into the deaths of children who were known to be at high risk of abuse, but whose deaths were not prevented. These texts do give some attention to the complexities of the movement and non-movement involved in (not) keeping them safe. They are replete with examples of families who avoided the services by going on the move, and accounts of where social workers and other professionals missed opportunities to do more to protect children while being in the same room as them in hospitals and offices and on home visits. But while described, the meanings and implications of these instances in terms of where they occurred and why and the mobilities involved are not adequately examined.

A telling example of this occurred in the case of a child from London who has come to be known as 'Baby Peter'. Peter died aged 17 months, with over 50 injuries on his body. He was known to have been physically abused in the past and he and his siblings were neglected. Serious consideration had been given to taking the children into care, and frequent announced and unannounced home visits were made by social workers. The family had some 60 contacts with social work, health and police during Peter's life. The inquiry report into why Peter was not protected includes the following scene:

> On 30 July 2007 all the children were seen on a planned home visit by the social worker on their own and with Ms A (Peter's mother). Peter was in the buggy, alert and smiling but overtired. His ear was sore and slightly inflamed. He had white cream on the top of his head and Ms A thought the infection had improved. Peter's face was smeared with chocolate and the social worker asked that it be cleaned off. The family friend took him away to do so and he did not reappear before the social worker left. Ms A said she

had a GP appointment and mentioned grab marks on Peter. She was worried about being accused of harming him.

(Haringey 2009: 13)

Three days later Peter was dead. Given the extent and severity of the injuries he had at the time of his death, which appears to have been caused by assaults incurred both before and after the social worker last saw him on the above occasion, he was carrying serious injuries at times when in the presence of professionals, but these were missed. We now know that the chocolate was deliberately placed on the child's face by his mother and her cohabitee and another man who were abusing Peter to conceal injuries. The presence of men in the home was kept hidden by his mother. In the above scenario the family friend was set up to not return the child in order to conceal his injuries. This typifies the problems professionals face in accessing children within the home and how in such cases the children's bodies have been covered up and moved about by parents and carers in tactical ways to conceal their injuries. The same happened to professionals. Parents have manipulated the placement of their bodies within rooms or on doorsteps to prevent them from properly seeing, touching, listening to or talking with injured children (for instance, London Borough of Brent 1985: 125–6). Professionals have effectively been rendered immobile, stopped from moving.

Key research questions to emerge from such scenarios are what would it have taken for that social worker to have walked across the room to properly see, touch, hear and examine the child, and to have insisted on looking around the home, including in the bathroom and bedrooms, steps which could have revealed the presence of men's residence in the home through shaving gear, toothbrushes and so on? There has, since the earliest days of child protection at the end of the nineteenth century, been a tradition of this kind of deeply investigative approach to child protection that probes into the most intimate parts of family's lives (Allen and Morton 1961), but clearly in this case, it was not followed. But because home visiting has been so neglected in research we have no systematic knowledge about how typical the absence of such an investigative approach is in practice. How could the professional have overcome the immobilisation that was occurring by firstly becoming aware of it and then by moving – quite literally – to a position of mobile practice which would have brought her into direct contact with the child and the reality of who was living in the home in a manner that could have resulted in their protection? These questions can only be adequately framed in the first place through the increased awareness of the centrality of movement provided by a mobilities perspective. And they can only be adequately answered through the use of social theory and research methods, which incorporate a mobile dimension (Ferguson 2009a).

The social worker would probably have felt significant anxiety and fear, and such feelings would have contributed to a freezing of the body which is part of what immobilises workers. Yet little attention has been given in research or policy to the depth of the feelings being experienced. Policy texts and much academic work ignore these emotions and practice is represented as though social workers just have to make their minds up rationally to do something and have an intention to engage directly with the child and get on with it. A triumph of rationality over emotion, mind over body is expected, indeed demanded. This constitutes a way of seeing welfare practice in terms of a linear model of cause and effect. Mobilities research, on the other hand, seeks to develop a theory of practice based on understandings of the contingencies that arise from the inter-connections between flows of bodies, information, organisational life and prac-tices. The 'lived body' (Merleau-Ponty 1962) needs to be (re)inserted into understandings of welfare practices. This means focusing on 'the recentring of the corporeal body as an affective vehicle through which we sense place and movement, and construct emotional geographies' (Sheller and Urry 2006: 216).

Following Ingold, the world of welfare practice needs to be viewed through the feet and not (just) the head. Social science, he argues, is 'head over heels' in that it biases what is 'seen' through the eyes, ears and the mind and ignores or downplays touch, the feet and lower body. What is needed is:

> a more literally *grounded* approach to perception [which] should help to restore touch to its proper place in the balance of the senses. For it is surely through our feet, in contact with the ground (albeit mediated by footwear), that we are most fundamentally and continually 'in touch' with our surroundings.
>
> (Ingold 2004: 330; see also Ingold 2000)

A core task of mobilities-aware research into welfare practice is to deepen under-standings of how the body and mind of the practitioner moving into the lives and (domestic) spaces of the other is affected by the visceral experience of doing the work, and how the senses and emotions impact on perception and workers' and service-users' capacities to relate to one another. A fundamental concern is with how the spaces within which practice goes on (such as the home) are used and moved within by service-users and how the (professional) body moves through those spaces, or becomes immobilised and fails to move (enough). Mobile research methods need to produce 'emotional geographies' (see Bondi *et al.* 2006) of welfare practices like social work, which cover all the sites on which it operates: the office, clinic, car, street, café, community centre and the home visit.

Researching social work's mobilities

I will now consider in more detail the form that mobile methods can take in researching welfare mobilities. I will include in this some observations from my recent experience of working with social work teams to capture the mobilities in their work. This must inevitably be partial due to limitations on space and the fact that the work is in progress and I am not yet in a position to report findings in any systematic form. To capture the mobilities of social work and welfare practices it is necessary to go with the 'flows' of how the practices are routinely enacted. Researchers need to shadow practitioners, following in their footsteps on the walks, drives and any other (mobile) ways in which social work is done. This means following the practitioner as she leaves the office, makes a journey by car or on foot, walks to the doorstep and (tries to) gain access to the service-user's home, walks into and within the home, and then leaves and does the return journey. The guiding methodological practice is for the ethnographer to particip-ate in patterns of movement, and observe and interview people preferably during it, or afterwards, or both. 'Mobilised ethnography' (Sheller and Urry 2006) involves participation in the 'natural' work that goes on, including patterns of movement as well as stillness while conducting ethnographic research. The basic idea is that 'the researcher can be co-present within modes of movement and then employ a range of observation, interviewing, and recording techniques' (Sheller and Urry 2006: 218).

Kusenbach (2003) describes this kind of method as a hybrid between partici-pant observation and interviewing and refers to it as the 'go-along'. To go-along in research means to accompany the subjects of research wherever they go that is relevant to the concerns of the study. The two main types are 'ride-alongs' (on wheels) and 'walk-alongs' (on foot). Kusenbach distinguishes 'go-alongs' from the technique of 'hanging-out' with many or all informants. The difference lies in the relatively static nature of 'hanging-out', when researchers study their sub-jects in a single or limited number of locations. This may include some move-ment along with them, but not necessarily systematic attention to the differing spaces and sites to which they go and the travel/movement/linkages between them. The key distinction is between studies of the social organisation of bounded settings – for example, as in the classic school ethnographies, asylums, or hospital emergency rooms – and the study of social phenomena, such as social work practice, that are by their nature spread over a number of locales and the spaces between them. Going-along enables the active exploration of research subjects' streams of experiences and practices as they move through, and inter-act with, their physical and social environment. The ethnographer is able to observe their informants *in situ* while accessing their experiences and interpreta-tions at the same time (Kusenbach 2003: 463). Such an approach fits with Marcus' (1998) influential work, which argued for a shift from participant obser-vation on one bounded site to multi-sited research, and ethnographies that can account for different places and the interconnections between them. The researcher then follows mobile bodies and objects through multiple sites.

Gaining full access and getting into the service-user's home with the profes-sional is the ideal. However, as I remarked earlier, just how far it is permissible for the researcher to go in observing the professional–service-user encounter is influenced by research ethics. Service-users must give consent to being researched, which means that it is only legitimate to enter the service-user's home on pre-announced visits with social workers once consent has been gained. This limits the reach of research into practice in situations where social workers are calling unannounced and are not expected or where they are expected and it is seen as potentially harmful or disruptive to the welfare of the service-user and the work on the case to have another person present.

When present at worker–service-user encounters, beyond participating in the civilities of everyday encounters, the researcher must remain a silent, passive observer, and the obvious benefit of being there is to be able to see, hear, smell and feel what goes on. This provides invaluable data on which to base subsequent interviews with the worker about their experience and why they did and said what they did, their feelings at the time and so on. Gathering the data through the use of audio and/or visual recording of the sessions should be considered and how advantageous that can be depends in some measure on what the research questions are. If the purpose is to analyse the talk and discourses produced by workers and service-users then the use of audio recordings is clearly very important (Hall and Slembrouck 2009). If it is to consider the unspoken as much as the spoken, like body use and placement and how physical movement occurs – such as did the worker look around the home, at what point did they do so, how did they make the request, if and how did they physically engage with the children, and so on – then producing visual recordings would be very useful. There is, however, great value in the researcher just observing (and making detailed field notes) and fewer risks involved in not using technology that is very obvious and which may be experienced by service-users and workers as intrusive and inhibiting.

Whether the researcher has been able to observe the actual worker–service-user encounter or not, the best time to do the research interviews is during the journey to the home before the visit occurs and as soon after the encounter has occurred as possible. This increases the depth that the inquiry can reach into the lived experience of the worker because that experience is alive for the worker on the way to the visit (they are literally working) and once they have stepped out of the visit the experience remains alive within them (and for the researcher if they were present at the casework). It is this 'aliveness' and closeness to the experience that enables this method to go beyond the limitations of studies based on retrospective accounts to comment on how social workers achieve what they say they do.

When the journeying to visits and back to the office is done in the practitioner's car my experience is that it provides a remarkably productive space for research. First, because the worker is going about their business, one is observing and discussing with them what they would be doing anyway, giving vital access to a key dimension of the work. There is huge scope for the development of research into welfare practice in cars using visual and audio methods to record how professionals and service-users relate to one another. Laurier et al.'s (2008) study of driver–passenger interactions in cars shows that driving and passengering are skilled social accomplishments. While a great deal of the time their research subjects spent in the car involved doing nothing extraordinary at all, the car was also a place where matters of life, love and death were discussed, intimate disclosures occurred and interpersonal support was given. Apart from the obvious differences between the car and other meeting places (such as clients' homes and interview rooms), social work in the car is qualitatively different from that undertaken elsewhere. This difference resides in three main areas: the reasons for and meanings of journeys in welfare (such as transporting an elderly person to new accommodation, or a child into care, or to an access visit with a parent); the effects of being in movement and the distractions and engagements and 'pause-ful' reflective conversation this enables (Laurier *et al.* 2008); and how seating arrangements and body placement in the car level-out power relations between professional and service-user and create trust and intimacy (Ferguson 2009b). As a consequence of these factors, service-users often disclose personal things they may not reveal elsewhere. As a social worker in my current study expressed it with regard to trying to work with young people:

> Well sometimes they won't engage, so if you can, kind of, pick them up from school in the car and maybe drop them home they might be more likely to … it's kind of a way of getting in isn't it? It can be quite a good time to talk things through as well.

These dynamics which influence disclosures in cars also occur in researcher–professional encounters during research interviews and research needs to take advantage of the opportunities that arise on 'ride-alongs' (see also Sheller 2004).

Compared to doing retrospective research interviews a considerable time after the event (days, weeks, even months, as happens), I have found that greater depth occurs even where I have remained outside, sat in the worker's car while they are inside the home. This is borne of the shared experience of going along and journeying together, discussing with the worker what their aims and expectations are and feeling the anticipation and emotions – very often rising tension – as the visit approaches and being able to see, hear and smell the kind of environment external to the home that the work is being done in and capturing glimpses of what might lie behind the door of the home. I have watched from a distance while workers have approached the front gate to be met by as many as three large dogs barking and aggressively trying to get at them.

In home-visiting work there is always significant walking to be done, even if the worker travels to the visit by car, and this tends to be around disadvantaged public places, having to negotiate unpleasant smells, poor lighting, aggressive dogs, human and animal excreta, as well as actual threats from service-users and/ or other residents. This means that social work involves walking in an atmosphere of tension and sometimes menace, pervaded by uncertainty, anxiety, fear and adventure. I have been struck by how deeply physical and emotionally demanding the work is even before the worker gets to meet the client and the extent to which even getting to the doorstep of the home where the service-user is often involves workers taking significant risks. I have accompanied social workers on foot along inner-city streets where they cannot drive for fear that their car will be damaged or stolen and they may be assaulted in the process, and to high-rise housing blocks where the level of danger they feel is such that they will not agree to leave their car and walk up to the flat unless a family member comes down to meet them and escorts them up the stairs/lift to the family home. Being with workers and interviewing them while they are having these kinds of experiences provides the basis for exploration of what effects these journeys have on their encounters with families in their homes and the demands made on practitioners' personal resources and capacities to perform and protect vulnerable people.

As I have been emphasising, highly consequential movements (and non-movements) take place in the service-user's home and a fundamental aim of mobile methods must be to document this. The journey back to the office or to the next home visit, be it on foot or in the car, is the ideal time and place to conduct the research interview about the worker's experience of the home visit. I have argued elsewhere that an important theoretical starting point for mobile research into social work and other welfare practices is an understanding that walks and other movements that are undertaken in the home are not the same as movements performed in other places, such as the street, the social work office, hospital ward or clinic. This is because of the nature and meanings of homes to those who reside in them, the (re)actions of those service-users who live in them to being visited and professionals' relationships to the service-users and experiences of their homes (Ferguson 2009a). Homes are complex spaces which carry deep meanings associated with intimacy and privacy which impinge on how freely professionals feel able to move in them, to directly engage with a child or check whether men/fathers are resident there, the condition of the children's bedrooms and so on. Home visiting is a deeply tactile, sensual experience, and research needs to explore the feelings that arise from bodily engagement with the homes and lives of others, especially when dirt and foul smells are present, as they so often have been and are in neglect cases (Ferguson 2004). Ingold (2007) refers to how walking outdoors is *enwinded*, meaning that it is inseparable from direct experience of the weather and fresh air. Pathways get formed through the interaction of (wet) weather and the impact of footprints repetitively made on the earth. Walks in service-users' homes go on in quite different enclosed environments characterised by the absence of (fresh) air and where there are no established pathways for practitioners to follow. It is the family's air, their atmospheres that must be breathed in by workers and the path that casework takes is always deeply influenced by the condition and reactions of service-users. A crucial yet neglected (or avoided) reason why professionals have failed to get close to and protect abused children is because of perceptions of their diseased condition and feelings of disgust, with a resulting professional avoidance of touch. The Baby Peter example discussed above is a tragic example in that, in the last days of his life, despite all the concern there was about injuries to him and his marked face being smeared with chocolate, not only did the social worker not touch him, but a paediatrician and a GP did not touch him or examine him either.

It is vital that research explores the full range of emotions and embodied experiences involved in welfare practice, including the meanings and problematic nature of touch. To fully capture this, interview methods can usefully incorporate attempts to access the unconscious dimensions of experience and (in) action and produce narratives which enable research subjects to bring to mind their primitive fears (of contamination, for instance) and what they are avoiding in the context of enquiring into their emotional and embodied experiences (Holloway and Jefferson 2000; Cooper and Lousada 2005). There are, of course, significant ethical issues at play here in terms of when it is legitimate and safe to touch a client, especially when it is a child. But in my experience of interviewing workers about how or if they move around the home to engage in tactile (or other) ways with children, there is significant variation in approach. Some do sometimes, some never do. Some regard it as a cultural thing ('We English are not comfortable with touching'), others as determined by character and personal preference ('I'm not a tactile kind of person'). This shows how mobile-oriented research must go beyond the movement of wheels and legs to include the entire body and the use of the arms and hands (see also Lewis 2001). Such an embodied research approach is crucial to clarifying what the norms and patterns of current practices are, providing for an assessment of their effectiveness and helping to reveal the enablers and barriers workers experience in performing the necessary movements which promote welfare and protect vulnerable citizens.

Conclusion

I have argued in this chapter that if we are to produce more accurate understandings of welfare practices it is crucial that we conceive of them as they are practised: on the move. This does not, of course, mean ceaseless movement. There is always a relationship between movement and non-movement, mobilities and immobilities, flows and flux (Adey 2006, 2009). I have shown how social workers move in a number of ways and the importance of these movements to protecting vulnerable children and adults. But there are times when social workers need to be still, such as when seated and listening attentively to their service-users, tuning in to their needs. Being seated at a desk/computer and keeping case records is also a requirement of good practice. Establishing how mobilities and immobilities shape welfare practices and the legitimacy of when movement and non-movement occur and how one affects the other needs to be at the heart of research into welfare. While I have focused on some of the dynamics of how mobile practices occur on different sites of practice – the office/organisation, the journey and the home visit – although analytically distinct, in practice they are all interconnected and what goes on at each site influences the other. Research needs to explore what are the organisational conditions that best promote the skill and ability of welfare practitioners to move? In social work this would include, for instance, enquiring into the presence of staff supervision and whether it gives workers the space to think about and discuss their bodily experience. The use of mobile research methods can produce the kind of movement-driven knowledge which can deepen understandings of the dynamics of relationships with service-users and how free or constrained professionals feel to move around and take control of encounters and what can immobilise them in performing the movements that are essential to doing effective welfare work.

Bibliography

Adey, P. (2006) 'If Mobility is Everything Then It Is Nothing: Towards a Relational Politics of (Im)mobilities', *Mobilities* 1: 75–94.
—— (2009) *Mobility*, London: Routledge.
Allen, A. and Morton, A. (1961) *This is Your Child: The Story of the National Society for the Prevention of Cruelty to Children*, London: Routledge & Kegan Paul.
Bondi, L., Davison, J. and Smith, M. (eds) (2006) *Emotional Geographies*, London: Ashgate.
Broadhurst, K., Wastell, D., White, S., Hall, C., Peckover, S., Thompson, K., Pithouse, A. and Davey, D. (2009) 'Performing "Initial Assessment": Identifying the Latent Conditions for Error at the Front-Door of Local Authority Children's Services', *British Journal of Social Work* 40(2): 352–70.
Buckley, H. (2003) *Child Protection Work: Beyond the Rhetoric*, London: Jessica Kingsley.
Cooper, A. and Lousada, J. (2005) *Borderline Welfare: Feeling and Fear of Feeling in Modern Welfare*, London: Karnac.
Cresswell, T. (2006) *On the Move: Mobility in the Modern Western World*, London: Routledge.
de Montigny, G. (1995) *Social Working: An Ethnography of Front-Line Practice*, Toronto: University of Toronto Press.
Dingwall, R., Eekelaar, J. and Murray, T. (1983) *The Protection of Children: State Intervention and Family Life*, Oxford: Basil Blackwell.
Ferguson, H. (2004) *Protecting Children in Time: Child Abuse, Child Protection and the Consequences of Modernity*, Basingstoke: Palgrave.
—— (2008) 'Liquid Social Work: Welfare Interventions as Mobile Practices', *British Journal of Social Work* 38(3): 561–79.
—— (2009a) 'Performing Child Protection: Home Visiting, Movement and the Struggle to Reach the Abused Child', *Child & Family Social Work* 14(4): 471–80.
—— (2009b) 'Driven to Care: The Car, Automobility and Social Work', *Mobilities* 4(2): 275–93.
Floresch, J. (2002) *Meds, Money and Manners: The Case Management of Severe Mental Illness*, New York: Columbia University Press.
Forrester, D., McCambridge, J., Waissbein, C. and Rollnick, S. (2008) 'How Do Child and Family Social Workers Talk to Parents about Child Welfare Concerns?', *Child Abuse Review* 17(1): 23–35.
Foucault, M. (1977) *Discipline and Punish: The Birth of the Prison*, Harmondsworth: Allen Lane.
Garrett, P.M. (2004) 'Social Work's "Electronic Turn": Notes on the Deployment of Information and Communication Technologies in Social Work with Children and Families', *Critical Social Policy* 24(4): 529–53.
Hall, C. and Slembrouck, S. (2009) 'Communication with Parents in Child Welfare: Skills, Language and Interaction', *Child and Family Social Work* 14(4): 461–70.
Haringey (2009) *Serious Case Review, Baby Peter, Executive Summary*, Haringey Local Safeguarding Board. Online: www.haringey.gov.uk/childa.htm.

Healy, K. (2000) *Social Work Practices: Contemporary Perspectives on Change*, London: SAGE.

Holloway, W. and Jefferson, T. (2000) *Doing Qualitative Research Differently*, London: SAGE.

Ingold, T. (2000) *The Perception of the Environment: Essays on Livelihood, Dwelling and Skill*, London: Routledge.

Ingold, T. (2004) 'Culture on the Ground', *Journal of Material Culture* 9: 315–40.

Ingold, T. (2007) 'Footprints through the Weather World: Walking, Breathing, Knowing', unpublished paper, via personal communication.

Kusenbach, M. (2003) 'Street Phenomenology: The Go-Along as Ethnographic Research Tool', *Ethnography* 4(3): 455–85.

Laurier, E. *et al.* (2008) 'Driving and "Passengering": Notes on the Ordinary Organization of Car Travel', *Mobilities* 3(1): 1–23.

Lewis, N. (2001) 'The Climbing Body, Nature and the Experience of Modernity', in P. Macnaughten and J. Urry (eds) *Bodies of Nature*, London: SAGE.

London Borough of Brent (1985) *A Child in Trust: Report of the Panel of Inquiry Investigating the Circumstances Surrounding the Death of Jasmine Beckford*, London Borough of Brent.

Marcus, G.E. (1998) *Ethnography through Thick and Thin*, Princeton: Princeton University Press.

Merleau-Ponty, M. (1962) *Phenomenology of Perception: An Introduction*, London: Routledge & Kegan Paul.

Munro, E. (2004) 'The Impact of Audit on Social Work Practice', *British Journal of Social Work* 34: 1075–95.

Parton, N. (2006) *Safeguarding Childhood: Early Intervention and Surveillance in a Late Modern Society*, Basingstoke: Palgrave Macmillan.

Pithouse, A. (1998) *Social Work: The Social Organisation of an Invisible Trade*, Aldershot: Ashgate.

Scourfield, J. (2003) *Gender and Child Protection*, Basingstoke: Palgrave.

Sheller, M. (2004) 'Automotive Emotions: Feeling the Car', *Theory, Culture & Society* 21(4–5): 221–42.

Sheller, M. and Urry, J. (2006) 'The New Mobilities Paradigm', *Environment and Planning A* 38: 207–26.

Smith, M. (2003) 'Gorgons, Cars and the Frightful Fiend: Representations of Fear in Social Work and Counselling', *Journal of Social Work Practice* 17(2): 154–62.

STAR (1900) *Stockton and Thornaby Branch NSPCC, Annual Reports*, London: NSPCC Archives.

Urry, J. (2007) *Mobilities*, Cambridge: Polity.

Webb, S. (2006) *Social Work in a Risk Society*, Basingstoke: Palgrave.

6 Connectivity, collaboration, search

Jennie Germann Molz

To reflect on mobile methodologies is to reflect on movement, in its various forms, not only as an object of knowledge, but also as a mode of knowing. In the Introduction to this volume, Büscher *et al.* remind us that the interlinked practices of investigating mobilities and mobilizing research techniques are 'not just about how people make knowledge of the world, but how they physically and socially make the world through the ways they move and mobilise people, objects, information and ideas'. Central to moving, knowing and making the world are the various technologies that mobilize people, objects and ideas, mediate social lives on the move, and at the same time enable new research techniques for investigating these emerging mobile phenomena. Like mobility, these new technologies constitute both an object of knowledge and a way of knowing that 'makes the world' in particular ways. What kind of world does mobility make, and make knowable? The aim of this chapter is to explore the terms of this performative relationship between mobility, technology and knowledge.

The empirical context for this discussion is the burgeoning trend of interactive travel, a mode of leisure travel that I have been studying for the past several years. Whereas researchers have studied business travellers' use of mobile technologies in relation to knowledge management and knowledge production (Holly *et al.* 2008; Jemielniak and Kociatkiewicz 2008), less attention has been paid to the way leisure travellers use mobile technologies as a way of creating knowledge and negotiating on-the-road 'know-how'. Leisure travellers are increasingly using mobile technologies such as laptop computers, MP3 players, GPS devices and mobile phones to research and plan their trips, network with other travellers, share advice and record, photograph and publish their experiences for the Internet public. The result is a proliferation of online travel blogs, networked backpacker communities, mobile travel guides, hospitality networking sites, travel discussion boards and the digital sharing of videos and photographs from travellers' journeys. These online social interactions also spill over into face-to-face encounters and physical places as interactive travellers search out a hostel recommended on a discussion board, crash on the actual couches of hosts they meet online, or take an urban walking tour narrated on their mobile phone.

The interactive travellers I focus on in my research are a diverse and loosely defined group of leisure travellers from several countries, including Australia,

Canada, Ireland, New Zealand, Norway, Poland, the United Kingdom and the United States. Many of these interactive travellers are young backpackers travelling the world during a gap year or on an early sabbatical from their careers. Others are recent retirees and some are families taking a year off from work and school to travel. While the travellers in my study are certainly not homogeneous in their backgrounds nor in their activities and attitudes towards travel, what they do have in common is their location at the intersection between corporeal and virtual movement. These travellers are not only physically on the move, but are constantly moving among overlapping virtual, imaginative, communicative and corporeal spaces of social interaction. And to a certain degree, I move with them, virtually travelling along by following their blog updates, watching the videos they post online, interacting with them via email and discussion forums, and meeting up with them in person. Like most mobilities researchers, my field site is thus multiple, fluid and shifting, constituted at the places where online, on-the-phone and face-to-face socialities intersect with the technical materiality, visual and narrative representations and embodied practices of interactive travel.

Studying social relations and mobility practices at this intersection raises some complicated methodological problems that require us to reflect on how interactive travel is implicated in a broader paradigm constituted by the relationship between mobility, technology and knowledge. What assumptions about knowledge, technology and mobility underpin mobile methodological approaches? And how, in turn, do these approaches engender particular knowledges, especially when the social phenomena under investigation – mobility and technology – are at the same time epistemological practices? I address these questions from two directions. First, I briefly trace the evolution over the past several decades of a special relationship between mobility and knowledge. This relationship has tended to focus on knowing and moving as solitary practices, an emphasis that I argue is now shifting towards more social modes of creating knowledge through mobility. Second, I consider these questions from the perspective of interactive travellers. If one of the drivers of tourism is a thirst for knowledge, as Crang (1997) has argued, then how are interactive travellers seeking and producing knowledge at these intersections between virtual and physical mobilities? In particular, I focus on three strategies that interactive travellers invoke to produce and legitimate knowledge: connectivity, collaboration and the algorithmic logic of search. As I will describe below, travellers make sense of their online practices and mediated social interactions through a matrix of electronic and social connectivity. This connectivity, in turn, allows them to collaborate with friends, family members and other travellers to manage, search and distribute knowledge about travel and about the world. I conclude by asking what mobilities researchers might possibly learn from the way interactive travellers produce knowledge in a mobile, mediated and networked social world.

Mobility and knowledge

Mobilities researchers who engage mobility not just as an object of knowledge, but also as a way of knowing, implicate themselves in an already complex historical narrative of mobility and knowledge. Since Herodotus, 'travel has been pursued for the sake of knowledge' (Adler 1989a: 1382). Consider the way travellers, theorists and philosophers alike have conferred movement with epistemic possibility:

> Travel provides food for the mind.
>
> (Thomas Cook, cited in Brendon 1991: 31)

> Up there [in an airplane] one is, as it were, suspended from earthly cares. Looking down from above the clouds one cannot avoid thinking.
>
> (Rojek 1993)

> Journeys are the midwives of thought.... Of all modes of transport, the train is perhaps the best aid to thought.
>
> (de Botton 2002)

> Travel and change of place impart new vigor to the mind.
>
> (Seneca, cited in Gmelch 2004: 1)

In this section, I briefly trace the way this relationship between mobility and knowledge has evolved especially, but not exclusively, within the context of travel and tourism in a way that has privileged solitary travel as a path to knowledge.

In her historical account of the emergence of touristic sightseeing, Adler (1989b) traces the way travel practices have been historically intertwined with ways of knowing the world, developing from the pursuit of intellectual discourse and educational improvement in the sixteenth and seventeenth centuries to an emphasis on scientific discovery in the eighteenth century to the eventual rise of modern sightseeing as a way of knowing and mastering the world. Adler describes in detail how travellers in the sixteenth and seventeenth centuries were advised to seek out wise interlocutors and engage in scholarly discourse as a way of knowing the world and cultivating a worldly self. By the late seventeenth century, however, travel writers began to emphasize seeing rather than speaking and listening as the best way of apprehending the world. During this period, travellers were engaged in the broader ethos of scientific inquiry that marked European societies in this era. Their sightseeing ventures involved collecting, categorizing and reporting on a variety of natural, cultural or architectural objects. Tourists faithfully recorded their observations to be delivered back home to scientific societies or published in scientific journals as part of a collaborative project to compile a 'universal history' and comprehensive accounting of the observable world, a point I will return to later.

The product of these tourists' efforts was predicated on what Adler refers to as 'an epistemological individualism'. The belief that seeing could produce a 'direct, unmediated, and personally verified experience' encouraged 'every man to "see", verify, and, in a sense, "create" the world anew for himself' (1989b:

11). Individual eyewitness became a superior way of accessing knowledge about the world. By the end of the eighteenth century, the emphasis on visuality was again redefined as the traveller's eye was cultivated as an instrument of aesthetic discernment rather than scientific reporting. Adler tells us that by this time, travellers emphasized the private, spiritual and emotional aspects of visuality. Travelling was still seen as a way of knowing the world, but sightseeing was no longer a public and emotionally detached form of objective appropriation. Instead, it was an avenue towards passionate engagement with sights and landscapes with a special emphasis on the individual traveller's spiritual experience. Thus, as travel moved from a scientific to an aesthetic appropriation of the world, 'sightseeing became simultaneously a more effusively passionate activity and a more private one' (1989b: 22). In other words, as travelling, seeing and knowing were becoming increasingly conflated projects, so too were they becoming increasingly solitary experiences.

While Adler's historical account is usually characterized as a genealogy of sightseeing – indeed, her key aim is to historicize the otherwise naturalized association of tourism with sightseeing – her analysis can also be read as a genealogy of the relationship between tourism and the production of knowledge. She argues that evolving tourist practices must be understood as part of the historical development of 'orientations toward the problem of attaining, and authoritatively representing, knowledge' (1989b: 8). In the 1980s and early 1990s, around the same time that Adler published 'Origins of Sightseeing', a similar convergence of moving, seeing and knowing became discernible in critical theory's privileging of a kind of 'intellectual nomadism' (Pels 1999: 63).

Notable in much of the writing of this time, including, among others, Said's 'travelling theory' (1983) and 'reflections on exile' (1984), Clifford's notion of theorizing as 'leaving home' (1989), Deleuze and Guattari's 'nomadic thinking' (1980) and Chambers' claims that thought 'wanders' and 'migrates' (1994), were emerging celebrations of the creative and intellectual productivity of movement, exile and homelessness. Within this discourse, mobile figures such as the *flâneur*, the exile, the stranger, the nomad and the traveller epitomized the modern condition, with travel providing 'some critical distance from which to better understand the world' (Oakes 2006: 238). Claims to the intrinsically mobile character of thinking thus legitimated the conflation between moving and knowing, imbuing the conditions of nomadism, travel, homelessness and exile with intellectual connotations (Pels 1999).

This discourse of nomadism has been subjected to intense criticism, not least for its tendency to elide the historical, cultural and geographical specificity of the mobilities and knowledges it aims to recuperate metaphorically (Kaplan 1996; Pels 1999; Jokinen and Veijola 1997). These critiques provide a much richer and more nuanced evaluation of this literature than I can address here, but what I do want to point out is the extent to which this association of moving and knowing idealizes the solitary traveller represented by the figures of the *flâneur*, the exile or the refugee. Just as Adler's historical account of tourism indicated that sightseeing became more personal and individualized by the eighteenth century, the critical theory outlined here bears out a similar atomization of the solitary-traveller-as-intellectual. As Kaplan notes, Said's 'Reflections on Exile', in particular, ultimately privileges 'a mystified figure – the solitary exile' (1996: 120); a figure that, as Said puts it, 'carries with it ... a touch of solitude and spirituality' (cited in Kaplan 1996: 120). In these discourses, creativity, knowledge and theory stem from estrangement, solitude and singularity – being 'existentially alone' (1996: 28).

These theorists have developed a richly compelling model of the relationship between knowing and moving that I find useful for understanding how interactive travellers engage in the production of knowledge while on the road. However, I want to contrast the solitary project described in these discourses with a more social and collaborative logic that I see emerging in practices of contemporary interactive travel. While many travellers in my study express a desire to travel alone or get away from it all, what is also evident, and in some ways more explicit, is the way interactive travellers engage mobile information and communication technologies in order to stay in touch and remain embedded in social networks while on the move. This emerging logic of mobility and knowledge revolves not around a solitary traveller, but around mobilizing a social network and knowledge community. I find this *social* logic behind mobility and knowledge intriguing, in part because of the rich collaborative and technologically mediated model it suggests for researchers developing mobile methodologies. In the following sections, I elaborate the way moving, knowing, networking and interacting coalesce in interactive travel around three important modes of knowledge production: connectivity, collaboration and search.

Connectivity

New mobile technologies keep travellers connected and linked in to their social networks in unprecedented ways. Even while they are physically on the road, interactive travellers are moving through complex digitally connected geographies of email, websites, social networking sites, discussion boards, podcasts, mobile applications and ubiquitous computing. In fact, the possibility of constant connectivity poses a threat to the modernist project of solitary travel or 'finding oneself' on the road and sceptics wonder whether young travellers are sacrificing authentic experiences by staying in constant touch with friends and parents back home (Murphy 2009). This anxiety is borne out of the discourses described earlier, in which knowing the world or the self is achieved through detachment and solitary mobility. But in the context of interactive travel, instant access and constant contact become the very basis for producing knowledge. As interactive travellers navigate through – and indeed produce – this digitally connected environment, they evoke connectivity as a way of making sense of their online presence and their interactive practices and as a foundation for the other strategies of knowledge-production – collaboration and search – that I will discuss later.

By sharing stories and photos in their blogs, exchanging information online and staying in touch with friends and family, travellers create what Bach and

Stark (2004) refer to as 'incipient knowledge communities'. In their analysis of non-governmental organizations' use of new interactive technologies, Bach and Stark argue that the adoption of new interactive technologies is not just an opportunity to work faster or more efficiently, but actually 'restructures interdependencies, reshapes interfaces and transforms relations' through which knowledge is produced (2004: 101). Mobile knowledge communities are premised on electronic connectivity, fluid networks and deliberative collaboration rather than conventional hierarchical models of information diffusion. The political aims of the non-governmental organizations in Bach and Stark's study may be quite different from the motivations behind interactive travel, but there is a similar impulse towards creating loosely integrated mobile knowledge communities through connectivity and interactive technologies. In contrast, then, to images of the solitary traveller freed (or stripped) of the banal rituals, obligations and commitments of social life, interactive travellers remain embedded in their social networks via digital technologies and electronic connections.

Over the past decade or so, the significance of connectivity within interactive travel has evolved from a primarily technical matter to a metaphor for networked and mobile sociality. When tech-savvy travellers began to publish travel diaries online in the mid-1990s, their websites were as noteworthy for the technical accomplishment they represented as for their content or layout. These travel blogs (although the term 'blog' had not yet entered the common lexicon) were more than travel diaries online; they were instantiations of the immediacy and interactivity of the Internet. In the early days of Internet connectivity and online publishing, the mere fact of being able to upload a website and communicate with a remote audience while travelling around the world was itself a remarkable feat. One of the first live travel blogs to appear online, 'A Hypertext Journal' posted in 1996 by digital artists Nina Pope and Karen Guthrie, was launched with the explicit goal of experimenting with new interactive technologies that allowed the travellers to stay connected while on the road.

Initially, interactive travellers saw connectivity as an end in itself, as evidenced by journal entries detailing the technological challenges of rigging electrical outlets to power up computers or splicing phone lines to get a modem connected. Travellers' online exchanges of information and advice about how to upload and maintain websites while on the road and in remote locations simultaneously positioned connectivity as an object of knowledge, as a means of sharing knowledge and as proof of technological know-how. Today, the proliferation of Internet cafés, wireless hotspots, free user-friendly travel-blog templates and photo-sharing sites has made connectivity somewhat less remarkable. As cheaper, easier and more reliable mobile and wireless connections have normalized ubiquitous access to the Internet, interactive travellers tend not to express the same sense of wonder and accomplishment over logging on to the Internet. Nevertheless, interactive travellers continue to create knowledge *about* connectivity, often on travel discussion boards where they debate over the best gadgets to pack, share advice on how to upload blog posts from a mobile phone or, as in a recent discussion thread titled 'It's 2008 people – how's the wi-fi out there?', canvass fellow travellers for first-hand information about the state of connectivity on the backpacker circuit.

The novelty of technical connectivity seems now to be overshadowed by the potential for social connectivity. Websites like Bootsnall.com, and social networking sites such as Couchsurfing.org, have become touchstones for interactive travel communities. For example, on Bootsnall.com, members can participate in discussion forums, access the latest travel news, find deals on travel insurance, download travel guides, plan itineraries and publish travel blogs. Couchsurfing. org, a hospitality networking site aimed at independent travellers, offers an alternative to commercial booking sites by connecting travellers with other members willing to host them for free in local destinations (Germann Molz 2007; Bialski 2009). Members publish detailed profiles that other members can search and evaluate in order to decide whether or not to visit or host that member. Not only do these profiles contain logistical and personal details about the member, but they also locate the member within a wider social constellation where members 'vouch for' each other and display their links to the members they are friends with in the network.

If knowledge is coupled to the practices that create it, then travellers' association of electronic connectivity with social connectedness produces knowledge in particular ways. For example, on Couchsurfing.org, online connections and the sharing of personal information are extrapolated into broader regimes of knowledge production, mobility and connection, made explicit in the website's mission statement:

> CouchSurfing seeks to internationally network people and places, create educational exchanges, raise collective consciousness, spread tolerance and facilitate cultural understanding.... CouchSurfing is ... about making connections worldwide.... We open our minds and welcome the knowledge that cultural exchange makes available. We create deep and meaningful connections that cross oceans, continents and cultures. CouchSurfing wants to change not only the way we travel, but how we relate to the world!
>
> (Couchsurfing.org)

This mission statement draws on the familiar assumptions that travelling is educative and mind-opening and that connections forged through travel thus result in new kinds of knowledge that go beyond logistical or technical know-how to include cultural understanding, collective consciousness and new ways of relating to the world. Members' comments also allude to the notion that connecting with a local host can unlock a supposedly more authentic knowledge of the traveller's destination. In these contexts, digital connections underpin not a solitary travel experience, but instead a highly networked and social encounter with people and places.

These discourses suggest that digital technologies shape, but certainly do not determine, the kind of knowledge produced through electronic connectivity. Instead, and this is important for mobilities researchers to keep in mind, mobility, knowledge and technologies are co-constituted within particular social contexts. Interactive travel communities might best be thought of, then, as hybrid bundles of corporeal and virtual mobilities, different kinds of technical, spatial and social knowledges (and differently valued knowledges), and electronic and social connections that implicate interactive travellers in the larger projects of collective and collaborative knowledge production that I discuss in the next section.

Collaboration

Buzzwords like 'smartmobs', 'wiki', 'crowdsourcing' and 'distributed collaborative intelligence' attempt to capture the socio-technical relations through which knowledge is produced and mobilized in technologically connected but geographically dispersed groups (Rheingold 2002; Howe 2006). Interactive travellers and the mobile knowledge communities they form are certainly included in this trend. Blogs, chatrooms and discussion forums become a public sphere where interactive travellers solicit, post and debate where to go, what to do, where to stay, what to eat or how to get around. Invitations posted on travel blogs encouraging readers to 'Follow along', 'Watch us wander', or 'Stow away on our trip' speak to an assumption that interactive travel is a collaborative project premised on the real-time sharing of stories, images and advice. Interactive travellers increasingly expect their friends, family members and other travellers to actively participate in shaping the narrative and the journey by posting comments or advice. 'That is the beauty of blogging,' one travelling couple writes online, 'it's a two way street' (theworldisnotflat.com).

Online, knowledge about travel, places, landscapes and cultures is collaboratively produced, consumed and contested. For example, travellers may post threads wondering whether a month is too long to spend in Germany, or how to spend a ten-hour layover in Singapore, or whether travel insurance policies cover malaria tablets. Of course, word-of-mouth has always been an important, informal way of producing and corroborating knowledge among travellers. Now, discussion forums mediate word-of-mouth across geographically dispersed and mobile communities of travellers, often decentring authorized knowledge sources such as published guide books or travel agents. Studies indicate that travellers are increasingly likely to research and book their trips online rather than through a travel agent (m-travel.com 2005) and some guidebooks, such as *Lonely Planet*, have introduced online versions while others have ceased publishing altogether as travellers increasingly turn to the Internet for travel information.

But the collaborative production of knowledge is not just about decentralizing structures of authority or even democratizing knowledge; it is increasingly about creating knowledge through 'distributed structures' (Bach and Stark 2004: 104). Travel-specific wiki projects are a good example of how this knowledge production is distributed. A wiki refers to a collaboratively created website, such as the online encyclopedia Wikipedia. In the context of interactive travel, projects like

Wikitravel.org, Wikimapia.org or VeniVidiWiki.eu rely on distributed collabo-ration to compile geographical and travel information. In other words, travellers themselves upload information, plot points of interest and edit the information on the websites. For example, Wikitravel is an open-source, collaborative website that aims to create a 'free, complete, up-to-date and reliable world travel guide' sourced, edited and consumed by travellers themselves. Wikimapia and VeniVediWiki, two websites offering collaboratively edited world maps layered onto Google Earth, similarly aim to create a 'surfable' or searchable annotated cartography of the Earth, an aspiration captured by Wikimapia's slogan: 'Let's describe the whole world!'

New models of knowledge production as mobile, distributed and collabora-tive enable the ambitious, indeed global, scale of these projects to blog, annotate and thereby 'know' the world. This impulse to map and describe the world in encyclopedic detail is not entirely unlike the collaborative descriptive enterprise that motivated travellers centuries ago to compile topographies and cosmogra-phies of the known world (Adler 1989b). Adler explains that throughout the sev-enteenth and eighteenth centuries, travellers' first-hand observations and amateur reports of 'facts' about the world were compiled into a 'heterogeneous assem-blage of physical, biological, ethnological, and political information' (1989b: 16). In this way, 'the world open to gentlemen-scholars gradually became exhaustively known and described' (1989b: 21). As with contemporary efforts to comprehensively describe the world through social collaboration, these earlier projects imagined, and indeed constructed, the world as a knowable, informa-tional entity.

This 'knowable' world called for a particular kind of 'knowing subject'. As Adler notes, 'the form of human subjectivity such travel ritual required, honed, and exalted was one which could "grasp" this vast new world of "things" without being overwhelmed by it' (1989b: 24). The comprehensive inventory of informa-tion produced by travellers needed to be organized and rationalized in an appre-hensible manner. Indeed, some eighteenth-century travellers called for catalogues that would rank sights and destinations in order of significance (1989b: 13). Perhaps what those travellers needed is something that contempor-ary interactive travellers now take for granted: a search engine. In the process of mapping and describing the whole world, collaborative projects like Wikitravel and Wikimapia (re)make the world as an informational and searchable entity. In this sense, as I will discuss next, the production of knowledge relies not just on social collaboration to compile information, but also on the algorithmic logic of search. Search not only rationalizes the vast excess of data and information posted on the web into usable knowledge, but also reimagines the interactive traveller's relation to other travellers and to the world.

Search

The intersecting online and offline practices I have described so far – travelling, blogging, editing wikis or participating in discussion forums – are manifestations of interactive travellers' mobile production of knowledge. At the same time, these interactive practices contribute to the excessive proliferation of information characteristic of the web. Thanks to the 'collaborative scalability' of open-source operating systems and interactive platforms, billions of users a year add a volume of data that is hundreds of millions of times larger than the content of the United States Library of Congress (Hyman and Renn 2007). But how do interactive travellers access and make sense of all that information?

The problem of processing digitized data into knowledge is certainly not unique to interactive travellers. Indeed, technological advances in capturing, storing and processing data have led some commentators to suggest that a paradigm shift in the production of knowledge itself is at stake. This is the premise of an article by *Wired* magazine's editor-in-chief Chris Anderson titled 'The End of Theory'. Anderson suggests that as data sets become increasingly large, comprehensive and digitized, the scientific logic of 'hypothesize, model, test' will be replaced by statistical algorithms designed to mine data for correlations and patterns (2008: 109).

At the end of his article, Anderson argues that the 'new availability of huge amounts of data, along with the statistical tools to crunch these numbers, offers a whole new way of understanding the world' (2008: 109). If the blogosphere's reaction to Anderson's prophecy of the 'petabyte' future is any indication, what this 'new way of understanding the world' might look like is hotly contested. In these debates, algorithms, and particularly Google's search algorithm, become central, if contested, instruments in the production of knowledge. Sceptical bloggers question Anderson's assumptions about the nature of the algorithms and data in question and suggest that he has been too quick to throw out models and theory as a basis for producing knowledge (see blog posts by Timmer 2008; Hurst 2008; Conway 2008). What most of these critics seem to take issue with is Anderson's suggestion that algorithms will replace theoretical models, as if algorithms were not themselves models. Anderson's assessment overlooks the extent to which data itself is socially produced, and the extent to which what counts as knowledge is enabled and contained within social contexts. It also overlooks the fact that, whether or not knowledge requires models and theories, it does require a knower. The production of knowledge is always social. To recuperate this emphasis on the social dimension – and social possibilities – of knowledge production, Bach and Stark argue that 'knowledge, unlike "information", cannot exist independently of a subject and cannot be conceived of independent of the communication network in which it is both produced and consumed' (2004: 109). The production of knowledge is never a purely epistemological practice.

The algorithmic logic of search does not merely process data into knowledge; it enables, at an ontological level, certain kinds of knowledges, certain objects of knowledge, and certain ways of knowing. In other words, our ability to compile huge amounts of data and to design increasingly powerful algorithms to sort, correlate, categorize and rank this data are not just changing the way we understand the world, they are bringing a new world into being. Thrift argues that the near-ubiquity of calculation and our increasing tendency to replace analytic solutions with 'brute computing force' parallels a cognitive history of computability (2007: 93). From the discovery of mathematical deduction to the inventions of filing systems in the nineteenth century and logistics in the twentieth century to the recent growth of surveillance technologies, developments in computation and calculation have 'produced a new sense of the world and new forms of representation of it ... by decomposing and recomposing the world in their own image' (2007: 93). If search represents a contemporary manifestation of computability that (re)makes the world in its own image, then how might interactive travellers make and make sense of the world in terms of a search logic? I would like to make three tentative proposals towards this question that might, at the same time, bring us back to my earlier argument that interactive travel involves a more social than solitary understanding of mobility and knowledge.

First, the logic of search, especially in the era of Web 2.0, is as much about sociality as it is about algorithmic models that process information. Algorithms assume that data is self-evident. For example, if I search for 'spiritual oasis', an algorithmic search engine will deliver relevant instances of the words 'spiritual' and 'oasis'. A social search engine, on the other hand, would deliver texts that have been tagged, bookmarked or ranked by other users as relevant to my search term. In this case, I might get links to websites and blogs about Bali or an ashram in India, even if those sites don't explicitly contain the terms 'spiritual' or 'oasis'. Web developers aim to integrate social search with social networking so that what counts as relevant is also determined by what one's social network thinks is relevant. Social search helps users wade through the excesses of information and content online by 'link[ing] social structures (who knows who) with knowledge networks (who knows what)' (Bach and Stark 2004: 110). This logic of searching is not just a way of producing, sharing or consuming knowledge, but a way of ordering knowledge communities.

Interactive travellers, in a similar way, use the premise of sharing knowledge not only as a way of finding or sharing travel information about the world, but as a way of organizing themselves as a mobile knowledge community. Travellers often share knowledge for the sake of sociality; and they are social for the sake of knowledge. For example, couchsurfers search the hospitality network's member database in order to connect to a local host who can provide insider knowledge about the traveller's destination, but who will also, presumably, be fun to chat and hang out with. The pure utility of reading blogs or surfing discussion forums is debatable. Sean Keener, a Bootsnall.com administrator, told *USA Today* columnist Laura Bly that 'for most people, someone else's blog is absolutely useless'. But he added that 'if you're planning an around-the-world trip, it can really build confidence to read how someone else is doing it' (cited in Bly 2004). Sharing knowledge about hostels and train schedules may or may not be useful for individual travellers, but the very practice of sharing knowledge does become the social basis for mobile knowledge communities like Bootsnall.com.

Second, the logic of search emphasizes customized knowledge with social contexts. If collaborative projects like those described in the previous section emphasize ambitions towards universal knowledge, search emphasizes the converse move towards personalization. Search algorithms are increasingly designed to 'know' the searcher. For example, if a user searched for 'outer space' yesterday and linked to a page about the solar system, then today's search for 'stars' is more likely to return information about the sun than about celebrities. When asked about the future of search, Marissa Mayer, Google's vice-president of search products and user experience, indicated that delivering increasingly personalized search results will rely on incorporating an individual's social network into the search process. She notes that Google will understand 'more about you and ... more about your social context: Who your friends are, what you like to do, where you are' (cited in Sherrets 2008). She suggests that automated information about the user's search history could be fused with social networking platforms in order to deliver an augmented personalized search built on 'implicit social connections between users who are like each other' (cited in Sherrets 2008). Amazon already uses a similar approach to suggest books to its customers based on common purchasing histories among customers. Relevance is determined less by search terms and more by what 'other people like you' have already bought. This kind of search is not just an act of processing data, but an act of self-performance and self-definition within one's social context. Personalized search is, perhaps ironically, an increasingly social practice that locates and identifies people within broader social networks.

Self-performance, social networking and the sharing of knowledge also intersect in travel blogs, discussion forums and social networking sites where travellers sort and evaluate information based on personality, trust and reputation. Travel blogs are elaborate performances of self where travellers lay out, often in intimate detail, their personalities and personal biographies. This is significant in terms of search because travellers seek information from other 'like-minded' travellers, which means that it matters whether the source of information is a young, independent, budget traveller or a middle-aged woman travelling solo. A blogger's self-performance underpins the relevance of the information and advice they provide. On discussion forums, travellers can use records of active participation and posters' reputations and profiles to evaluate the content and relevance of their posts. And on Couchsurfing.org, a much more complex system of vouching for and policing members' reputations is in place to help travellers determine whom they want to host or visit (see Germann Molz 2007). Reputation, trust and the credibility of information evolve through ongoing social interactions in these online venues.

Third, I wonder how interactive travellers might extend a logic of search from the virtual to the physical world. Travellers move through blended geographies composed of websites, Internet cafés, blogs, GPS data, location-aware mobile platforms, annotated geographies like Wikimapia and hyperlinked spaces (Germann Molz 2006). The proliferation of mobile portals between the virtual world and the material world has significant consequences for the way we understand and relate to place (see Kohiyama 2005). Researchers have argued that mobile technologies do not just operate in space, but actually structure the space, making it navigable, knowable, consumable or legible (Brewer and Dourish

2008). To what extent might a logic of search inflect the way travellers navigate through and understand places as blended, networked geographies where embodied access and informational access to those same places overlap? Will travellers come to *expect* their physical environment to be hyperlinked, responsive and searchable? As information-rich interactive tourist geographies emerge through the social practices of connecting and collaborating, searching may become as central a travel metaphor as exploring or discovering.

Conclusion

Throughout this chapter, I have explored how ontological and epistemological practices are intertwined within mobility. I have argued that the relationship between mobility, technology and knowledge is performative, using the examples of connectivity, collaboration and search to show how interactive travel practices bring the world into being as a knowable entity. My objective has been to encourage mobilities researchers to reflect critically on the intersection between travel, technology and knowledge and to situate themselves/ourselves within the historical context in which mobility has developed a special relationship to knowledge. In particular, I have highlighted the way mobilities researchers might understand the terms of this relationship as shifting from an emphasis on the solitary traveller-as-knower to a more social and interactive mode of producing knowledge through mobility. As Hine suggests, negotiating our theoretical and methodological response to new social phenomena can open up a space for 'reflexive engagement with our own practices' by encouraging us to examine our 'epistemological and methodological commitments afresh' (2005: 9). This reflexive engagement is particularly significant when studying social phenomena – such as mobility and technology – that are at the same time epistemological practices; in other words, that are both objects of and ways of knowing.

I have thus sought to underscore the hybrid socio-technical nature of knowledge. By describing how interactive travellers translate electronic connectivity into social connectivity, how they collaboratively produce and police knowledge and how they perform social networks and mobile communities through and around knowledge, I have proposed that this nexus of technologies, mobilities and knowledge structures the world within particular desires for and understandings of sociality. New information and communication technologies and new social media platforms, such as blogs, discussion forums and social networking sites, may afford new ways for travellers to connect and collaborate with each other, but what makes this mediation and production of knowledge meaningful is the fact that there are other travellers, friends and family members at the other end of the line. Mobile modes of connecting, collaborating and searching thus constitute not only ways of knowing, but a new empirical realm of mobile social life.

In reflecting on interactive travel and its lessons for mobile methodology, I am reminded of Crang's analysis of the parallels between tourists' photography practices and 'the academic gaze' (1999: 253). The similarities between touristic and academic practices of travelling, gathering data and presenting knowledge, he notes, are striking; 'Indeed so are the framing of an academic gaze and the way it too shapes places into sites of knowledge' (1999: 253). For travellers and for academics, knowledge is not an objective or independent entity to be discovered; rather knowledge is intricately connected to the mobile and technological practices that create it. As we mobilize our research techniques, whether physically or digitally, we are helping to create the very worlds we seek to know.

Bibliography

Adler, J. (1989a) 'Travel as Performed Art', *American Journal of Sociology* 94(6): 1366–91.

—— (1989b) 'Origins of Sightseeing', *Annals of Tourism Research* 16: 7–29.

Anderson, C. (2008) 'The End of Theory: The Data Deluge Makes the Scientific Method Obsolete', *Wired Magazine* 16(7). Online: www.wired.com/science/discoveries/magazine/16-07/pb_theory (accessed 10 February 2009).

Bach, J. and Stark, D. (2004) 'Link, Search, Interact: The Co-evolution of NGOs and Interactive Technology', *Theory, Culture & Society* 21(3): 101–17.

Bialski, P. (2009) *Intimate Tourism: Enquete dans un reseau d'hospitalité*, Limoges: Solilange.

Bly, L. (2004) 'Travel Blogs: They Can Make the World Go Round', *USA Today* (16 March 2004). Online: www.usatoday.com/travel/columnist/bly/2004-03-11-bly_x.htm (accessed 10 December 2009).

Brendon, P. (1991) *Thomas Cook: 150 Years of Popular Tourism*, London: Secker and Warburg.

Brewer, J. and Dourish, P. (2008) 'Storied Spaces: Cultural Accounts of Mobility, Technology, and Environmental Knowing', *International Journal of Human–Computer Studies* 66: 963–76.

Chambers, I. (1994) 'Leaky Habitats and Broken Grammar', in G. Robertson, M. Mash, L. Tickner, J. Bird, B. Curtis and T. Putnam (eds) *Travellers' Tales: Narratives of Home and Displacement*, London: Routledge.

Clifford, J. (1989) 'Notes on Theory and Travel', *Inscriptions* 5: 177–88.

Conway, D. (2008) 'The Hubris of "The End of Theory"', blog posting. Online: http://blogs.nyu.edu/blogs/agc282/zia/2008/06/the_hubris_of_the_end_of_theor.html (accessed 13 December 2008).

Crang, M. (1997) 'Picturing Practices: Research through the Tourist Gaze', *Progress in Human Geography* 21: 359–73.

—— (1999) 'Knowing, Tourism and Practices of Vision', in D. Crouch (ed.) *Leisure/ Tourism Geographies*, London: Routledge.

de Botton, A. (2002) *The Art of Travel*, London: Hamish Hamilton.

Deleuze, G. and Guattari, F. (1980) *A Thousand Plateaus*, trans. B. Massumi, London: Continuum.

Germann Molz, J. (2006) 'Travels in Blended Geographies: Technologies, Mobilities and "New" Tourist Destinations', paper presented to 'Mobilities, Technologies and Travel' workshop, Roskilde University, Roskilde, Denmark, 20 April 2006.

—— (2007) 'Cosmopolitans on the Couch: Mobile Hospitality and the Internet', in J. Germann Molz and S. Gibson (eds) *Mobilizing Hospitality: The Ethics of Social Relations in a Mobile World*, Aldershot: Ashgate.

Gmelch, S.B. (2004) *Tourists and Tourism*, Long Grove, IL: Waveland Press.

Hine, C. (ed.) (2005) *Virtual Methods*, London: Berg.

Holly, D., Jain, J. and Lyons, G. (2008) 'Understanding Business Travel Time and Its Place in the Working Day', *Time & Society* 17: 27–46.

Howe, J. (2006) 'The Rise of Crowdsourcing', *Wired Magazine* 14(6). Online: www.wired.com/wired/archive/14.06/crowds_pr.html (accessed 12 December 2008).

Hurst, M. (2008) 'In Theory', blog posting. Online: http://datamining.typepad.com/data_mining/2008/06/theory---in-reply.html (accessed 13 December 2008).

Hyman, M. and Renn, J. (2007) 'Toward an Epistemic Web', paper presented at the 97th Dahlem Workshop on 'Globalization of Knowledge and its Consequences', Berlin, 18–23 November 2007.

Jemielniak, D. and Kociatkiewicz, J. (2008) *Management Practices in High-Tech Environments*, Hershey, PA: Thomson Gale.

Jokinen, E. and Veijola, S. (1997) 'The Disoriented Tourist: The Figuration of the Tourist in Contemporary Cultural Critique', in C. Rojek and J. Urry (eds) *Touring Cultures*, London: Routledge.

Kaplan, C. (1996) *Questions of Travel: Postmodern Discourses of Displacement*, Durham, NC: Duke University Press.

Kohiyama, K. (2005) 'Mobile Communication and Place', *Vodafone Receiver* 13. Online: www.vodafone.com/flash/receiver/13/articles/index06.html (accessed 1 December 2008).

m-travel.com (2005) 'Number of Bookings through Agents on the Decline', *m-Travel.com and Travel Distribution News*. Online: www.m-travel.com/news/2005/10/number_of_booki.html (accessed 12 December 2008).

Murphy, D. (2009) '10 of the Best Ways to Travel', *Guardian* (3 January 2009). Online: www.guardian.co.uk/travel/2009/jan/03/dervla-murphy-travel-tips (accessed 12 February 2009).

Oakes, T. (2006) 'Get Real! On Being Yourself and Being a Tourist', in C. Minca and T. Oakes (eds) *Travels in Paradox: Remapping Tourism*, Lanham, MD: Rowman & Littlefield.

Pels, D. (1999) 'Privileged Nomads: On the Strangeness of Intellectuals and the Intellectuality of Strangers', *Theory, Culture & Society* 16(1): 63–86.

Pope, N. and Guthrie, K. (1996) 'A Hypertext Journal'. Online: www.somewhere.org.uk/hypertext/journal/index.html (accessed 1 December 2008).

Rheingold, H. (2002) *Smart Mobs*, Cambridge, MA: Basic Books.

Rojek, C. (1993) *Ways of Escape*, London: Routledge.

Said, E. (1983) *The World, the Text, and the Critic*, Cambridge, MA: Harvard University Press.

—— (1984) 'Reflections on Exile', *Granta* 13: 159–72.

Sherrets, D. (2008) 'Google's Marissa Mayer: Social Search is the Future', *Venture Beat* (31 January 2008). Online: http://venturebeat.com/2008/01/31/googles-marissa-mayer-social-search-is-the-future (accessed 14 December 2008).

Thrift, N. (2007) *Non-Representational Theory: Space, Politics, Affect*, London: Routledge.

Timmer, J. (2008) 'Why the Cloud Cannot Obscure the Scientific Method', blog posting (25 June 2008). Online: http://arstechnica.com/news.ars/post/20080625-why-the-cloud-cannot-obscure-the-scientific-method.html (accessed 13 December 2008).

Websites

www.couchsurfing.org (accessed 5 June 2009).
www.theworldisnotflat.com (accessed 2 February 2009).
www.venividiwiki.eu (accessed 15 January 2009).
www.wikimapia.org (accessed 15 January 2009).
http://wikitravel.org/en/Main_Page (accessed 15 January 2009).

7 Travel Remedy Kit

Interventions into train lines and passenger times

Laura Watts and Glenn Lyons

> As in life, what matters is not the final destination, but all the interesting things that occur along the way.
>
> Tim Ingold, *Lines: A Brief History* (2007: 170)

Decisions concerned with government investment in transport, whether a road is built or rails are laid, are informed by the cost versus economic benefit of such investment, calculated on the basis of appraising a model of the proposed transport system. Luggage-carrying, individual and embodied passengers waiting for a train are translated into economically modelled passengers, who are rational actors in a calculative transport system. In this chapter we explore substantive differences between this aggregated economic model of the passenger and a sensory, affective model of the embodied passenger arising from social research methods – such as ethnography, focus groups and interviews. How might 'remedies' for the affective qualities of a passenger's train journey translate into benefits within the economically modelled version? At stake is a rethinking of what constitutes the *economically modelled passenger*, hence making it a potentially better model upon which transport appraisal and government investments might be made. It is through a novel *Travel Remedy Kit* that we propose our intervention, demonstrating how substantive improvements in the experience of individual journeys might also manifest as economic benefits in the aggregated, economically defined world of transport appraisal.

To set this chapter in context it is necessary to appreciate the orthodox thinking of transport appraisal, summarized (albeit rather simplistically) as follows. Travel is seen as a means to an end – a means of getting somewhere in order to do something at the destination. The 'means to an end' is an inconvenience – something to be minimized. It follows that quicker journeys are preferred to slower ones: less time spent on the inconvenience leads to more time to do something else. Travel time is seen as unproductive time, and any saved travel time is assumed to be reinvested in (economically) productive activity. This chapter stems from a three-year research project, concerned with 'Travel-Time Use in the Information Age', that has sought to challenge this orthodoxy by arguing that travel is more than just a 'means to an end' and, importantly for transport policy, the experience of travel time can in fact be productive (Lyons and Urry 2005). For example, 55 per cent of passengers according to our questions in the 2004 *National Rail Passengers Survey* of 26,000 passengers claimed their travel time was of some use, and a further quarter (23 per cent) said the time spent on the train was very worthwhile. Travel is not a waste of time for most passengers (72 per cent), but is of use and perhaps economically productive.

Not only does this question the value attributed to saved travel time, but it also questions whether investment in quicker journeys is the only means of yielding benefits in a transport system; investment in enhancing passenger productivity on-the-move may also have benefits – economic and otherwise. Indeed, as we will go on to show, not only is there the possibility of getting 'more' out of the time spent travelling, but there is an opportunity to create an experience of 'speeding up' a journey that is in addition to, and distinct from, reducing the clock time taken through transport infrastructure improvement.

Economically modelled passengers in transport appraisal are created through a process of translating the messy socio-material world of the traveller and their baggage into a series of calculative relations; a body is flattened into a formula according to the following general tenets (see Lyons and Urry 2005):

- passengers experience a universal clock time;
- they take action on the basis that any time in motion is wasteful, and would be valuable if recovered;
- if they travel outside of work they do so in their own time which they can value – they have a willingness to trade time for money;
- when travelling in the course of work they do so in relation to time owned by their employer – time that is valued according to the wage they are paid;
- individual passengers do not matter in an economic appraisal – attention is paid to the overall population of model passengers, the aggregate.

To help make clear the distinctive features of this 'appraised' passenger experience, as distinct from the features of a sensory, social and situated passenger experience created through social research, we will highlight the differences in their spatiality – the differences in their contingent possibilities for movement.

Both versions of the passenger move from departure to destination, from A to B, along a line – their spatiality is more or less linear. Lines are not all the same, however, as Tim Ingold has recently explored (Ingold 2007). Ingold attends to the differences between a line as a planned series of joined dots from point A to point B, to a free-flowing line or trail that has no beginning or end, that passes through places A and B as it responds to circumstances en route.

Within the 'flattened' tenets of economic 'transport appraisal', individual passengers move from a point of departure to a point of arrival in the shortest possible time, and ideally that would be no time at all. It is a world constituted by clock time and money, creating a line that can be plotted on a graph. The line of the journey is essentially uniform, it has no particular characteristics or quality of experience, and ends when the passenger arrives at the destination. Such a line moves over a largely unmarked world, racing from location to location in an attempt to achieve pure transportation: the quickest, straightest path (Ingold 2007: ch. 3). The passenger on such a line is static and unengaged with the world until the destination, the point of activity and re-entry back into the economic world. For the economically modelled passenger (travelling in the course of work) nothing happens en route, everything happens before and after. So there appears to be no possibility for valuable activity when travelling – or when waiting in the moments in between.

What now follows is an introduction to the design and implementation of the Travel Remedy Kit, which we will argue is a remedy kit for both improving individual embodied travel and, crucially, economically modelled travel in transport appraisal schemes.

Travel Remedy Kit

The Travel Remedy Kit is an intervention- and interview-based piece of empirical research, loosely based on the concept of personalized travel planning in transport studies, which seeks to encourage individuals to discuss and rethink their travel choices and behaviours with the prospect of some changes taking place to the benefit of the individual and society (Parker *et al*. 2007).

Through the national rail survey, a nationally based ethnography of bus and train travel-time use, six focus groups and interviews with industry stakeholders, we had gathered evidence for the extraordinary richness and importance of passenger activity on the move. For example, the national rail survey questions revealed that 13 per cent of passengers had planned 'a lot' for their journey, whereas 47 per cent had done so 'not at all', and passengers who considered their travel time to have been wasted were more than twice as likely to have done no advance planning (70 per cent) compared with those who considered their travel time to have been very worthwhile (31 per cent) (Lyons *et al*. 2007). Together with our other results this suggested that, through advantageous advanced planning, we could intervene in passenger travel time by providing particular artefacts and suggested interactions designed to positively affect the passenger and their travel environment.

We worked with six participants in the south-west and north-west of the UK who volunteered to have a familiar journey by train 'remedied'. The journeys included commuter, leisure and business categories of travel. We also invite the reader to reflect on how the Travel Remedy Kit might reconfigure their own journeys by public transport.

The kit comprises two elements: a deck of 34 cards (see Figures 7.1 and 7.2), constituting the results of our national rail survey, focus groups, stakeholder interviews and ethnography; and a travel pack of personalized items designed, with use of the cards, for the specific passenger and journey. The complete deck of cards, which we do not have the space to present here, and instructions for use can be downloaded from www.built-environment.uwe.ac.uk/traveltimeuse.

The Travel Remedy Kit method involves three stages: design of the kit, travelling with the kit and a final debrief and discussion of its effectiveness.

Figure 7.1 Deck of cards used to design and personalize the Travel Remedy Kit, with its container box.

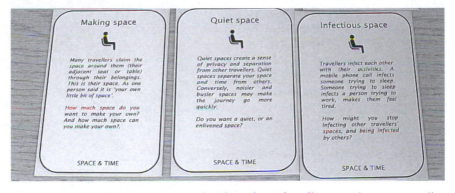

Figure 7.2 Three of the Travel Remedy Kit cards used to discuss and re-conceptualize the participant's journey.

Design your Travel Remedy Kit

We began by shuffling the deck of cards, which was divided into suits: the first two suits emphasized the story of the journey, the final suit constituted objects that could be included in the Travel Remedy Kit. Then we took one card at a time and invited the participant to reflect on the implications and significance of those ideas, activities and artefacts for the journey they wanted to remedy. If a card didn't seem relevant they discarded it. We asked the participant to place that card on the table in relation to all the other cards in order to build up a visual representation and story of the journey (see Figure 7.3). Card by card we began to articulate the mundane and everyday aspects of travel, which were deemed initially to be unimportant but became otherwise. Through this process we worked with participants to reconceptualize the journey, moving from an articulation of specific problems to a discussion of what would be ideal – and the potential remedies necessary to create that ideal.

We always opened our discussion of the participant's journey with the two cards: *Imagine Departure* and *Imagine Arrival*. We asked the participant to place them at either side of the table in front of us, to create an initial tableau. These two cards concerned the discontinuous moments of planning, expectations for the journey and sense of arrival. They made present to the participant how much of the journey, such as booking tickets, packing bags and planning a route occurs before or after actual arrival and departure (Watts 2008).

Then we invited participants to turn over a card from the shuffled deck and reflect on its significance for their journey.

Figure 7.3 Photographic collage of Steve's tableaux of cards, as he laid them out during the initial interview.

Boredom

People travel with mobile phones, polystyrene cups of tea, suitcases, bicycles, newspapers, books, laptops and tickets. They walk and wait at stations and stops (Bissell 2007); sit in trains and buses, and imagine, plan, think, work and relax as they pass beneath flashes of storm and electricity pylons. Unlike the economically modelled passenger, the embodied newspaper and mobile-phone-carrying passenger is not static when travelling but highly active. Only a very small percentage of passengers (2 per cent) in our national rail survey spent most of their journey being bored – in direct contrast to an industry stakeholder who, when interviewed, perceived train travel as 'boring ... dead boring'. Boredom is considerably less likely when passengers have imagined and planned their journey; those who had done no advanced planning in our survey were more than twice as likely to be bored than those who had not.

Turn over a card...

Make the Transition

In transport appraisal, distance is an anathema, since time taken to transcend distance represents inactivity, a waste of time and a loss of money. The ultimate transport network would involve no time and hence no distance at all. It would act as a point-to-point, instantaneous translation between departure and destination, more commonly referred to as a teleport. Yet various commentators in transport studies have questioned teleport as a passenger ideal (Graham 1997; Mokhtarian and Salomon 2001). In our earlier focus groups we asked passengers if they would prefer to teleport to their destination and the responses were, after some consideration, quite negative (Jain and Lyons 2008; Watts and Urry 2008). Travel was important planning and 'sorting things out in your head' time:

> Yeah, definitely, I like to have the time. I don't want to teleport, 'cause otherwise you end up going from meeting to meeting to meeting, and you've not had time to think about the next meeting, and you just go *ergh* [rolls eyes] like that. So, yeah, I like the time.
>
> (Claire, business traveller, response to *Make the Transition*)

Typically, those in the focus groups wanted to spend at least 20–30 minutes travelling to and from work (with the range being from 10 to 60 minutes). Spatially, rather than a line that tends to zero length, as in the transport appraisal model, the ideal length of the commuting passenger's line is actually 20–30 minutes. From ethnographic work, what also matters is the sense of ongoing movement, without stopping, through the world. It is movement that creates the ambiguity of place, the liminality and a valued sense of creativity, possibility and transition. This 'transition time' was an important creative time for many (Jain and Lyons 2008).

Turn over a card...

Routes

> I discovered another route, which is rather an adventure…
>
> (Huw, commuter, response to *Routes*)

Participants spoke of finding sometimes longer but more scenic routes, detours to pass favourite landmarks, and how they took different paths depending on the season or weather. Passengers do not move as though joining the dots between origin and destination, they move in particular and selective ways through places (Ingold 2000; Massey 2005). Passengers are actively engaged with the world, and adapt with the weather, seasons, traffic and changing circumstance. Rather than moving point to point, passengers are 'wayfarers' who make a trail that is ongoing and defined by the movement itself (Ingold 2007: ch. 3). As wayfarers, passengers move in and through the world engaged in situated actions (Suchman 1987, 2007), planning and re-planning. They have to interact with the social and material world in order to travel, and unlike the transport appraisal model are not effortlessly carried from point to point by the transport system.

Turn over a card…

Stretch/Compress Time

> The journey in the morning is really, really quick. The journey in the evening is really, really slow … Sometimes [in the morning] I just sit and look out of the window, and think. And sometimes I want to do that plus I want to send a text, plus I want to do some reading, or all of those things … And before you know where we are we're approaching [the station] and I've got to get my coat on.…
>
> (Huw, commuter, response to *Stretch/Compress Time*)

Time may tick slowly for a passenger standing in a vestibule, unable to sit on a crowded train. Whereas for a passenger sitting in the same carriage, on the same journey, thinking and looking out at the scenery, jotting down ideas in a note-book, time may tick fast. Travel time is made in travel-time use. The corollary of this is that the experience of travel time can be stretched or compressed, depending on the activity of the passenger. To create the experience of a journey passing more quickly, then, does not necessarily require a shorter clock time, but could involve compressing passenger time through the enactment of particular practices (Watts 2008). Generally, the more activities undertaken, the faster time passes. Travel time is compressed by intensive travel-time use (including looking out of the window and thinking) and stretched by inactivity. Making a journey 'speed up' (as part of an embodied sense of time) could be achieved through investment in supporting travel-time use, and not only through investment in reducing the clock time of the journey (although clock time still defines what can be 'fitted into a day').

Turn over a card…

Things to Hand

> Phone and headphones, because that's my mp3 player. Book. And usually
> something to graze on, drink and eat. And ... my laptop ... usually put eve-
> rything on the table. I quite like, you get to set out your little space in front
> of you, that's the whole thing ... And it's ... having those things at hand
> that allows stretching and compressing time...
>
> > (Steve, business traveller, response to *Things to Hand*)

Passengers are not simply bodies sitting in a seat but include their belongings
distributed through space: their bags are on seats and under seats, feet are in
aisles, smells permeate through a carriage and mobile phones connect passengers
to places outside the train (Green 2002; Hulme and Truch 2005; Watts 2008).
Passengers are always bodies plus their belongings. These 'distributed passengers' configure themselves in different ways: as packed passengers and unpacked
passengers (Watts 2008). Packed passengers are equipped for waiting at the
station or stop, with items such as newspapers and mobile phones to hand
(Bissell 2007; Gasparini 1995). Unpacked passengers in a seat are a reconfiguration of those same artefacts suitable for travel-time use; they are able to conduct
multiple activities on the move, such as read a book, drink some tea, gaze in
thought at the changing landscape. The possibility for activity on the move
not only reduces the potential for boredom (as we have discussed), but more

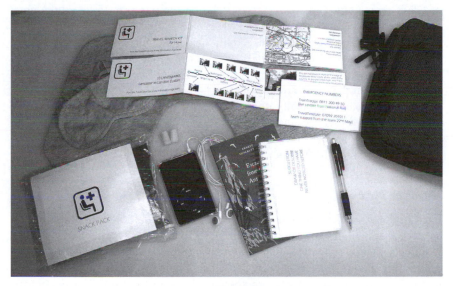

Figure 7.4 Some of the possible contents of the Travel Remedy Kit with its bag, including: instruction booklet, snack pack, inflatable pillow, eye cover, ear plugs,
music and game player, book, notebook and pen, emergency number and
landmark guide.

importantly unpacked passengers are configured to make time pass more quickly. As Steve says, all those things at hand allow you to compress your travel time.

Turn over a card...

Ultimately, the discussion of all 34 cards and their visual tableaux formed the first intervention into the participant's journey. By attending to the mundane, to the familiar, we altered how the journey was understood and imagined. The major form of intervention was the actual Travel Remedy Kit. This small shoulderbag contained a series of carefully selected, hand-crafted items designed for that particular person and their particular journey; an enticing, carefully orchestrated set of things to do, see, hear and taste, en route (see Figure 7.4).

Travel with your Travel Remedy Kit

The plan

The crucial part of each Travel Remedy Kit was the concertina set of step-by-step instructions. This small booklet opened up to guide the traveller during every moment of the journey from door to door, to remedy the whole experience and help create the participant's ideal journey. In the plan, we suggested a new route to walk to the train station, or a bus to catch, or a different route to drive there, always supported by a personalized map. When we suggested taking a bus we included a map to the bus-stop, the timetable and the cost of the ticket. We suggested where to park the car and the best way to pay for parking. Then we made suggestions for where to wait at the train station, where to buy a good cup of tea or coffee and perhaps where to stand on the platform to board the quiet coach of a train.

Once on board, we suggested activities suitable for different parts of the journey, tailoring what to do when they want to stretch or compress their travel time. We always suggested how to unpack the Travel Remedy Kit into a productive shape, given the space around them.

The plan opened up, finally, to directions for onward buses, a walk or some other transport to their destination. We still continued to suggest where to wait and what to do when en route, and always provided helpful hints (and even a telephone helpline) for the unexpected.

Munch and brunch

Each bag came with a specially made 'snack pack' with favourite morsels from baklava to chocolate-covered ginger biscuits. To remedy a participant's journey required a nuanced understanding of how they travelled and what their particular desires for an ideal journey were. However, perhaps surprisingly, the ideal journey for all our participants was not very different from their current experiences, and not unachievable by careful preparation or un-addressable by the transport sector – although we emphasize that transforming travel is non-trivial, and passengers and the industry must, together, be actors in such transformation.

Special things, special things for the journey ... you know, might have made something at home, or buy it from the nice sandwich shop.

(Claire, business traveller)

Writing

We explicitly asked each participant to describe or draw one thing they had never noticed on that journey before. Almost every participant talked about using a notebook as an extremely flexible device, able to support activities from diary-writing to drawing.

Apart from [starting] the diary ... also asking me to draw something, notice something ... And as I was drawing it, I could remember the details ... So this was precious, this particular exercise ... What I learned was that I shouldn't just do one thing, on the journey, that I could diversify my activities; that the journey is an opportunity to do a number of things.

(Maryam, commuter)

Music player

Listening to music was, perhaps not unsurprisingly, a crucial part of travel-time use for many of our participants. For others, a music player that also supported audiobooks and games provided an important diversity of activities.

I think I'll probably get a [music player] now, because I'm convinced that I'll use it ... I felt that it was more my journey. I guess that was because it was planned, you sort of planned it.... But it became less of a journey ... less of an ordeal ... And I sort of found if I was getting bored, there was something I could do. I could listen to something else. So that helped. And it made it go much more quickly. So it seemed a much quicker journey.

(Derek, business traveller)

Mobile office

Pertinent to the costs versus benefits approach of transport-scheme appraisal is the result from the national rail survey that 86 per cent of business travellers, a particularly influential group in economic appraisal due to the high value of their time, believe that, in terms of their paid employment, there is some work that can easily be undertaken on the train (Lyons *et al.* 2008).

My ideal office is on the train ... especially if I've got things to work out [and I'm] at that point when you're just getting creative with it. It's my most creative place to work because it's that, you get a bit stumped, and you get to look out of the window for half an hour ... see things...

(Steve, business traveller)

That passengers are potentially obtaining substantive economic benefit from what they do while travelling has the potential to affect the economic model of passengers, and hence the outcome of transport appraisal calculations upon which policy and investment decisions are made. Transport appraisal contests it is only concerned with the value of travel time *saved*, not with the value or nature of travel time *spent*; however, we suggest that the benefits of travel may be calculated only if both are considered. The economically modelled passenger needs to include some measure of activity while moving from A to B.

Debrief your Travel Remedy Kit

After participants had experienced their remedied journey, we conducted a post-journey interview a few days later to discuss how effective the kit was. The cards and their layout (reproduced in a photograph, such as Figure 7.3) were discussed in an unstructured interview, which we opened by asking the person to tell us the story of their remedied journey. We then explored particular artefacts or moments that arose as meaningful during the discussion.

The following are what appeared to be some of the most effective and important remedies for improving the passenger experience.

Landscape guide

Scenery was often crucial to the desire to stretch or compress time. When passing through places that held less meaning or interest participants wanted to move faster, whereas they wanted to savour other places and views through the window. As wayfarers constituting the line of their journey, rather than inactive passengers being carried along, they wanted to move more slowly and attentively through some places and inhabit them for longer. From the national rail survey, gazing through the window or people-watching was the second most undertaken activity across all passengers (18 per cent), alongside reading for leisure (34 per cent) and working and studying (13 per cent) (Lyons *et al.* 2007; Watts and Urry 2008).

We created a personalized landscape guide with photographs taken from the train and information on visible and often unusual landmarks by which the train passed.

> But to be honest once I've looked for my landmarks, read my book, drawn some pictures, made a few notes, we're there! ... But it went very quickly. It was great. And I was there before I knew it.... It was fun actually. It was quite fun. Other people were just sitting there, reading, or looking at their mobiles, and I've got plenty to do.
>
> (Julia, leisure traveller)

Viscous time

Compressing travel time requires strategizing so that the right moments are compressed and stretched. From ethnography and discussions with participants, we noted that the early part of a journey is more easily compressed than the later part when passengers are tired. It is this later part of a longer journey that often needs the most 'remedy' and, moreover, could lead to the greatest benefit in terms of the embodied experience of an improved and potentially 'faster' journey.

> Third hour, I was still very keen to listen to things [on the music player] ... I had a go at some of the games ... I got the pillow out for about the last hour, and I felt a bit self-conscious, but it was very comfortable, it was very good ... So I enjoyed it a lot, it was very good. It certainly made the journey seem quicker. I was sort of 'there' you know...
>
> (Derek, business traveller)

Adaptation

Through the use of the Travel Remedy Kit passengers became much more active participants in their journey. Rather than passively accepting their circumstances, the toolkit pointed to ways for them to manage their travel time, and in so doing make their journey pass more quickly or slowly (although not by the measure of clock time). In essence, the Travel Remedy Kit was a wayfarer's toolkit for making a train journey as a trail (following Tim Ingold's analogy discussed earlier). It comprised technologies for engaging in different ways with the world while moving; it transported and transformed participants from potentially bored and inactive passengers into equipped and alert wayfarers making a trail from A to B.

> I was a bit more alert at the end of the journey ... because usually I'm in a bit of a daze at the end of the journey.
>
> (Claire, business traveller)

The Travel Remedy Kit also seemed to affect passengers in the longer term. Although designed for one journey, it often shifted how they engaged with travelling more generally. Through the kit, participants were not only equipped for wayfaring, but became wayfarers (at least for a time afterwards). As one of the participants said:

> Taking notice of it as a journey, as opposed to something that you just do ... If you see what I mean ... I wouldn't ever remember my bus journey as I go to and from work, because it's just always the same. Whereas this made it all different.
>
> (Claire, business traveller)

Conclusions

The Travel Remedy Kit method was designed to create journeys that were more beneficial to passengers, and where travel time might be stretched or compressed. The kit equipped and transformed inactive passengers into wayfarers, providing a rich possibility for different interactions with the train-world, different activities and ways of making travel time variable. These benefits to the passenger in the form of increased pleasure, productivity and the sense of passing time came without the cost of infrastructure investment to speed up the journey. So what are the implications for transport appraisal and the economically modelled passenger?

First, the ideal length of a journey does not tend to zero. The line of movement from A to B has an ideal length and its duration can be an important place for valuable creative work or transition time, and often provides an opportunity for economically or personally productive activity. Travel time has some value to passengers and therefore should be valued. However, all these benefits are not currently included in the transport-appraisal-modelled passenger (travelling in the course of work). If these benefits were to be included, it might broaden notions of how transport investment can yield passenger, and thus economic, benefits. The model should not be confined to the presumption that these economic benefits can only occur through reducing journey times, but should recognize that they can also occur through enhancing the experience of passenger travel time.

Second, there can be an experience of 'saving' travel time, and of compressing the journey duration, when the passenger is considered as an active participant in making their travel time. They are not passively carried along but are participants in travel alongside the transport infrastructure. A different kind of time from clock time can be saved, but it is one that is not yet present in the world of the economically modelled passenger.

The role of transport economic appraisal is to adequately represent the cost versus benefit of a transport scheme. The benefit, and the cost, is rendered a monetary one through assumptions about travel time and how saved travel time is valued. The question is one of value and, of course, what is present in the model to be valued. As a reminder, transport appraisal is about assessing the cost of *changing* the transport system and passenger experience and the benefits that accrue from such change. We propose that when considering improvements there be a move away from a model of passengers as inactive during travel, to one where the passenger is active, and that the quality of that activity can be improved through investment. This move to include something of the material and embodied aspects of the passenger experience, albeit still through economic translation, is in order to accommodate the benefits of travel time that the Travel Remedy Kit demonstrates are possible. In other words, appraisal should allow for transport improvements, and their benefits, that are not confined to altering the operation of the transport service itself. The activities of passengers, their travel-time use, should be within scope for being changed and appraised. Such *use-modelled passengers* would, we suggest, need to include certain tenets. They would:

- have an ideal duration for the journey rather than an assumed ideal of zero duration;
- value their travel time as a site of creativity and transition or preparation, which can be augmented through different activities; and
- conduct productive activities on the move that are dependent on the environmental qualities of the moving and waiting places in which they work.

In order to increase the productivity of passengers, both in terms of economically productive work and in terms of their travel-time use, the creation of an environment with the necessary *affect* is needed. As has been shown throughout our project, how people feel about, and engage with, the world around them is crucial to productive as well as pleasurable travel time. Improving travel time then becomes not only a matter of infrastructural investment to reduce clock time, it also becomes a matter of investing in ways to help passengers become wayfarers, supporting activities and affective environments where it is possible for passengers to unpack, become active and engaged, and so compress or stretch their travel time.

Simply, *use-modelled passengers* open up the possibility for affective (and effective) transport interventions and investments.

The current transport appraisal model of passengers as purely transported and inactive is ostensibly a view derived from very careful calculations and judiciously considered assumptions, and yet it is a view that seems removed from the richness of the travel experience. We contest that this removal strongly brings into question whether the current economically modelled passenger as a focus for transport economic appraisal is sufficiently 'fit for purpose'. The Travel Remedy Kit research method demonstrates not only how passengers can be, and often are, well equipped as wayfarers to make productive use of their time, but that it is possible to make interventions into travel time that are highly beneficial to passengers but of low cost to the industry. We propose a move to *affective transport appraisal*, where attention and ultimately investment in transport policy expands to include the *making* of travel time, as well as the simple *saving* of travel time.

Acknowledgements

We thank our colleagues on the 'Travel-Time Use in the Information Age' project: John Urry, Juliet Jain and David Holley. We would also like to thank all the participants throughout our research, whose voices made this account possible.

Bibliography

Bissell, D. (2007) 'Animating Suspension: Waiting for Mobilities', *Mobilities* 2(2): 277–98.

Gasparini, G. (1995) 'On Waiting', *Time and Society* 4(1): 29–45.

Graham, S. (1997) 'Telecommunications and the Future of Cities: Debunking the Myths', *Cities* 14(1): 21–9.

Green, N. (2002) 'On the Move: Technology Mobility, and the Mediation of Social Time Space', *The Information Society* 18: 281–92.

Hulme, M. and Truch, A. (2005) 'The Role of Interspace in Sustaining Identity', in P. Glotz, S. Bertschi and C. Locke (eds) *Thumb Culture: The Meaning of Mobile Phones for Society*, Piscataway, NJ: Transcript Verlag/Transaction.

Ingold, T. (2000) 'The Temporality of the Landscape', in *The Perception of the Environment: Essays in Livelihood, Dwelling and Skill*, London: Routledge.

—— (2007) *Lines: A Brief History*, London: Routledge.

Jain, J. and Lyons, G. (2008) 'The Gift of Travel Time', *Journal of Transport Geography* 16(2): 81–9.

Lyons, G. and Urry, J. (2005) 'Travel Time Use in the Information Age', *Transportation Research Part A* 39: 257–76.

Lyons, G., Holley, D. and Jain, J. (2008) 'The Business of Train Travel: A Matter of Time Use', in D. Hislop (ed.) *Mobile Work/Technology: Changing Patterns of Spatial Mobility and Mobile Technology Use in Work*, London: Routledge.

Lyons, G., Jain, J. and Holley, D. (2007) 'The Use of Travel Time by Rail Passengers in Great Britain', *Transportation Research Part A* 41: 107–20.

Massey, D. (2005) *For Space*, London: SAGE.

Mokhtarian, P.L. and Salomon, I. (2001) 'How Derived Is the Demand for Travel? Some Conceptual and Measurement Considerations', *Transportation Research Part A* 35(8): 659–719.

Parker, J., Harris, L., Chatterjee, K., Armitage, R., Cleary, J. and Goodwin, P. (2007) *Making Personal Travel Planning Work: Research Report*, London: Department of Transport.

Suchman, L. (1987) *Plans and Situated Actions: The Problem of Human Machine Communication*, Cambridge: Cambridge University Press.

—— (2007) *Human–Machine Reconfigurations: Plans and Situated Actions*, 2nd expanded edn, New York/Cambridge: Cambridge University Press.

Watts, L. (2008) 'The Art and Craft of Train Travel', *Journal of Social and Cultural Geography* 9(6): 711–26.

Watts, L. and Urry, J. (2008) 'Moving Methods, Travelling Times', *Environment and Planning D: Society and Space* 26(5): 860–74.

8 Mobile, experimental, public

Monika Büscher, Paul Coulton, Drew Hemment and Preben Holst Mogensen

Mobile methods can enable powerful new insights, as the contributions to this book illustrate. In this chapter we argue that mobile methods can also help to advance sociology 'beyond societies' (Urry 2000), a move necessary as social relations are increasingly shaped by global flows and movements and 'society' is failing as a unit of analysis to provide analytical grasp of how the social is co-constituted by and constitutive of the material, environmental and technological. However, our enthusiasm for mobile methods is due to more than the theoretical advances they enable.

The authors of this chapter are a social scientist–designer and computer scientist working in participatory socio-technical innovation, an engineer–designer and Nokia Champion, and an artist–curator and director of the international *Futureverything* (previously *Futuresonic*) festival where participants explore emerging social-technology innovations. We find synergy in connecting our different forms of engagement in socio-technical change. Against a background of – in our experience – extremely fruitful interdisciplinary collaborations between prospective technology users, technology designers, artists and social scientists, and joint orientations towards both 'basic' and 'applied' research, we show how mobile methods in the context of engaged experimentation can identify directions for desirable innovation (for example, genuinely supporting existing and emergent work practices, creating new media content and added value for customers and companies, and technologies that fit with people's visions of the 'good life'). At the same time, the mobile, experimental, public approach we describe yields some sense of, and some control over, unintended consequences of socio-technical change for all involved.

The chapter is structured as follows. First, a discussion of key motivations for mobile, experimental, public research provides some background to our argument. We then turn to examples to make the potential of a mobile, experimental, public approach concrete, beginning with Coulton's 'Mobile Radicals' projects, which often involve large-scale experimental public release of mobile 'beta' technologies. Several issues arise here, but we focus on changing conceptions and practices of location privacy and community involvement as particularly important. The next example, drawing on ethnographic observations during a participatory innovation project with police and fire-service professionals, develops this inquiry, broadening our concern with location privacy to explore increasing possibilities for surveillance. Third, examples of art and design interventions open up potentially disruptive spaces of play and mass participation.

At several junctures, mobile methods are showcased in their potential to take debate beyond utopian/dystopian binaries and into informed shaping of socio-technical possibilities and dangers. Mobile methods can drive the emergence of a new kind of public 'experimentality' (Szerszynski *et al*. 2008), which could be key to the 'collective experimentation' needed to address complex contemporary socio-technical challenges such as, for example, CO_2 emissions from transport and the threat of Orwellian surveillance that accompanies 'intelligent transport solutions' to this challenge (Wynne and Felt 2007; Dennis and Urry 2009). Mobile, experimental, public methods from our examples might enable new forms of control in socio-technical innovation.

Background

Mobile methods are intrinsically experimental. Mobility 'broadens the mind', not least because it immerses people in new situations (Germann Molz, Chapter 6) and provides multiple perspectives and multi-sensory impressions. In contrast to scientific experimentation that seeks to systematically isolate causal factors and reduce complexity for analysis, experimentation in and through mobility 'goes along with' complexity and emergence. It fosters open-ness to uncertainty, situatedness, feedback effects and reflexivity. Researchers on the move naturally learn to appreciate that analysis 'is not [meant] to set up a relation of external contact or correspondence between subjective states of mind and objectively given conditions of the material world, but to make one's way through a world-in-formation' with eyes open to the processes and practices of formation (Ingold and Vergunst 2008).

Mobility and its non-representational implications for analysis set our approach apart from earlier calls for experimental sociology (Greenwood 1944). The kind of experimental sociology we seek is closer to Dewey's 'experimental method in politics' (1927), gearing analysis into the dynamic relational complexities and situated actions of world-making, providing important insight into the interactions between everyday creativity and socio-technical innovation. The potential for emergence at this juncture is caught well by the ethnomethodological concept of 'another next first time', which describes the ordered, yet improvisational, contingent and reflexive character of social life (Garfinkel 2002). Studying the indigenous practices or 'ethnomethods' of how people creatively, reflexively make social life orderly, ethnomethodologists engage in an 'alternate' sociology that has been influential for a range of theoretical orientations. Their insights resonate with feminist concepts of 'performativity', Foucauldian notions of 'governmentality', and – extending analytical attention to the role of material and technological agencies in world-formation – actor-network theory and agential realism (Barad 2007). Most importantly, the notion of 'another next first time' highlights the simultaneous orderliness *and* creativity of everyday-life-in-the-making (see also Prigogine 1997), locating important opportunities for innovation at the level of everyday practice.

Mobile methods are good at knitting together the different material, technical, social, temporal and spatial scales at which everyday actions take effect. A particularly fertile aspect of this is captured in the notion of 'experimentality' (Szerszynski *et al.* 2008), where at one level, experimentation is a top-down technology of government, while at other levels, it manifests as a source of uncertainty, bottom-up creativity and emergence: 'Thanks to the incessant intensification and growing scale of technologies and technosciences, as Krohn and Weyer first put it in 1988, nowadays "society [and the larger environment] is the laboratory"' (Wynne and Felt 2007: 52; addition in original). In the name of progress and global economic competitiveness, people have become experimental objects, their movements mapped, tracked and interrogated, subject to actuarial 'qualculations' – a combination of qualitative judgement and calculation based on the increase of 'addressable' data about individuals (Thrift 2008) – for insurance, marketing, transport efficiency and security purposes, their food, medical interventions and energy enhanced or created through instrumental application of science and technology. But from the instrumental application of science to these domains spring innumerable experiments in the wild, with both positive and negative, intended and unintended consequences. A positive example is the unanticipated up-take of Short Message Service (SMS) text-messaging capabilities by predominantly young mobile-phone users. Initially intended as an exclusive business service emulating the success of paging technologies, the stampede of unexpected users gave rise to rapid innovation in technology and service models, enabling the use of SMS for everyday communications (Taylor and Vincent 2005). A more problematic example is the greenhouse effect of CO_2 emissions. For good or ill, such examples of unanticipated opportunities and problems reveal that experimentation inevitably breeds a lively mix of interactions where uncertainty is not residual but immanent. Against this backdrop we argue that it may be advantageous to accept this unruly element of experimentation, its uncertainties and the potential for creative improvisation and work with it rather than against it. However, this is not easy. Wynne and Felt ask: 'if everyone is in principle a guinea-pig, then who is participant in the experimental design, and interpretation – and who has right to its veto?' (2007: 68). They identify 'a need to embrace an ethic of non-control', and recommend development of 'collective experimentation' practices, enabling citizens to participate in the production of science and technology, not just their 'application' or 'implementation'. This is not meant as another strategy to counter public resistance to science and technology innovation, nor is it just a sign of democratic generosity. The very power and morality of science and technology innovation depend on responsible alignment with social innovation. But while we agree with Wynne *et al.*'s call for collective experimentation, we find that 'embracing an ethic of non-control' involves discovery of different meanings, modes and methods of control rather than wholesale abandonment of control. Mobile methods – 'moving along with' members of the public likely to be touched by technology as they carry on their everyday business (Kusenbach 2003; Ingold and Vergunst 2008; Büscher 2005) 'moving in' with prototype technologies (see example two below), and 'being moved by' experiences, observations and conversations that arise along the way – are different methods of 'control', understood not as a quest for mastery but as a moral, multi-sensory and collective strategy of taking fine-grained responsibility for innovation, placing researchers, designers and practitioners into the flow where technological innovations meet social practices, allowing them to experience, evaluate and react to the myriad frictions, troubles and opportunities that arise.

Towards collective experimentation

We now argue that, and show with examples from information technology how, mobile methods can help introduce useful new conceptions and practices of 'control' into the public realm and mobilize everyday creativity for collective experimentation.

Mobile Radicals

In chemistry, radicals are highly reactive atoms or molecules. Mobile Radicals – a group of artists, engineers, researchers and designers – similarly seek reactions, but of a social kind. By releasing novel mobile technologies into the wild they stimulate emergent user experiences and behaviours. The release of these projects into the wild also utilizes emergence in that new services/applications are announced on Paul Coulton's Forum Nokia blog (http://blogs.forum.nokia.com/blog/paul-coultons-forum-nokia-blog) which is likely to initially reach a global audience of digitally literate technophiles, but from there spread 'virally' through other social networks, attracting diverse and in some cases very large groups of people (mobile game widgets Bombus and Boom! attracted over 1.5 million users).

LocoBlog (www.locoblog.com), for example, is being used by a growing global group of participants. It is a location-based service that allows people to upload geo-tagged images taken with their mobile phones to an Internet site, where the images are placed on an interactive map using the Google maps API (application programming interface) (Figure 8.1a). This has inspired new ways of 'blogging' or documenting movement, quite different from older formats of images inserted into text as in traditional blogs or micro-blogging services such as Twitter. LocoBlog was initially released in July 2006 (Bamford *et al.* 2007) and although personal location-based services have been proposed and investigated by researchers since the establishment of GPS as a dual-use system in 1996 which opened it up for non-military applications, it was the first such system made available to the general public that was operable on the mobile phones they were likely to own.

The relative accessibility of LocoBlog soon attracted a 'long tail' of participants from many parts of the globe as shown in Figure 8.1b. The long-tail effect is evident in a variety of activities such as economics (Anderson 2006) and culture (Watts 1999; Shirky 2003) and describes the power law curve profile

Figure 8.1 (a) LocoBlog; (b) LocoBlog user locations.

reflecting how a wide range of niche activities can be supported within a business or social network. Where it comes to goods and services that people actively seek, the Internet has enabled a step change in reaching significant numbers, mainly because it dramatically reduces the cost of search (Brynjolfsson *et al*. 2006; see also Germann Molz, Chapter 6). Moving through a vastly diverse universe of offers has become much easier. However, search has not eliminated chance. Through recommendation systems and social networks, people are increasingly discovering niche items, or items they may not have known to want, but which on serendipitous discovery become desirable.

Capitalizing on such serendipitous discovery, the LocoBlog designers were able not only to follow emergent-use patterns of the service and adapt it accordingly, they were also able to challenge preconceived notions often promoted by the mainstream media that users would be very concerned by the security implications of revealing their location. In fact, LocoBlog illustrated the opposite effect in that the first entry most users made was their home location and in the case of one user actually blogging the address (Bamford *et al*. 2007). Indeed, this willingness to reveal location information is illustrated in the growing popularity of Google Latitude. But perhaps this readiness to publish private information indicates worrying naivety on the side of users? Not necessarily. Mobile methods of experimental public release, of closely following emergent-use behaviours and of ongoing development of the technologies in response to such behaviours open up new questions about location privacy. For example, embodied experience of location privacy extended into virtual environments gives rise to user demand for 'editability' after upload (implemented in LocoBlog after users' requests) and for the ability to moderate the granularity of location information (e.g. street, city, country, implemented in Google Latitude). Moreover, more fine-grained practical 'ethnomethods' of negotiating location privacy in interaction with others are emerging, such as when location-tracked gaming makes possible face-to-face meetings between strangers and players produce delicate excuses to avoid such meetings (Licoppe 2009). These socio-technical and social innovations are beginning to enact the new kinds of sensitivities and senses around location privacy that Thrift expects to evolve around ever more pervasive computational qualculation (2008), and they arise, to a large extent, in community interactions.

The user-activity profiles of Mobile Radicals services resemble the power law distribution seen on services such as Wikipedia in that almost all activity is generated by a relatively small number of users (Weinberger 2007). For example, LocoBlog now has over 4,700 photographs overall, with two users producing over 900 (one of them Paul), five over 100 photographs (one of them Monika) and over 80 users having created fewer than ten photographs (Figure 8.2a). This activity profile is also evident in another Mobile Radicals project: m3Dcam (www.m3dcam.com) which allows mobile-phone users to create 3D anaglyph photos which can be viewed in 3D using red–cyan glasses (another long-tail activity) before uploading to a community site for rating. Thus far the project has generated 35,467 images by 13,950 unique users. If we considered a simple average this would be two to three images per user. However, as Figure 8.2b clearly shows, this average user is not the norm and the majority of users only make one entry and a relatively small group generate in excess of ten images.

The importance of this profile comes to the fore, particularly for a site like m3Dcam, when the user-generated content is rated and images are displayed according to rank. If the whole community is allowed equal ranking rights then a few unscrupulous users could take poor-quality images and rate them highly to get their name displayed high in the rankings. This would upset high-volume users who are striving to create high-quality images for display. A similar effect was observed in games, where early ranking systems divided the average score by the number of players, thus favouring low-use players over those trying to develop their skill over repeated plays. Therefore, to manage the community, we provide special ranking privileges to high-end users to moderate user-generated ratings, and ensure both continued use by highly committed users and that high-quality images are seen by new users entering the site. In this way the community continues to grow in largely self-regulating ways, highlighting dangers for operators managing their community from a Gaussian perspective, overemphasizing the importance of average users in a normal distribution (Taleb 2007).

Managing community involvement requires care. But it is not a matter of leadership in any simple sense. Instead, it is a matter of moving with and of being moved by the community members' efforts and actions. The examples

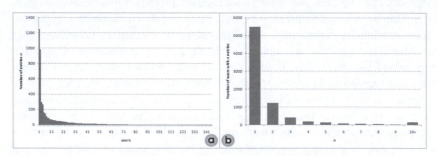

Figure 8.2 (a) User entry activity for Locoblog; (b) user entry activity for m3Dcam.

above practically illustrate some of the benefits obtained from moving from the small 'controlled experiments' traditionally used in technology usability labs to real-world experiments if we are to understand and engage with emerging practices of using, creating and making media social in the sense of augmenting people's ways of finding and appreciating content through technologically augmented social connections and conversations. The mobile, experimental and public Mobile Radicals approach plugs designers into the everyday creativity of new user communities but requires careful balancing through community management. In addition, we use the concept of perpetual beta. 'Perpetual beta' means that technology is not a product but a process. The overall design may be changed or subtly 'tweaked' in response to emergent-user practices, recognizing the integral role of social innovation and providing communities with mechanisms for inventing and negotiating acceptable new practices, senses and sensitivities as witnessed in LocoBlog where greater facilities for online editing of blogs was requested by the community.

Although LocoBlog and m3Dcam both support some forms of virtual community of strangers with shared interests (Rheingold 1993), they are principally centred on the individual user and do not provide for collaborative creativity on a shared project. A further Mobile Radicals project, *LocoMash* (www.locomash. com), was created to support such group creativity using a similar concept to LocoBlog but inspired by the Mass Observation movement of the 1950s to enable collaborative photo mapping of events and festivals. An important design consideration when providing this type of service for festivals and events is that it supports simultaneous production and consumption (Cheverst *et al*. 2008) normally through presenting the real-time evolution of the project on large public displays as shown for the Roskilde Rock Festival in Figure 8.3a. In this type of experience activity profiles are perhaps less interesting than emergent live behaviour around particular locations that may be attracting interest and, using the time and location of the entries, it is possible to generate real-time heat maps

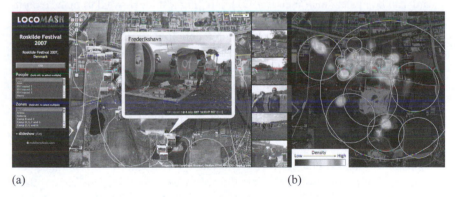

(a)   (b)

Figure 8.3 (a) Roskilde LocoMash; (b) Roskilde LocoMash entries heat map (colour versions at http://blogs.forum.nokia.com/blog/paul-coultons-forum-nokia-blog/2008/10/22/mobile-user-generated-content-at-fn-tech-day).

that highlight fluctuating audience densities as shown for Roskilde in Figure 8.3b. This form of information could be valuable for festival visitors to decide where to go and for festival organizers to manage mobilities in real-time. This possibility is also explored in the next section.

Mobilizing IT

In the next example, a focus on professional work through mobile methods has given rise to a different, but kindred practice. Figures 8.4 and 8.5 show frames from ethnographic video at a 'living lab' during the 2007 Tall Ships' Races in Aarhus, Denmark. Living labs are experimental 'mobilizations' of prototype technologies in as realistic as possible situations (Büscher *et al.* 2008; Schumacher and Niitamo 2008). The living lab and ethnographic study at the Tall Ships' Races was part of a four-year project (PalCom) that brought emergency professionals together with computer scientists and social scientists to design a computer architecture that supports people in 'making computing palpable'. Computer architectures – the structures for communication and connection between computational devices, services and user interfaces – are an advanced 'basic research' area for computer science. Equally, for social science the question of how people grasp complex processes and make them 'palpable' is a fundamental research question, a preoccupation of phenomenology, ethnomethodology and science and technology studies (Lynch 1993). However, these 'basic' research questions are best approached through 'applied', empirical, mobile, experimental, public research, because people's interactions with infrastructures are fleeting, often experienced in mobility and emergent in interaction with technology.

Cars, mobile phones, cameras, geographical positioning devices (such as GPS), radios, public displays – most now use computation. A design challenge is not just how people might use these individual devices, but also how they might create 'assemblies' nomadically, to suit current needs and circumstances. In this respect Mark Weiser's otherwise pioneering vision for 'ubiquitous' computing can be misleading (Weiser 1991). His 'highest ideal [was] to make a computer so imbedded, so fitting, so natural, that we use it without even thinking about it' (www.ubiq.com/ubicomp), which technology designers have frequently interpreted as a call to make the computer 'invisible' (Norman 1991). To protect users from complexity, designers hide computing by embedding it, making it 'autonomous', self-healing, and context-aware (Kephart and Chess 2003). These approaches can be powerful and have been used in the prototype PalCom architecture. However, the team also found that these 'invisibility' mechanisms can impede what they seek to support. Weiser's – and our – ultimate concern is not the literal invisibility of technology, but 'invisibility-in-use', synonymous with the phenomenological notion of 'ready-to-hand' (Heidegger 1962). Perhaps paradoxically, invisibility-in-use requires the ability to make things visible or otherwise palpable. The PalCom living lab at the Tall Ships' Races was a mobile, experimental, collective innovation process, designed to enable real-world nomadic assembly of technologies to support collaboration between the police,

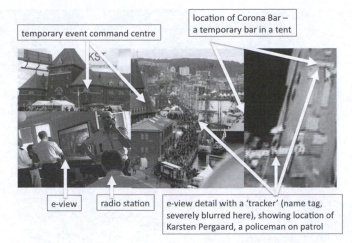

Figure 8.4 Working with PalCom prototypes at the 2007 Tall Ships' Races (source: figure from ethnographic video: Monika Büscher).

fire services and emergency medical staff. The team also wanted to explore how people might practically make computing palpable and invisible-in-use with support from a prototype PalCom architecture.

'E-view', a large touch display that gives control over a model of the harbour area populated with live input, is a core part of the assembly of mobile cameras, networks and location-tracking devices put together for the duration of the Tall Ships' Races all around the harbour area. It is located in the temporary command centre in the harbour customs house. Satellite photography has been draped over the terrain to show real surfaces and 3D structures are inserted based on GIS information. Some are temporary, such as the Corona Bar tent highlighted in the somewhat blurry detail from ethnographic video in Figure 8.4. Some ground personnel are carrying GPS camera phones and their movements are tracked in the model. Karsten Pergaard, a police officer on patrol, is shown at the bottom of Pier 1, for example. The model also shows live information from webcams (Figure 8.5), camera phones and Automatic Identification Systems carried by ships (showing their location).

Throughout the Tall Ships' Races, this assembly of technologies was used alongside traditional technologies, such as radios, maps and pen and paper. The aim of the living lab was not to replace old ways of working, but to explore and shape socio-technical futures and help develop new technologies through social innovation. Developing and implementing working prototypes of cutting-edge technologies through experimentation in real contexts like this makes it possible to explore not only how such technologies perform under real-world conditions. It also enables prospective users to 'colonize' socio-technical futures and shape new working cultures, not just through discursive deliberation, but also through embodied, hands-on everyday creativity. An example of how emergency

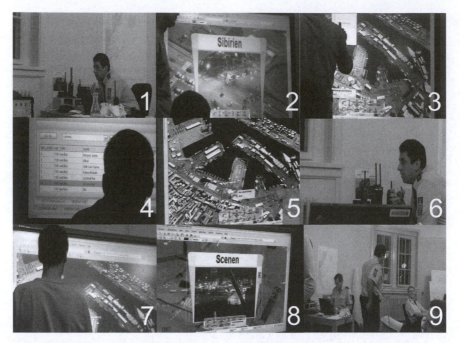

Figure 8.5 The Corona Bar incident. Frames from ethnographic video.

professionals do incident response 'for another next first time' – that is, in many ways as they always do it but with new tools – will illustrate this process.

8:30 pm. Music is thumping through the open windows of the command centre: Police chief Amrik is fielding two calls for action: a radio report of dangerous pedestrian behaviour at a major road crossing after the end of a concert on Pier 3 and a report about a fight in a 'Corona Bar' (1). His job is to mobilize a response. As Amrik talks, he looks at e-view and Jesper, a computer scientist from Aarhus University, brings forward live feed of the road crossing (Sibirien) from one of the cameras connected into 'e-view' (2). Seeing the situation, Amrik seems happy with the response already underway. The fight at Corona Bar is more troublesome: no-one knows where the bar is. Most staff are local, but do not know the locations of temporary venues. Overhearing again, Jesper opens up the GIS inspector, types in 'Corona' and searches (3&4). The tent is highlighted in the model, but Jesper also moves the cursor to allow Amrik to see the tent's location from his chair (5&6, detail in Figure 8.4). This puts Karsten Pergaard closest to the scene, and Amrik asks him to attend. Jesper returns to the screen just as Karsten's tracker shows him arriving at the Corona Bar (7), and he pulls forward a camera view of the now emptying concert area (8). Indicating satisfaction with the attention given to the two incidents, Amrik gets up and begins to chat about how boisterous but peaceful the crowds are (9).

This glimpse into the quiet management of small disturbances at a large entertainment event reveals how new technologies are creatively appropriated into such work. Combining GIS search facilities with live information about the movement of personnel made it possible to address the situation swiftly. In discussion with the professionals, this potential was greatly appreciated. Its corollary – the fact that mobile patrol personnel were visible to colleagues, in effect open to mobile surveillance – was seen as a novel aspect in need of careful management. Moreover, it is closely intertwined with aspects of how technology is being made invisible-in-use, which the example makes amenable to study at least in outline. First, Jesper's actions are critical to this process. He knows when and how to mobilize which elements of the assembly. His sensitivity to the work process of addressing the situation and Amrik's trust in him are the result of a long collaborative process that has moved researchers and practitioners in and out of each others' contexts many times (Büscher *et al.* 2008; Büscher and Mogensen 2009). The resulting mutual understanding enables collaborative shaping of emergent new socio-technical working cultures, often without the need to explicitly highlight innovations, such as new ways of knowing that incidents are being attended to (for example, through seeing Karsten's tracker arrive at the Corona Bar in e-view). A second contributing factor is the PalCom architecture. It supports assembly of devices and services and live inspection through an 'extrovert programming style' that enables people to drill down into computational processes (Gjerlufsen *et al.* 2009). Over months of preparation and the days of extensively supported appropriation at the Tall Ships' Races, computer scientists and practitioners used these palpability mechanisms (Büscher and Mogensen 2009), enabling trust in the technology – for example, the accuracy of location information.

In subsequent evaluation meetings, the designers, Amrik and his colleagues discuss new ways of working and design implications of their experience. Next iterations of e-view are implemented during living labs at the 2008 and 2009 Skanderborg Music Festivals. Here the team also explore the festival visitors' role. Most carry mobile phones, with the potential to make their locations available through Bluetooth (as in LocoMash above and Loca: Set to Discoverable discussed below; see also Ahas, Chapter 11). Trials of mapping crowd movements are perceived to be useful, not just by event managers and emergency staff, but also by festival visitors, who appreciate the visualization of hotspots and the peace of mind of having their location known in case of an emergency. At the same time, as both staff and visitors grasp how technological augmentations broadcast traces of their movements (to e-view and phone records) without them being physically aware of who can see their location, concerns about surveillance are being raised.

A treacherous bargain?

These are serious concerns, especially when considered with a view to 'intelligent' transport, an area where mobile surveillance could reach truly Orwellian proportions. In *After the Car*, Kingsley Dennis and John Urry (2009) think through integrated 'intelligent transport' technologies:

> 'Smart cards' would control access to ... mobility. And software systems will 'intelligently' work out the best means of [travel] ... physical move- ment ... would be subject to rationing.... How the issue of personal mobil- ity is dealt with will in part determine whether and how people live their lives down the line, in small-scale localism, in a Hobbesian war of all against all, or in Orwellian systems of digital surveillance.
>
> (Dennis and Urry 2009: 157–64)

In personal communication Dennis and Urry add 'The digital nexus system would need to be subject to energetic democratic control in order to make it less obvi- ously Orwellian.' The question is, what form should such democratic control take? A combination of the above approaches towards collective experimentation provides some traction. However, citizens and designers need more methodo- logical innovation to engage large communities collaboratively and practically, to enable people to question the invisibility and to grasp the complexity of the tech- nologies involved. The aim should be to make it possible to materialize and colo- nize futures, and to experience intended and unintended consequences realistically enough to understand them. This might allow citizens to also begin to invent new ways of engaging with the technologies that might more democratically mitigate undesirable consequences, such as the potential for locoblogging or wearing trackers to lead to mobile surveillance and unwanted disciplinary pressures.

The final example adds inspiration from an artistic perspective. From a series of art–design interventions that have explored a range of phenomena related to locative media, social networking and mass participation, conducted in the context of the *Futureverything* festival and other international art and technology events, we describe two that are particularly revealing with regard to location privacy and the threat of surveillance of mobile behaviour.

Art-design intervention: Loca and Futureverything

Computers have become social interfaces for sharing digital media and collabo- rating to build online communities and folksonomies. Mobile and 'locative' media that combine distributed computing with various forms of sensing make possible new forms of experiences where digital content is accessed by moving through hybrid environments. They enable people to collectively participate in sampling their life, city and environment, producing new kinds of datasets and data visualizations, and opening up new opportunities for engagement in the mediated environment. This has been the site of artistic experimentation with innovative methodologies for participatory observation and mapping, which, when combined with the ability to share information globally and instantly, creates an unprecedented capacity for participatory mass observation. At a very large scale, social distributed media lead to interesting transformations. The massive uptake of social media has led to the growth and proliferation of databases and libraries that we access and update in the course of our everyday lives, often incidentally. This leads to new opportunities and a society both more at ease and also challenged by ever greater levels of personal disclosure; a new way, indeed, of being social.

As seen, questions of surveillance and location privacy are posed by mobile media. This is a particular issue in locative media, which are predicated on disclosure of location. We are interested in how artist-designers can work as disruptors, opening up disruptive spaces of play. One of the many forms this can take is to amplify and exemplify a socio-technical aspect, or possible futures, so that it may be occupied, lived and therefore better understood.

Loca: Set to Discoverable was an experiment in pervasive, user-generated surveillance, which aimed to equip people to deal with the ambiguity of locative media. By deploying a network of Bluetooth nodes in downtown San Jose, the project team was able to track and communicate with anyone carrying a Bluetooth device set to 'discoverable'. Over seven days at the ZeroOne/ISEA2006 festival more than 2,500 people were detected more than half a million times, enabling the team to build a detailed picture of their movements. People were sent Bluejacking messages – 'We are currently experiencing difficulties monitoring your position: please wave your network device in the air' – from a stranger with intimate knowledge of their movements. We drew inferences based upon the movement of people and by responding to urban semantics, the social meanings of particular places: 'You walked past a flower shop and spent 30 minutes in the park, are you in love?' Over the course of the week the messages became gradually more sinister, 'coffee later?' changing to 'r u ignoring me?'. Upon accepting the message, people were invited to visit the project stand in the main exhibition centre, where they were given a printed log of the times and places they were detected, which in some cases were over 100 m long.

Loca: Set to Discoverable aimed to expose the disconnect between people and the digital trails they leave behind, and to provoke people to question the networks they populate. Responses to Loca have been many and varied, from the confiscation of a Loca node by the San Jose Police Department, to an animated debate on BBC World Service with Shami Chakrabati, Director of Liberty and one of the UK's leading civil-liberties advocates, and a discussion in Seoul, South Korea on how issues of privacy, surveillance and disclosure play out very differently outside Europe and North America. Some people learned for the first time how Bluetooth functioned, and a few were compelled to switch their Bluetooth device to undiscoverable. Others have been inspired to explore the creative possibilities of locative media.

This work on locative media and locative arts energized interdisciplinary thinking around the social and the city. A subsequent curatorial project conducted at the *Futuresonic* 2008 festival in Manchester, England, *Social Networking Unplugged*, sought to investigate the virtual mobilities of social networking.

Social technologies create an extension of socio-technical space, and new ways for people to find the stuff that interests them, link up with others and share. Social technologies can refer to technologies created and maintained by social networks, such as communities of developers and users working collaboratively with open-source tools, as well as 'Web 2.0' social media applications such as Facebook, and the Internet itself. However, the reach of social technologies is much deeper. When you use your credit card, you are using a social technology. Each time we buy something we let the company know where we are and what we are buying. An electronic profile is created for each one of us and the aggregated information is used to shape services and place products on supermarket shelves. This in turn shapes the choices available to us, and the society we live in. The social is more than a set of preferences or links entered online. There is also the dark matter of unknown composition that cannot easily be counted or given an IP address, but which we know is there because of its gravitational effects on visible culture.

Social Networking Unplugged featured 20 world premiers, UK firsts and commissions. Artists were commissioned to devise artworks which play with notions of social networking, and involve various publics in constructing spaces of social interaction. The artworks held up a mirror to the phenomenon of social technologies, and ranged from gallery pieces to ambient happenings in public space, online and offline artspaces and participatory workshops. Some directly addressed online social networking and virtual worlds, for example by recreating interaction metaphors from online social networking websites in a physical, offline form. Others went in search of the social in other ways, such as by playing with social norms and expectations in public places, creating 'free' and 'open' spaces for social interaction in Manchester, or exposing seams between online and offline personas. Like injecting one substance into another to trigger a chemical reaction, the Social Networking Unplugged theme came from mixing an interest in virtual worlds and online social networking with an interest in presenting social and participatory artworks in unexpected city spaces. The exhibition at the *Futuresonic* 2008 festival aimed to pull the plug in order to take the new socio-technical spaces apart, see how they work and put them together in new ways. Here art offers new perspectives on the ways in which people collaborate to make or use technology.

For example, the art and performance group *plan b* wanted to explore how people use social media for self-expression and representation. *MySpace – YourSpace – OurSpace* was an 'unplugged', offline, cut-and-paste alternative to MySpace (www.myspace.com). A shop window was dressed as if it was the page of a new social networking Internet site, inviting people to create their own space. This space was no virtual space, however, but a section of the window, filled by a 5 cm deep A5 card box (Figure 8.6) that people could decorate to express themselves.

A range of materials were provided, including found and bought objects, paper, magazine cuttings, beads, cardboard and glue, and people showed great skill at creating personal MySpaces. *plan b* were the API of the project, working with live users, but also on behalf of remote users, trying to fulfil their requests to prepare MySpaces for them. Project participants could also send messages to

Figure 8.6 plan b's *MySpace – YourSpace – OurSpace* at the *Futuresonic* festival 2008.
(source: With permission from the artists, Daniel Belasco Rogers and Sophia
New. www.planbperformance.net/myspace.htm).

one another using a messaging system consisting of cards for writing on and
envelopes attached to the rear of each box. The project was inspired by the
assemblages of Joseph Cornell, the vitrines of Marcel Duchamp, Pollock's Toy
Theatres and Victorian shadow boxes.

A team of ethnographers observed the ways in which the replacement of
virtual mobilities with physical mobilities (of creating material user profiles,
moving them into a physical display grid, and physically writing and posting
messages between them) shaped the way people acted, interacted and reflected
upon the nature of virtual mobility and social networking online (see also Lan
et al. forthcoming). In the *plan b* artwork, for example, one participant asked the
artists to remove their box from the window. This led to a discussion about what
it meant to 'delete' the 'user's' 'data'. To remove the box from view but save it
out of sight would be equivalent to how data is managed in many online social
media sites. The artists decided they wanted to go further, and completely disas-
sembled the box, recycling its contents among the materials available to other
uses. Another observation was the effort required to manage the paper-based
messaging system that depended upon artists and participants physically placing
messages and retrieving them, highlighting not only how much structuring, sys-
tematization and information transportation takes place in messaging systems,
but also how carefully negotiated and visible social conventions of privacy are
around physical messages stored in envelopes as opposed to electronic mail or
text messages.

Discussion

Our aim here was to explore synergies between three independent sets of mobile, experimental and public methods of research in socio-technical innovation, with a twofold motivation. On the one hand, we seek conceptual advances to carry sociology 'beyond societies', most importantly to study the entangled character of the social and the technical and to better understand the integral role of social innovation in socio-technical change. On the other hand, the creative marginality (Urry 2000) afforded by our interdisciplinary collaborations between art, design, engineering, social science, everyday and professional practice enables us to blur the boundaries between 'basic' and 'applied' research and contribute to the development of collective experimentation approaches. The three main dimensions of synergy are that this work is mobile, experimental and public in complementary ways.

By mobile we mean that our approaches are, firstly, interested in movements of people, goods, information and ideas as well as the effects of such movements – LocoBlog, for example, asks 'where do people physically go, what do they see, how do they value their experiences?' Moreover, new ways of experiencing and managing technologically augmented physical mobilities become amenable to study, such as the movement of police officers or festival visitors on the ground and their traces in digital displays, as well as databases and phone records. Virtual mobilities can be studied, such as interactions between people with shared interests via social networking technologies, and the formation of virtual communities. To analyse these empirical phenomena and to inform innovation, we use a variety of mobile methods – from 'radical' design interventions to ethnographically informed participatory design, to playfully disruptive artistic interventions. These methods are mobile not just in the sense that they make researchers move with physically or virtually mobile subjects, we also use the notion of mobile methods more metaphorically in the sense that we seek to be moved by people, that is, we seek to sensitize ourselves to the subtleties of their actions, interactions and reflections, and to the opportunities and implications of these subtleties for design and socio-technical innovation.

This work is experimental in the sense that careful observation and analysis are folded into iterative interventions that, in turn, stimulate emergent and unpredictable reactions (Dewey 1927; Szerszynski *et al.* 2008). In sometimes very large-scale collaborations, we seek to create partial desirable socio-technical futures and experimentally colonize them, to understand opportunities and dangers, materialize the former and counteract the latter – not just through academic sociological critique or top-down design, but through stimulating awareness, ongoing public reflection and social innovation. Attempts at collective experimentation like this provide new forms of control. A more messy, but also more immediate, experiential and publicly shared sense of opportunities and dangers arises, and – through what one might call 'perpetual involvement' – all participants can develop and share their skills for realizing technological potential more responsibly. So, for example, the PalCom living lab revealed a need for expert support in utilizing ubiquitous computing technologies. Creating new professional working cultures that can capitalize on the potential of ubiquitous computing is clearly not a matter of handing new technologies to the professionals with instructions. The living lab made it clear that the creation of new roles – emulating the support enacted by Jesper – may be necessary. Similarly, the involvement of festival audiences in LocoMash, PalCom, Loca: Set to Discoverable or MySpace – YourSpace – OurSpace allows members of the public to develop a more concrete sense of how their movements may be mapped, tracked and interrogated, fostering understanding and social innovation.

Finally, this work is public, drawing inspiration from Michael Burawoy's call for public sociologies that 'enrich public debate about moral and political issues by infusing them with sociological theory and research' (2004: 1603). But this is more than a matter of feeding scholarly discourse into debate. Research and, for that matter, innovation requires 'engagement' and commitment to 'placing relations among science, technology, and public interests at the centre of the research program' (Sismondo 2007: 21). This makes research and innovation 'hybrid' in the sense that analysis, design and everyday practice become so intermingled as to be inseparable, making them 'mutually instructively descriptive' (Suchman and Trigg, quoted in Garfinkel 2002: 101) for scientists, engineers, designers, artists and practitioners.

Mobile, experimental, public research makes a more empowered 'public experimentality' conceivable. By this we mean a public demand for and a sense of entitlement to be involved in the production, not just the implementation of advanced science and technology, as well as the confidence and capability to contribute constructively. Such sentiments can be highly effective in mobilizing more democratic participation in collective experimentation. They are visible in social movements of 'deep democracy' approaches to development (Appadurai 2001), open-source and Web 2.0 social technologies and the environmental movement (Clifford and King 1996). Reconnecting sociology and design to such social movements could be a powerful move (Urry 2000).

Acknowledgements

We would like to thank the EU Commission IST programme, Nokia, Arts Council England, British Council, AHRC, *Futureverything* and University of Salford for supporting parts of the research described here. Personal thanks for inspiring debate go to Will Bamford, Amrik Chadha, Michael Christensen, John Evans, Tony Gjerlufsen, Theo Humphries, Margit Kristensen, Morten Kyng, Patrizia Marti, Jesper Wolff Olsen, Mike Raento, Dan Shapiro and John Urry.

Bibliography

Anderson, C. (2006) *The Long Tail: How Endless Choice Is Creating Unlimited Demand*, London: Random House.
Appadurai, A. (2001) 'Deep Democracy: Urban Governmentality and the Horizon of Politics', *Environment and Urbanization* 13(2): 23–43.

Bamford, W., Coulton, P. and Edwards, R. (2007) 'Space–Time Travel Blogging Using a Mobile Phone', in M. Inakage, N. Lee, M. Tscheligi, R. Bernhaupt and S. Natkin (eds) *Proceedings of the International Conference on Advances in Computer Entertainment Technology – ACE 2007*, Salzburg, 13–15 June 2007, pp. 1–8.

Barad, K. (2007) *Meeting the Universe Half-way: Quantum Physics and the Entanglement of Matter and Meaning*, Durham, NC: Duke University Press.

Brynjolfsson, E., Hu, Y.J. and Simester, D. (2006) 'Goodbye Pareto Principle, Hello Long Tail: The Effect of Search Costs on the Concentration of Product Sales', *MIT Center for Digital Business*, Working Paper. Online: http://papers.ssrn.com/sol3/papers.cfm?abstract_id=953587 (accessed July 2009).

Burawoy, M. (2004) 'Public Sociologies: Contradictions, Dilemmas, and Possibilities', *Social Forces* 82(4): 1603–18.

Büscher, M. (2005) 'Social Life under the Microscope?', *Sociological Research Online* 10(1). Online: www.socresonline.org.uk/10/1/buscher.html (accessed 19 September 2009).

Büscher, M. and Mogensen, P. (2009) 'Matereal Methods', in M. Büscher, D. Goodwin and J. Mesman (eds) *Ethnographies of Diagnostic Work: Dimensions of Transformative Practice*, London: Palgrave.

Büscher, M., Kristensen, M. and Mogensen, P. (2008) 'Making the Future Palpable: Notes from a Major Incident Future Laboratory', *International Journal of Emergency Management* 5(1–2): 145–63.

Cheverst, K., Coulton, P., Bamford, W. and Taylor, N. (2008) 'Supporting (Mobile) User Experience at a Rural Village "Scarecrow Festival": A Formative Study of a Geolocated Photo Mashup Utilising a Situated Display', in N. Henze, G. Broll, E. Rukzio, M. Rohs, A. Zimmermann and S. Boll (eds) *Mobile Interaction with the Real World 2008 – MIRW 2008 – Mobile HCI Workshop*, Amsterdam, 2 September 2008, pp. 27–38.

Clifford, S. and King, A. (1996) *From Place to PLACE: Maps and Parish Maps*, London: Common Ground.

Coulton, P. *Forum Nokia Blog*. Online: http://blogs.forum.nokia.com/blog/paul-coultons-forum-nokia-blog (accessed 19 May 2010).

Dennis, K. and Urry, J. (2009) *After the Car*, London: Polity.

Dewey, J. (1927) *The Public and its Problems*, Athens, OH: Ohio University Press.

Garfinkel, H. (2002) *Ethnomethodology's Programme: Working out Durkheim's Aphorism*, New York: Rowman & Littlefield.

Gjerlufsen, T., Ingstrup, M., Olsen, J.W. and Kyng, M. (forthcoming) 'Mirrors of Meaning: Supporting Understandability through Inspectable Runtime Models', *IEEE Computer* (special issue on Models@Run.Time).

Greenwood, E. (1944) *Experimental Sociology: A Study in Method*, New York: King's Crown Press.

Heidegger, M. (1962) *Being and Time*, London: Blackwell.

Ingold, T. and Vergunst, J. (2008) *Ways of Walking: Ethnography and Practice on Foot*, Aldershot: Ashgate.

Kephart, J.O. and Chess, D.M. (2003) 'The Vision of Autonomic Computing', *Computer* 36(1): 41–50.

Kusenbach, M. (2003) 'Street Phenomenology: The Go-along as Ethnographic Research Tool', *Ethnography* 4(3): 455–85.

Lan, K., Voilmy, D., Büscher, M. and Hemment, D. (forthcoming) 'The Sociality of Stillness', in L. Mondada, P. Haddington and M. Nevile (eds) *Being Mobile: Movement as Social Action*, New York: Walter de Gruyter.

Licoppe, C. (2009) 'Recognizing Mutual "Proximity" at a Distance: Weaving Together Mobility, Sociality and Technology', *Journal of Pragmatics* 41(10): 1924–37.

Lynch, M. (1993) *Scientific Practice and Ordinary Action*, Cambridge: Cambridge University Press.

Norman, D.A. (1991) *The Invisible Computer*, Cambridge, MA: MIT Press.

Prigogine, I. (1997) *The End of Certainty*, New York: Free Press.

Rheingold, H. (1993) *The Virtual Community*, Reading, MA: Addison Wesley.

Schumacher, J. and Niitamo, V.P. (2008) (eds) *European Living Labs: A New Approach for Human Centric Regional Innovation*, Berlin: Wissenschaftlicher Verlag.

Shirky, C. (2003) *Power Laws, Weblogs, and Inequality*, essay first published 8 February 2003 on the 'Networks, Economics, and Culture' mailing list. Online: www.shirky.com/writings/powerlaw_weblog.html.

Sismondo, S. (2007) 'Science and Technology Studies and an Engaged Program', in E.J. Hackett, O. Amsterdamska, M. Lynch and J. Wajcman (eds) *The Handbook of Science and Technology Studies*, Cambridge, MA: MIT Press.

Szerszynski, B., Koerner, S. and Wynne, B. (2008) 'Experimentality 2009/10. Description of a Research Programme', unpublished draft, available from Bronislaw Szerszynski (bron@lancaster.ac.uk), www.lancs.ac.uk/ias-experimentality.

Taleb, N. (2007) *The Black Swan: The Impact of the Highly Improbable*, New York: Random House.

Taylor, A.S. and Vincent, J. (2005) 'An SMS History', in L. Hamill and A. Lasen (eds) *Mobiles: Past, Present and Future*, Godalming: Springer, pp. 75–91.

Thrift, N. (2008) *Non-representational Theory: Space, Politics, Affect*, London: Routledge.

Urry, J. (2000) *Sociology beyond Societies*, London: Routledge.

Watts, D.J. (1999) *Small Worlds: The Dynamics of Networks between Order and Randomness*, Princeton: Princeton University Press.

Weinberger, D. (2007) *Everything Is Miscellaneous: The Power of the New Digital Disorder*, New York: Times Books.

Weiser, M. (1991) 'The Computer for the 21st Century', *Scientific American* (September): 94–104.

Wynne, B. and Felt, U. (eds) (2007) 'Taking European Knowledge Society Seriously', *European Commission*. Online: http://ec.europa.eu/research/science-society/document_library/pdf_06/european-knowledge-society_en.pdf (accessed 19 November 2009).

9 Reassembling fragmented geographies

Lorenza Mondada

The 'mobility turn' within social science (Cresswell 2006; Laurier 2003; Urry 2007) has acknowledged the centrality of mobility in the contemporary world; it has also emphasized the theoretical importance of mobility for questioning assumptions about place, foundations and stability. Despite this booming interest, little is known about the detailed practices through which mobility as a social action is achieved, and through which temporal and spatial coordination within mobile, dispersed, fragmented networks is accomplished.

Taking an ethnomethodological and conversation-analytic perspective, this chapter focuses on the practices by which participants coordinate movement and action at a distance. The analysis is based on video data recorded in a call centre providing motorists with breakdown assistance, a perspicuous setting for the study of temporal and spatial coordination. Coordination is central to the organization of persons moving in different places. It is generally recognized as a pervasive need of contemporary mobile life – as shown by the use of mobile phones to 'micro-coordinate' imminent meetings (Katz and Aakhus 2002; Ling 2004: ch. 4).

Ethnomethodological and conversation-analytical studies examine practices of coordination, including how people announce where they are in the openings of mobile phone calls (Arminen and Leinonen 2006; Laurier 2001; Relieu 2002) and how friends or acquaintances coordinate their movements in familiar places, sometimes discovering accidental co-proximity and negotiating the opportunity for meetings on such occasions of discovery (Licoppe 2008). By contrast, in this chapter I focus on a professional setting and on the diverse skilled practices through which unacquainted participants negotiate their respective locations in unfamiliar places, discovering and then resolving multiple contradictions arising from discrepant place formulations.

Coordination can be supported by mobile and stationary phones but also through various other communication technologies. Their use in professional and institutional settings to support mobile collaborative work and services has been described within workplace studies (Luff *et al.* 2000) identifying complex 'centres of coordination' (Suchman 1996) where professionals are distributed across different locations, working across multiple and fragmented spaces (Luff and Heath 1998). This chapter focuses on the use of phone and Internet technologies in call centres providing breakdown assistance to travellers. In these activities, the detailed, embodied practices participants use to produce relevant place formulation (Psathas 1986; Schegloff 1972a) rely not only on talk but also on the use of computers, documents and maps in order to provide for the urgent dispatch of help to the right place (Fele 2007).

Call centres are a perspicuous setting (Garfinkel and Wieder 1992) for the study of coordinating practices at a distance. They have been studied as typical examples of delocalization, of de- and restructuration of work at various spatial scales, and of 'glocalized' organizations (Breathnach 2000; Bristow *et al.* 2000). From a micro-analytic perspective, the vital role of call centres and emergency call services for communication in emergency situations has been studied (Baker *et al.* 2005; Whalen 1995; Zimmerman 1992). Such studies have found that successful help dispatch relies on the production of place formulations carefully made relevant to the problem and to the intervention that is called for: as Meehan (1989) puts it, callers have to produce a 'police-locatable location'. This location can be relatively straightforward to produce – for example, when people are asking for help from home and give their address (although even in this case problems can emerge, as shown by Whalen *et al.* 1988). However, it can also be very difficult to establish – for example, when the call is issued from unknown places, from places that do not have a standard address or from mobile phones (Bergmann 1993). This chapter focuses on practices and resources mobilized by callers and call-takers to coordinate mobile motorist help-seekers, stuck in and calling from often remote places that may be unfamiliar to them, and the breakdown assistance personnel sent to their location.

The study of these lay and professional practices of bringing together immobilized persons and mobilized assistance personnel shows that geographies are mobile, mutable and multi-layered. Partial, occasioned geographies are locally achieved for the practical purposes at hand. The study reveals how general assumptions of place as a stable, uniquely describable location can become problematic. Despite – or indeed, as we shall see, *because of* – their assumption of a common, objective, pre-existing world, participants can create multiple fragmented, contradictory geographies through talk and action. Geography is here considered in a praxeological perspective (cf. Laurier in press), as a matter of 'writing' places or 'geo-graphy'. Geographies are assembled through participants' practices of formulating, describing and naming places, offering possibly relevant landmarks and distance calculations, mentioning place names, postal codes and highway exit numbers, reconstructing itineraries and checking locations on the Internet, etc. Whereas often common formulation of spaces and places is unproblematic, practices of space-making can also produce multiple incompatible geographies, which change in the course of the ongoing negotiation. This chapter focuses on such 'reality disjunctures' (Pollner 1987), detailing the practices and resources mobilized by different participants to discover and resolve critical disjunctures, actively assembling a shared geography, a world seen in common.

Data and methodology

The chapter focuses on the activities of a call centre specialized in bringing help to Spanish tourists travelling in France and encountering problems with their car – either vandalized, robbed or broken down in an incident. The call centre, located in a large French town, employs bilingual Spanish–French call-takers who not only answer calls from help-seeking motorists, but also dispatch assistance, contacting professionals and directing them, and organizing alternative travel solutions where vehicles are incapacitated.

The chapter is based on the analysis of a single case of a triangular phone call connecting a call-taker, a help-seeker and a mechanic dispatched to help him. During the call, the participants first take for granted that they are sharing a common understanding of the location of the help-seeker and seek convergence; they then progressively discover that they have created distinct, fragmented, divergent geographies. They eventually manage to assemble a shared geography, which prompts them to abandon their joint attempt at breakdown assistance and initiate a new network.

In order to work on the detailed practices through which mobile action in space is understood and coordinated here, the analysis distinguishes between the *participants' methods* (Garfinkel 1967) of assembling the relevant geographies and the *researchers' methodology*, which permits their reconstruction on the basis of naturalistic video recordings.

On the one hand, the focus is on members' mobile methods for (re)assembling a common geography. Participants organize their actions through practical 'ethnomethods' that achieve a shared geography's local intelligibility and accountability (Garfinkel 1967), for example, by using place formulations and by indexing references like 'here' or 'there' with contextual information and through their positioning in the sequential unfolding of narratives. In this perspective, participants 'methodically' organize their action, adjusting to the specificities of the context and, in a systematic way, relying on micro-practices that make them competent members of their group.

On the other hand, the focus is on the researchers' methodology for reconstructing the callers' and the call-taker's work from various video sources documenting both talk on the phone and activity at the computer (Mondada 2008a). The activities in the call centre have been videotaped by two cameras, one focusing on the call-taker and the other on her computer screen. These two cameras document the call-taker's work consisting of talking on the phone but also mobilizing material and technological resources, such as paper documents, computerized forms and Internet pages. A detailed analysis of her work as it unfolds in time, moment by moment, enables an understanding of the way in which 'reality disjunctures' remain opaque or emerge as problematic within calls and the methods through which the participants manage this. This analysis requires not only various video sources but also their transformation into a detailed transcript making available the sequential and temporal unfolding of the call and of the participants' actions.

The chapter aims at contributing to mobilities research in various ways. First, it provides insight into intersecting physical and virtual (im)mobilities, with:

- a caller physically immobilized in an unfamiliar place by a broken-down car and virtually mobile and partially present in the motoring assistance call centre (and later at the mechanic's location) through a mobile phone;
- a mechanic living in the area and mobilized to provide assistance;
- a call-taker physically immobilized or 'tied to' a stationary telephone and a computer, but virtually mobile, able to travel to locations with Internet mapping software and present in both the help-seeker's and the mechanic's location through her voice and the mobile phone connection.

Second, by exhibiting the production and resolution of geographical reality disjunctures, the chapter describes important indigenous mobile methods of coordinating movement and assembling geographies. Third, mobile research methods of 'moving with' the participants by capturing and transcribing members' methods throughout the unfolding coordination attempt make it possible to study the practices by which the participants work through the case, mobilizing various resources, such as talk, the computer, pre-formatted text files and a route-planner website.

The call's opening

We join the action at the opening of the triangular call: Elena, the call-taker (C-T) has decided to connect the help-seeker, Jordi (JOR), and the car mechanic (MEC) dispatched to help. This decision is important. First, it shows that the call-taker considers that the problem has to be solved by all the participants and not only by her as a call-taker and help-dispatcher. Second, it establishes a new participation framework (Goodwin and Goodwin 2004) within a phone call between three participants, consequential for the way in which turn-taking will be organized (Sacks *et al.* 1974). Moreover, turn-taking is also sensitive to the fact that Jordi has been identified as supposedly speaking only Spanish and the mechanic as speaking only French; consequently Elena has announced she will act as a mediator and translator for both. The opening of this three-way conversation is the moment where the participants' categories are established and defined relative to the organization of talk and of activity (Sacks 1972; Schegloff 1972b).

(1) (cad75)*
* Please find transcription conventions detailed at the end of the chapter.
 1 C-T: allô?
     hello?
 2 MEC: [ouIh,
     [yeah,
 3 JOR: [si,
     [yes,

4 C-T: oui bah on est en conférence, eh:: señor, yo estoy con
          yes ehm we are connected, eh:: sir, I am with
5   el señor de la grua.
          the mechanic of the crane.
6   (0.6)
7 JOR: si:h,
          yes:h,
8   (0.4)
9 C-T: eh: necessi- (.) que el lo esta buscando hace tiempos °me::m°
          eh: need- (.) who has been searching you for a while °me::m°
10   no- y no lo encuentra
          no- and doesn't find you
11   (1.2)
12 JOR: pues (.) aqui estoy en la- en la plaza del pueblo estoy,
          well (.) here I am in the- in the square of the village I am,
13   (1.0)
14 JOR: en la plaza se llama carl de gaulle
          in the square called carl de gaulle
15   (0.4)
16 C-T: y- allô monsieur?
          and- hello sir?
17 MEC: oui,
          yes,
18 C-T: il me dit qu'il est dans la place charles de gaulle.
          he tells me that he's in the square charles de gaulle.
19   (0.6)
20 MEC: >°ah oui mais je sais pas où elle est moi,°<
          >°oh yes but I don't know where it is, as far as I am concerned°<
21   (0.2)
22 MEC: j'ai fait plusieurs places,
          I went on various squares,
23   (0.4)
24 MEC: je me suis déplacé à pied parce que- en fait,
          I walked because- actually,
25   quelle couleur elle est la voiture?
          what colour is the car?

The peculiar participation framework between three participants and in two languages is immediately established by Elena's initial summons (Schegloff 1972b) (1) which can be possibly heard as being in French as well as in Spanish, and which is indeed responded to in overlap by the mechanic (2) and by Jordi (3) together, each in his own language. The next turn is organized by orienting to this particular feature (cf. Heller 1982; Mondada 2004), with a first slot produced in French, addressed to the mechanic, and a second slot in Spanish, addressed to Jordi – within what Auer (1984) calls a participant-related code-switching, adjusting to the recipient by speaking his favourite language. Jordi responds (7) and the call-taker continues addressing him, summarizing the previous exchange she had with the car mechanic who cannot find him (9–10).

This formulation of the problem occasions a description of Jordi's location: 'aqui estoy en la- en la plaza del pueblo' (12). Using two definite articles, this description supposes that all of the participants share the identification of the village and that the village has only one square. Nevertheless, this description is not followed by any response (13); after a long pause, Jordi reformulates and repairs the description by providing the name of the square ('en la plaza se llama carl de gaulle' (14)), thus orienting to a possible identification problem for the co-participants. Elena translates this last specification, which does not mention the name of the village, thus still considering it as recognizable and taken for granted (18).

Although this kind of place formulation projects its recognition by the co-participants, it is responded to by the mechanic with a disclaimer, within a negative formulation ('je sais pas' (20)), followed by a description of his last movements (22, 24), mentioning him walking through various squares. Again, the identification of the village is taken for granted and not mentioned, although the mechanic's description supposes that it has many – and not only one – squares. The fact that the car mechanic is walking (and not driving) within the village and his question about the colour of the car – orienting to its possible visible access and identification – both suppose the co-presence of Jordi and himself in the same place (Schegloff 1972a: 83–4). Here, the mechanic engages in the coordination of mobile trajectories within the local space, at the geographical scale of the village.

In sum, in the opening of the call, although the participants suppose the shared identification of the village, some discrepancies are emerging in their descriptions. They diverge from each other in the way in which they refer to one unique or to several square(s); and they exhibit a discrepancy between the announcement of Jordi's location, which projects as a *preferred response* its recognition by the car mechanic and the latter's negative, *dispreferred response* (Pomerantz 1984). The latter manifests a further discrepancy, between the fact that the mechanic is supposed to know the local geography and his claim not to know (Mondada in press).

The emergence of spatial discrepancies

Reality disjunctures occur when participants offer divergent, discrepant and even contradictory versions of what they consider themselves to be the same facts (Pollner 1987). What emerges from these versions is not a unique territory but multiple geographies. This is consequential for the coordination of mobile actions – the mechanic being supposed to meet Jordi – which relies on the supposition of a common geography.

As the call goes on, more spatial discrepancies emerge:

(2) (cad245)
1 MEC: e[h::: mais ils sont- mais ils sont à cadillac même?
e[hm:: but are they- but are they in cadillac itself?

```
 2 JOR:  [(        )
 3 MEC:  dans dans la ville?
         in in the town?
 4       (0.8)
 5 C-T:  oui, i me dit qu'il e:st en plei::n dans la place en fait.
         yes, he tells me that he's in the middle of the square actually.
 6       (0.9)
 7 MEC:  oui mai:s quelle place? (.) y a y a y en a: y en a dix, (.) de places
         yes but in which square? (.) there's there's there are ten, (.) squares
 8 C-T:  la place:: charles de gaulle,
         the square:: charles de gaulle,
 9       (0.5)
10 JOR:  oui,
         yes,
11       (1.3)
12 C-T:  voilà
         that's it
13       (0.3)
14 MEC:  il es- il est à proximité d'une grande route?
         is he- is he near a big road?
15       (0.6)
16 C-T:  EH::: señor esta cerca de una:: de una:: via grande?
         EH::: sir are you near a:: a:: big road?
17       (1.4)
18 JOR:  no es un pueblo MUY pequeño, (0.2) es un pueblo muy pequeñito
         no it's a VERY small village, (0.2) it's a very very small village
```

A recurrent method used by participants to search for a solution to the localization puzzle consists of asking questions about the place: the car mechanic does this in lines (1), (7) and (14). These questions evoke different spatial granularities and move across various geographical scales: questions can concern a very local detail or can come back to a greater level of generality, showing the instability of what can be taken for granted and the search for a common ground.

The first question (1, 3) problematizes the identity of the town (note that the car mechanic refers to a 'ville', a town, and not to a 'village') and receives an affirmative response from Elena (5), who repeats Jordi's initial description in a form enhancing the centrality and unicity of the square (5). After a pause (6), the mechanic asks a new question, explicitly pointing to the contradiction between the singular and the plural reference to the square (7). The call-taker's response does not address this issue, but just repeats the name of the square (8), ratified by Jordi (10). The next mechanic's question (14), translated by Elena (16), refers to a landmark but receives a negative response ('no' (18)). It is followed by an expansion mentioning a spatial feature, 'pequeño' (18), intensified by the stressed 'muy' and then by the diminutive 'pequeñito', which is opposed to 'grande', used by the car mechanic.

The co-participants mention a series of contradictory features, which do not occasion frontal disagreements but generate misaligned next turns – i.e. turns that do not implement the projected preferred next action, but often answer on a different referential level than the one supposed by the question (cf. Drew 2006). The sequentiality of talk is organized by a non-cumulative series of questions, each adjacency pair question/answer (Schegloff 2007) tending to be disconnected from the previous (see, for instance, the question in line 14). Thus, fragmented geographies generate a fragmented sequentiality of talk.

Furthermore, another discrepancy appears, concerning the name of the village:

(3) (cad102)
```
 1 C-T:   et, le village c'est cadillac c'est ça?
          and, the village is cadillac isn't it?
 2           (0.4)
 3 MEC:   ca[dillac.
 4 JOR:     [oui,
            [yes,
 5           (0.5)
 6 JOR:   cadigliac, (0.5) en, (0.2) fra:n- (0.4) fran:sa::fran,
 7           (1.8)
 8 JOR:   freinsavail,
 9           (0.6)
10 MEC:   °qu'est-ce qu'il a dit?°
          °what did he say?°
11 C-T:   EN en fransa- fransadé: euh:: (.) cadillac quelque chose en fait,
          En en fransa- fransadé: ehm:: (.) cadillac something actually,
12         c'est pas cadillac toute seu- tout seul ça::
           it's not cadillac all alo- all alone it::
13           (0.3)
14 MEC:   ah:, (0.3) ah:::. voilà
          oh:, (0.3) oh:::. that's it
```

Place names are a central resource for referring in a unique way to a place – in addresses as well as, more generally, in geographical descriptions. They can also be sources of ambiguities and misunderstandings. In this transcript, Elena checks the name of the village (1): her question is formatted as a request for confirmation, projecting a positive response. A positive response is indeed produced by the mechanic repeating the name (3), and by Jordi saying 'oui' in overlap (4).

However, at this point the sequence is not closed. After a lapse (5), Jordi repeats the place name (6) and, after a new pause, adds a complement of the name, first in the form of a preposition ('en') introducing the second part of a compound name, delayed by some difficulties and corrections of its pronunciation (6–8). This expansion is addressed by the mechanic, who initiates a repair (10), occasioning its translation by Elena (11) – relating the opacity of the name to Jordi's non-native pronunciation (and not to the mechanic's lack of know-ledge). Elena repeats the last part of the place name, displaying a few hesitations (11) and then resuming the compound form by the gloss 'cadillac quelque chose' (11), reinforced by the negative claim 'c'est pas cadillac toute seu-tout seul' (12). These ad hoc glosses of the name preserve its compound structure, although treating its form as opaque. This information is received by a change-of-state token (Heritage 1984) by the mechanic (14). What follows next (not reproduced here) is a long sequence of spelling out of the name, which does not produce any result.

Although proper names are supposed to offer secure and unique grounds for reference, their use in interaction can generate intense negotiations (De Stefani 2009). Here, the mention of the place name does not produce a unicity of the place reference but contributes to the opacity of the spatial formulations prof-fered by the participants. The last transcript shows a destabilization of the geo-graphical landmarks supposed to be shared by the participants: non-congruent versions are exchanged and a lack of recognition of the place that was first taken for granted is exhibited.

From talk to talk-cum-Internet search

The Internet is one resource co-participants methodically mobilize in order to search for a solution to location problems. Here, it is available only to the call-taker, since she is the only one located in an office and since both Jordi and the mechanic are moving about in public space, using only their mobile phones, in the absence of other artefacts such as GPS or maps. Turning to the Internet has a series of consequences for the organization of the ongoing interaction: Elena engages in an alternative form of navigation and of spatial inquiry, which allows her to reconstruct Jordi's itinerary and location in a way that is both autonomous from the ongoing conversation and finely articulated with it. Engaging in a form of parallel simultaneous activity – a multi-activity (Mondada 2008a) – also means various forms of engagement and disengagement from talk.

In the following, I focus on the moments at which Internet searches are initi-ated by the call-taker and at which their results are publicly announced: their sequential finely tuned positioning within the context of the ongoing talk shows how they are performed as a possible solution to the problems and misunder-standings as they emerge within the course of the action.

Turning towards the computer and initiating the first search

During the beginning of the call, Elena is bodily oriented towards the phone, in a way that embodies her attention to the conversation and her exclusive use of verbal resources to deal with the case. Three minutes after the beginning, she turns to her PC. In the following analysis, I focus on the sequential environment of this reorientation within the workspace, embodying shifting relevancies by turning to alternative methods for dealing with the case. The analysis is based on a refined version of transcript 2, integrating multimodal details that concern both the gestures and body postures of the call-taker and her actions on the computer, visible in the movement of the mouse and changes on the screen:

(4) (cf. transcript 2)

```
 1  C-T:   voilà: e- à peu près à vingt kilometres de bordeaux i me dit
            here it is: e- about 20 km from Bordeaux, he tells me
 2          (1.5)
 3  MEC:    alors là:: je sais pas. j'sais pas où i sont *hein. là
            at this point I don't know. I don't know where they are. there
     c-t                  >>was leaning on the phone*sits up-->
 4          je suis in*capable de:
            I am unable to:
     c-t            ->*scratches head-->
 5          (0.5)
 6  MEC:    e[*h:::* mais ils sont- mais ils sont à cadillac même? (.)* &
            e[h::: but are they but are they in cadillac properly? (.) &
            ->*,,,, *looks at and manipulates her papers -------------*
 7  JOR:    [(       )
 8  MEC:    &*dans dans la ville?         *
            & within the town?
     c-t       *...hand to keyboard....*
 9          *(0.8)
     c-t    *goes with her mouse on intExplo-->
10  C-T:    OUI, i me dit qu'il e:st en plei::n dans
            YES, he tells me that he's in the middle of
11          la place en *fait.
            the square actually.
                            *selects www.mappy.com/BtoB/mappy/v2/--->
12          (0.9)*
     c-t      ->*
13  MEC:    oui mai:s quelle place? (.) y a *y a [y en a: y en a]&
            yes but which square? (.) the're the're [there are there are]
     scr                                *mappy appears-->
14  C-T:                                          [°e::::::::::::]
15          &dix, (.) de* places
            ten, (.) of squares
     scr            -->*
```

The call-taker announces extra information concerning Jordi's position (1), which is received by the mechanic in a dispreferred way (Pomerantz 1984; Schegloff 2007) displayed by a delay (2) and a new disclaiming of knowledge, produced in a series of three negative epistemic formulations (3–4).

This is the point at which the call-taker changes her body position: until then, her posture was focused on the phone; from then on, she stands up, scratches her

head, assumes a thinking face, turns her gaze to the table covered with documents, and grasps a sheet of paper. This circular gaze on her desk – inspecting
her work environment searching for possible resources to mobilize for the solution to the case – ends on the computer: the call-taker moves her hand towards
the keyboard and the mouse, engaging in another activity than the conversation,
which continues in a parallel fashion. This transition towards multi-activity
(Mondada 2008a) exhibits the search for an alternative solution, mobilizing
resources other than talk.

During the discrepant moment in which she announces Jordi's localization
('en plei::n dans la place' 10–11), and the mechanic reaffirms that there are
plenty of squares (13) (cf. above), she selects a website, www.mappy.com,
which proposes both itineraries and maps.

Typing the first search

The typing of the first search is undertaken while the phone conversation continues: it displays both an alternative practice searching for a solution and its
orientation to the ongoing talk. Two sources of knowledge are simultaneously
mobilized, each one mutually formatting and recycling the detailed outputs and
relevancies of the other.

On the website, the call-taker selects an itinerary form where she has to type
the departure and the arrival point. The writing of these two names is performed
bit by bit, initiated, suspended and continued in a way that is sensitive to the
sequential organization of the interaction and to Elena's subsequent engagements
and disengagements from talk.

```
(5)  (cf. the end of transcript 2 above)
  1           *(1.4)*
     scr   *a new itinerary form appears*
  2 JOR:  no es un pueblo MUY peque*ño, (0.2) es un pueblo muy pequeñito
          no it's a very VERY small village, (0.2) it's a very very small village
     c-t                               *in the field «departure town» types
                                        «cadillac»-->
  3 MEC:  et qu'est qu'y a* autour de lui. (.) autour de lui y a
          and what is there around him. (.) around him there is
     c-t              -->*
  4        ( ) il faudrait qu'il me dise ce [qu'il y a autour de lui.
           ( ) you should tell me what [is there around him.
  5 C-T:                                  [que-que mas ve- ve
                                          [wha- what more do you se- see-
  6        algun hote:l, algun resta:urante: algo asi?
           any hote:l, any restaurant: something like that?
  7        (1.2)
  8 JOR:  e::l restaurante::
          the:: restaurant::
```

```
 9 VOI:   <((beside JOR)) la table gourmande>
10 JOR:   la table, (.) gourmande
11        (1.1)
12 C-T:   voilà. le restaurant la table gourmande
          that's it. the restaurant 'la table gourmande' (='the greedy table')
13        (0.2)
14 C-T:   *non? ça vous   dit   ri*en?=
          no? it doesn't tell you anything?=
          *continues to type «en»*
15 JOR:   =gourmande (  )#
          #see Figure 9.1, image 1
16        *(0.9)
   c-t    *types «fronsadais»-->
17 MEC:   qu'est-ce que que c'est la table gourmande.* c'est qu*oi?
          what's the table gourmande. what is it?
   c-t                                             -->*ENTER----*
18 C-T:   *c'est* un restaurant,
          that's a restaurant,
   c-t    *displays a long list of possibilities*
19        (1.2)
20 MEC:   c'est^un re- *c'est^un: c'est^un restauran:t,# c'[est:?
          that's a re- that's a: that's a restauran:t, that['s?
   c-t                 *chooses the first item on the list: «cad en fr»->
                       #see Figure 9.1, image 2
21 C-T:                                                [ouais::
                                                       [yeah::
22 JOR:   c'est un restau*rant, (.) °oui°.
          that's a restaurant, (.) °yes°.
   c-t                   ->*
23        (0.4)
24 MEC:   c'est un restaurant?
          that's a restaurant?
25        (0.2)
26 JOR:   [ouih,
          [yeh,
27 C-T:   *[°oui°
           [°yes°
          *goes in the field «town destination» and types «bordeaux»-->
28        (1.0)
```

This first search consists of typing a departure point and an arrival point
(Figure 9.1, image 1). Elena does not type two names straight away: she inserts
them bit by bit. The first one (Cadillac, line 2 on) is inserted while Jordi points
to the contradiction between 'grande' and 'pequeño' (see above, transcript 2)
(2). At the completion of this turn, Elena remains silent, engaged in her search,

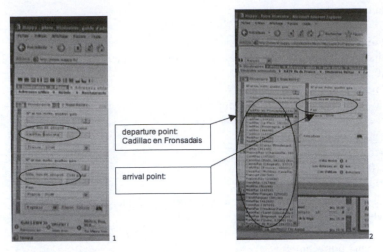

Figure 9.1 Internet route mapping: Cadillac-en-Fronsadais–Bordeaux.

while the mechanic initiates a new sequence, asking for a landmark (3). Elena translates it, as well as Jordi's and his wife's answers (12). At the end of this sequence, while she checks the recognizability of the landmark requested by the mechanic, she continues to type the second part of the place name (14 and 16). The car mechanic shows that he does not recognize the given landmark (17) and extends the sequence with a series of questions initiating repair.

During this post-sequence extension, Elena carries on with her search on the Internet. She realizes it in a discontinuous way, showing her distinctive orientation towards the first part of the sequence – where she suspends her typing and engages again in the conversation and translation – and the second part – where she continues with her search, disengaging from the translation, and letting Jordi answer the mechanic directly, while she participates minimally in this exchange (21).

When she has typed the first name, the form automatically offers a set of possibilities in a long list (18, Figure 9.1): she selects the first one, which is 'Cadillac en Fronsadais', before she carries on typing the name of the arrival town (Bordeaux – which has been mentioned just before, see transcript 4, line 1).

Thus, this excerpt shows how the call-taker and the mechanic engage actively in a search procedure, mobilizing different resources and methods: both trying to reconstruct Jordi's itinerary, the former navigating within the Web and the latter asking questions.

Announcing the results of the first search

At this point, Elena has not yet launched her Internet search (she has not yet pressed the 'Enter' key). However, interestingly, even *before* the search has begun, she uses the output of her selection of the place name in the list to make a

first announcement (31–2). In this way, she confirms the name previously given
by Jordi, but treated as obscure and unrecognizable by the mechanic: the place
name acquires a new status, being checked and shared by another person.

(6)　(continuation of transcript 5)
27　C-T:　*[°oui°
　　　　　　[°yes°
　　　　　　*goes in the field «town destination» and types «bordeaux»-->
28　　　　(1.0)
29　MEC:　ah ah ah ah ah ah ah alors là je- je sais pas où
　　　　　　　　　　　　　　　　so here I- I don't know there
30　　　　c'est là h[ein?
　　　　　　it is there [isn't it?
31　C-T:　　　　　　　[a- attendez je v-* je vois ici
　　　　　　　　　　　　[w- wait I s- I see here
　　　　　　　　　　　　-->*
32　　　　sur euh::::# sur le logiciel, y a:　　[(.) cadillac en frRONSADAIS
　　　　　　on ehm::: on the screen, there is: [(.) cadillac en frONSADAIS
　　　　　　#see Figure 9.2, image 3
33　MEC:　　　　　　　　　　　　　　　　[oui
　　　　　　　　　　　　　　　　　　　　[yes
34　JOR:　te digo:, (.) la salida cuarenta de-
　　　　　　I tell you, (.) the exit forty of-
35　　　　(1.1)
36　JOR:　°burdeos pari:s°,
　　　　　　°bordeaux pari:s°,
37　C-T:　cadillac en fronsadais, c'est pas ça, c'est pas votre: euh:::
　　　　　　cadillac en fronsadais, that's not that, that's not your ehm:::
38　　　　(0.8)
39　C-T:　c'est pas prés de v- d'où *vou- d'où vous êtes* monsieur?#
　　　　　　it's not near where y- where you- where you are sir?
　　　　　　　　　　　　　　*...............*mouse on ENTER-->
　　　　　　#see Figure 9.2, image 4
40　　　　(0.7)
41　MEC:　(alors;ah non), >je connais pas ce nom *là.< (0.2)*
　　　　　　(well;oh no), >I don't know that name.< (0.2)
　　c-t　　　　　　　　　　　　　　　　---->*ENTER-*

As the call-taker types the arrival town, the car mechanic expresses quite vig-
orously his ignorance about the place where Jordi is supposed to be (29–30). In
the next turn, Elena responds and orients to the sequential consequences of his
stance in a timed way (31): first, she asks him to wait, in overlap, orienting to the
time of the progression of the interaction and thus to the consequential projec-
tions of the mechanic's turn. Second, she announces: 'je vois ici sur euh::::: sur
le logiciel' – making the first explicit reference to her parallel activity on the

the Internet form before sending it: the mouse goes on the ENTER
from Cadillac-en-Fronsadais to Bordeaux   button

Figure 9.2 Uncertainty about place names is reflected in parallel activities on the computer.

computer (Figure 9.2), which both makes this activity public and introduces the Internet as an authoritative source of the announcement projected at that point.

The announcement simply consists of reporting the place name (32), which seems to be no news to Jordi (34–6) but is not responded to by the mechanic. The name is repeated by Elena (37) with a peculiar format, a negative interrogative, which projects a negative answer. Moreover, it uses a place formation that contains a personal pronoun, 'votre:' (37), projecting a name that is not uttered, and instead is transformed into another personal construction, 'près de v-', also repaired in 'd'où vous êtes' (39). The mechanic's answer again expresses a negative epistemic stance (41).

Elena's spatial references select what Schegloff (1972a) calls *Rm* (relative to members) *formulations*: they are the simplest form, being preferred when relevant, and they express a strong possessive relation between the person and the place. In Sharrock's terms (1974), they refer to the fact that the person 'owns' the place, with strong situated implications concerning the local knowledge this person is supposed to have. The subsequent self-repairs produced by the call-taker operate, within the emergent turn, a revision of these presuppositions: they transform the reference to a strong possession ('your place') into a mere co-location. Thus, the first announcement is produced in a context in which the epistemic authority of the mechanic is being progressively downgraded. The very fact that this announcement exploits an intermediary result, coming from the selection among various options for the village's name; focusing on a first basic operation, the identification and verification of the name, shows that the place name itself is still being questioned, neither recognized nor shared by the participants. In this uncertain context, the first announcement reveals a new authoritative source confirming the existence and the form of the place name.

On this basis, a second announcement, based on the result of the search, expands the first:

(7) (continuation after *c.*15 lines)
55 MEC: et (.) et c'est + quoi ça?+ °au juste°. c'est *le nom du::# (0.2)
       and (.) and what's that? actually. is that the name of:: (0.2)
  c-t   *mouse on «Cad en F»*
      # see Figure 9.3

```
scr    >>display 1st half+2d half-+
             of the screen---+
```

56   c'est le- c'est * le nom de quoi ça.   * de la vi:lle::? d'une:=
        it's the- it's the name of what this one. of the town? of a:?=

```
c-t                  --->*mouse on postal code-*
```

57 C-T: =oui, c'est le nom du village où mon client se trouve, il es:t
             =yes, it's the name of town where my client is, it's:

58   c'est le département-, c'est tren- le code postal
        that's the department that's thirt- the postal code

59   c'est trente trois deux cent quarante.
        is thirty-three two hundred forty.

60   (1.8)

While the mechanic is asking a new very general question, various events happen on the call-taker's screen: the result of her search appears progressively, on the first half of the screen, then on the second half (55). Her 'reading' of the screen is embodied in the mouse movement on the screen, underlining the place name, then the postal code, written on the same line (Figure 9.1, image 1). This embodied 'reading' is an action sensitive to what is projected by the question being asked by the co-participant; its output is verbally exploited by Elena to produce an answer (57), confirming the name of the village and offering a new space description, first locating it within the region (58), then offering a more precise indication, in the form of the postal code (58–9). This information is not taken up by the mechanic, in the observable absence of his answer (60) (Schegloff 2007).

Thus, in this second announcement, the identification of the place is expanded with information concerning the postal code. It is delivered in a turn formatted in a more formal way by the call-taker ('c'est le nom du village où mon client se trouve' (57)), who refers to Jordi with a category ('client') contractually bound to her, reminding the mechanic of the institutional context of the search.

The mouse underlying the place name

Transcription of the previous screenshot

Figure 9.3 Cursor movements and highlighting of 'Cadillac-en-F'.

Progressively, the spatial knowledge accessible to Elena is expanded; she acquires epistemic authority as the mechanic's is downgraded, in an emergent shift of positions.

Various announcements (two of four are analysed in detail here) are produced in a methodic and systematic way: first, they are constrained by the timed progressive activation of the Internet page, the typing of relevant data, the selection among eventual options, as well as the timed display of the required Internet pages by the computer. 'Internet search' is a gloss that compacts these various operations, which are all distinct and timed achievements; detailed transcripts of these operations unpack not only the complexity of the actions performed, but also their timely sequential organization sensitive to the structure of the ongoing talk.

Second, they are produced as a response to claims of ignorance about the name (transcript 6: lines 29, 30) or to very general questions denoting non-recognition of the name (transcript 7: lines 55, 56). Thus, they use the information on the screen in a timed way to respond to what is taking place in the talk and to the absence of recognition on the part of the mechanic.

Third, they constitute an authoritative source of information for the call-taker, progressively empowering her and allowing her to counter the claims of the car mechanic. Elena modifies the distribution of knowledge within the group, provoking a shift of epistemic identities within the course of the interaction: the authority was first attributed to the participants moving about and searching within the proximate space; it is then attributed to the remote one, searching and navigating within the Internet space. Situated knowledge of space, such as Jordi's experiential one and the mechanic's regional one, is dismissed in favour of more abstract and disentangled knowledge.

Elena's announcements use different kinds of place formulations (place names, *Rm formulations* and postal codes). They manifest the active search for a relevant, adjusted and recipient-oriented formulation among an alternative set of spatial landmarks – which are nonetheless not recognized by the car mechanic. For example, the postal code is a spatial landmark offering a unique identification of the place; although being possibly 'correct', it is sequentially revealed to be 'irrelevant' to the car mechanic, who apparently does not know the code. The postal code refers to an 'administrative geography' that is readily available on the Internet but that is not necessarily used by local people. Thus, the search for a common ground is pursued by invoking other landmarks that could reconcile Jordi's and the mechanic's geographies.

Initiating the second search

After this first Internet search, a second one is initiated by the call-taker, while the participants use an alternative method to solve the problem: the reconstruction of Jordi's journey. As for the context of the first search, the sequential environment of the second is characterized by strong disagreements about the village location:

(8)
> scr   *((screen is still on the Cadillac–Bordeaux itinerary, transcript 7))*
> 1 MEC: et: il a fait combien de kilomètres pour arriver a cadillac?
>   and: how many kilometres did he drive for arriving in cadillac?
> 2   (0.7)
> 3 C-T: eh:: il e- il a pris, donc il était sur autoroute, il a pris
>   ehm:: he h- he took, well he was on the highway, he took
> 4   la sortie quarante, il a::: fait cinq kilomètres de la sortie.
>   the exit forty, he did:: drive five kilometres from the exit.
> 5   (0.6)
> 6 MEC: combien il a fait?
>   how many did he?
> 7 C-T: c̲inq
>   f̲ive
> 8   (0.7)
> 9 MEC: CInq?
>   FIve?
> 10 C-T: oui.
>   yes.
> 11   (1.1)
> 12 MEC: °ah. je voi- je vois pas.°
>   °oh. i se- i don't see.°
> 13   (0.6)
> 14 MEC: parce que: (0.5) euh: cadillac est:: loin de la- de::
>   because: (0.5) ehm: cadillac is:: away fro- from::
> 15   est loin de l'autoroute là
>   is far away from the highway there
> 16   (0.6)
> 17 MEC: cadillac est à::*::
>   cadillac is:
>   c-t   *looks at her screen--->
> 18   (0.5)
> 19 MEC: euh:: j's'pas moi::euh:* cadillac [*il est à:: [j'pas:: vin- &
>   ehm:: i don't know i:: ehm: cadillac [is:: i don't know tw- &
> 20 C-T: [*-ttendez je [vais voir,
>   [-wait a minute i'm looking,
>   c-t   -->*..........*moves mouse, scrolls screen-->
> 21 JOR: [( )
> 22 MEC: & vin-* vingt kilomètres à peu près
>   & tw- twenty kilometres more or less
>   c-t   ->*
> 23 JOR: °pues hombre°
>   °well men°
> 24   (1.3)

25 MEC: *alors là, là je vois pas,* hein   *
            well here, here i don't see, don't you
      c-t   *clicks on new search--*new page appears*
26 C-T: d'acc[ord.
            ok[ay.
27 MEC: [sor- sortie quarante ça n'existe pas *hein,
            [ex- exit forty doesn't exist does it,
      c-t   *types--
28   (0.5)
29 MEC: sortie quarante, ça n'existe* pas hein.
            exit forty, it doesn't exist does it.
      c-t   -- 'cadillac' for departure- *'cad en frons' for arrival-->

The excerpt begins with a disagreement about the distance between Cadillac and the highway. The mechanic asks how many kilometres Jordi has been driving (1) and when Elena responds on his behalf (3–4), offering a number of kilometres ('five'), he reacts with surprise (9), offering a contradictory version ('far' 14–15). The competitive versions of the distance are produced within different formats: Elena offers a quantified formulation, whereas the mechanic utters first a qualitative estimate and then engages in a search (17) for the number of kilometres. This search is oriented to both by Jordi (21, 23) and by Elena: the latter turns to her computer as soon as the mechanic's word search is projected by the spatial preposition 'à' (17), and announces an action intended to help it (20). As the mechanic utters the number of kilometres ('vingt', 19, 22), Elena scrolls down the page where the itinerary Cadillac–Bordeaux appears not only in a textual format (cf. image 1, transcript 7 above) but also as a map. After having uttered a very different number of kilometres than Elena (20km versus 5km), the mechanic ends up again with a disclaimer of knowledge (25). In the meantime, the call-taker initiates the search for a new itinerary, prompted by these contradictory claims.

Thus, Elena's Internet search is undertaken in a context where open contradictions emerge, and where divergences are radicalized, negating the very existence of the place announced by Jordi. Geographies become not only divergent but also incompatible. In this context, coordinated mobility between the mechanic and Jordi is not possible any more: reality disjunctures make mobile coordination impossible.

The search undertaken by Elena is sensitive to this extreme disagreement: until this moment, the participants treated Cadillac and Cadillac-en-Fronsadais as two names referring to the same place; in the context of increasing contradictions, Elena searches for the distance between these two names, thus considering that they might be different places. The result indicates that indeed there are more than 60km between them and that, consequently, Jordi and the mechanic are not at all in the same place. The geography of proximity of the call's beginning is radically reconfigured: places initially treated as identical are revealed to be far apart.

Annnouncing the result of the second search

Shortly after having discovered the result of her search, and after the completion of a long exchange between Jordi and the mechanic, Elena announces the result of her discovery that the mechanic's place (Cadillac) and Jordi's one (Cadillac-en-Fronsadais) are two distinct places (Figure 9.4):

(9)
```
 1 MEC:  [mais ils sont où, ils sont où là.]
         [but where are they, where are they there.]
 2 C-T:  eh- je vois ici, ils v- ils sont à soixante kilomètres
         eh- I see here, they v- they are 60 km
 3       de cadillac en fait h.
         from cadillac actually h.
 4       (0.4)
 5 MEC:  ils sont à comBIEN?
         are they at how many (kilometres)?
 6 C-T:  soixante kilomètres, d'après le logiciel.
         sixty kilometres, according to the software.
 7       (0.4)
 8 MEC:  <AH:::::, (0.7)> vo[ilà.
         <OH::::, (0.7)> here [it is.
 9 C-T:                      [parce qu'*y  a* [cadi#ll  *ac, et-* et- et
                             [because there's [cadillac, an- and- and
                                    * ... *points scr*, , , , , *
         #see Figure 9.4, image 6
10       cadi*lla*c #en * fron*sadais
         cadillac# en fronsadais
              *.. *points*, , , , *
         #see Figure 9.4, image 7
```

The announcement of the solution takes the form of a recipient-oriented location, 'sixty kilometres from cadillac' (2–3), orienting to the mechanic's location in Cadillac and supposing that Jordi is *not* there. This solution is responded to by the mechanic's surprise. The call-taker provides for a last

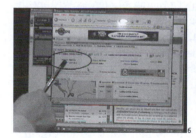

Figure 9.4 Discovering that there are two different places called 'Cadillac'.

expansion, in the form of an account stating the reason for the problem, the existence of two different villages, in the same region, the same distance from Bordeaux, one with a simple name, Cadillac, and the other with a compound name, Cadillac en Fronsadais (9–10). Geographies are reconciled, within a recomposed unique and shared vision of space, which makes the mechanic's and Jordi's coordination useless – Elena will call another mechanic, closer to the village where Jordi is.

Conclusion

In this chapter, I highlighted a range of practices dealing with divergent geographies, fragmenting and reassembling heterogeneous spaces, on the basis of a single-case analysis – focusing on a triangular call that has been video-recorded in a call centre between a call-taker, a caller seeking help and a car mechanic dispatched to bring help. The call begins with co-participants holding the supposition of a shared perspective on the world (Schutz 1962). It continues with the progressive discovery of discrepancies in the co-participants' spatial formulations, and it ends with them reassembling a common geography.

Mobility concerns here different layers of organization: mobile spaces are not just created by the positions of participants scattered in different places, moving around and trying to coordinate their movements at a distance, but also by the transformations of their assumptions, expectancies, taken-for-granted suppositions and space formulations – and ultimately of the geography relevant to their actions.

Methodologically, the analysis provided in this chapter has focused on the resources mobilized by the participants: a detailed sequential analysis, proceeding step by step within the unfolding of the action, allows us to reconstruct the way in which they define their practical problems, the resources they use to manage them and the practices within which they eventually solve them. This sequential analysis has shown the importance of the sequential environments in talk and gesture in which actions are performed – taking into account not only the actions of the participants engaged in the phone call, but also of the actions of the call-taker engaged in her multi-activity.

These features show the need for a careful transcription of both talk and other actions, a precise notation (Mondada 2008b, 2008c) of their temporal relationships, and a detailed articulation of the computer practices (such as writing the address, entering what has been typed, scrolling down an option menu, choosing an option, moving to the next field in the form, and so on). Local resources and local relevancies for these actions include not only participants' gestures but also the transformations of the pages appearing on the computer screen and their precise temporality. On this basis, a reconstruction of the practices through which spatial locations are produced, checked, understood, searched for and confirmed is made possible.

The analysis reveals the methodic practices by which participants organize their mobility across epistemic and embodied spaces. They not only move from one place to another: through their disagreements, negotiations and changing formulations they also produce mobile geographies.

In the case I analysed, the call-taker coordinates the action in the field remotely, to which she has no direct but only mediated access through talk and through the Internet; operating at a distance, the space made relevant by her practices is an abstract one, focused on place names, distances and postal codes. The help-seeker has direct access to his spatial environment, although he has no general knowledge of the geography of the region, having only the experience resulting from his journey across the territory. The car mechanic, also moving within the field, has local knowledge of the region, but does not make sense of the fragmented indications given both by the call-taker (e.g. the postal code) and the help-seeker (e.g. the highway exit number). So, all the participants are confronted with fragmented geographies: their attempts to articulate their perspectives, and to integrate their different fragments, produce incongruities and make mobility coordination impossible. At the end of the call, a unique geography, recognized and accepted by all of the participants, is reassembled, confirming the impossible reconjunction of Jordi and the mechanic. This shows that geography is actively achieved by the participants, being space ('geo-') 'written' ('-graphy') by their practices, being on the move as they constantly modify its coordinates, landmarks and relevancies.

Space transformations are deeply related to knowledge transformations: in the case described here, positions within space are articulated with epistemic positions as well as with identities. The car mechanic is a 'local guy', contacted by the call centre both for his professional activity and for his proximity: he is supposed to 'own' the knowledge (Sharrock 1974) of the local territory. Thus, his action is strongly related to epistemic rights and obligations (Heritage 2002; Heritage and Raymond 2005), since participants orient to who accountably knows, how they know what they know, the rights they have to talk about what they know, etc. These orientations are associated with membership categories (Sacks 1972): orienting to a relevant category produces inferences and expectancies about the knowledge the person is supposed to have. In the case analysed in this chapter, the consequentiality (Schegloff 1991) of the first categorization of the mechanic as a 'local guy' is progressively reconsidered, as he repeatedly contributes with negative turns-at-talk, registering the incongruence between categorial inferences and sequential development. Parallel to this, another transformation affects the call-taker's epistemic position, evolving from a 'not-knowing' to a 'knowing' stance (Mondada in press). In this sense, mobile spatiality also implies mobile identities.

Thus, the analysis of indigenous mobile methods proposed in this chapter shows how participants actively and practically achieve space within talk and other multimodal conducts in social interaction. It also shows that issues about space and mobility are strongly related to the local achievement of knowledge, embodied perspectives, epistemic stances and persons' identities.

Transcription conventions

Talk has been transcribed according to conventions developed by Gail Jefferson (Sachs *et al.* 1974):

[	overlapping talk
=	no gap between turns (latching)
(.)	micro-pause
(2.3)	length of pauses in seconds
,	continuing intonation
.	final intonation
?	interrogative intonation
:	vowel lengthening
.h	aspiration
°okay°	lower voice
ex<u>tra</u>	accentuated segment
exTRA	louder
>well<	faster
par-	truncation of a word
((laugh))	comments
< >	delimitation of phenomena noted between (( ))
&	continuation of current turn
( )	uncomprehensible segment
(y'know)	uncertain transcription
(see;clear)	multi-transcription

An indicative translation is provided line per line. It aims at facilitating the reading of the original.

Multimodal details have been transcribed according to the following conventions (see Mondada 2007 for discussion):

* *	delimit descriptions of one speaker's gestures and actions
+ +	delimit descriptions of another speaker's gestures and actions
*--->	gesture or action described continues across subsequent lines
*--->>	gesture or action described continues until and after excerpt's end
---->*	gesture or action described continues until the same symbol is reached
>>--	gesture or action described begins before the excerpt's beginning
....	gesture's preparation
----	gesture's apex is reached and maintained
,,,,,	gesture's retraction
c-t	participant doing gesture is identified in small characters when (s)he is not the speaker or when the gesture is done during a pause
scr	description of what appears on the computer screen
im	image
#	refers to the exact moment within the talk in which the image has been taken.

Bibliography

Arminen, I. and Leinonen, M. (2006) 'Mobile Phone Call Openings: Tailoring Answers to Personalized Summons', *Discourse Studies* 8(3): 339–68.

Auer, J.C.P. (1984) *Bilingual Conversation*, Amsterdam: Benjamins.

Baker, C., Emmison, M. and Firth, A. (eds) (2005) *Calling for Help*, Amsterdam: Benjamins.

Bergmann, J.R. (1993) 'Alarmiertes Verstehen: Kommunikation in Feuerwehrnotrufen', in T. Jung and S. Müller-Doohm (eds) *'Wirklichkeit' im Deutungsprozess. Verstehen und Methoden in den Kultur- und Sozialwissenschaften*, Frankfurt: Suhrkamp, pp. 283–328.

Breathnach, P. (2000) 'Globalisation, Information Technology and the Emergence of Niche Transnational Cities: The Growth of the Call Centre Sector in Dublin', *Geoforum* 31(4): 477–85.

Bristow, G., Munday, M. and Gripaios, P. (2000) 'Call Centre Growth and Location: Corporate Strategy and the Spatial Division of Labour', *Environment and Planning A* 32(3): 519–38.

Cresswell, T. (2006) *On the Move: Mobility in the Modern Western World*, New York: Routledge.

De Stefani, E. (2009) 'Per un'onomastica interazionale. I nomi propri nella conversazione', *Rivista Italiana di Onomastica* XV(1): 9–40.

Drew, P. (2006) 'Mis-alignments between Caller and Doctor in "Out-of-Hours" Telephone Calls to a British GP's Practice', in J. Heritage and D. Maynard (eds) *Communication in Medical Care*, Cambridge: Cambridge University Press.

Fele, G. (2007) 'La rinuncia all'agency: forme di cooperazione e di interazione sociale tra gli operatori dell'emergenza', in A. Donzelli and A. Fasulo (eds) *Agency nell'interazione umana*, Roma: Meltemi, pp. 173–93.

Garfinkel, H. (1967) *Studies in Ethnomethodology*, Englewood Cliffs, NJ: Prentice-Hall.

Garfinkel, H. and Wieder, D.L. (1992) 'Two Incommensurable, Asymmetrically Alternate Technologies of Social Analysis', in G. Watson and R.M. Seiler (eds) *Text in Context: Contributions to Ethnomethodology*, Newbury Park, CA: SAGE, pp. 175–206.

Goodwin, C. and Goodwin, M.H. (2004) 'Participation', in A. Duranti (ed.) *A Companion to Linguistic Anthropology*, Oxford: Blackwell, pp. 222–44.

Heller, M. (1982) 'Negotiations of Language Choice in Montreal', in J. Gumperz (ed.) *Language and Social Identity*, Cambridge: Cambridge University Press, pp. 108–18.

Heritage, J. (1984) 'A Change-of-State Token and Aspects of its Sequential Placement', in J.M. Atkinson and J. Heritage (eds) *Structures of Social Action*, Cambridge: Cambridge University Press, pp. 299–345.

Heritage, J. (2002) 'Oh-prefaced Responses to Inquiry', *Language in Society* 27: 291–334.

Heritage, J. and Raymond, G. (2005) 'The Terms of Agreement: Indexing Epistemic Authority and Subordination in Assessment Sequences', *Social Psychology Quarterly* 68: 15–38.

Katz, J.E. and Aakhus, M. (eds) (2002) *Perpetual Contact: Mobile Communication, Private Talk, Public Performance*, Cambridge: Cambridge University Press.

Laurier, E. (2001) 'Why People Say Where They Are during Mobile Phone Calls', *Environment and Planning D: Society and Space* 19(4): 485–504.

—— (2003) 'Technology and Mobility', *Environment and Planning A* 35: 1521–27.

—— (in press) 'Ethnomethodology/Ethnomethodological Geographies', in R. Kitchin and N. Thrift (eds) *The International Encyclopedia of Human Geography*, Amsterdam: Elsevier.

Licoppe, C. (2008) 'Recognizing "Mutual Proximity" at a Distance: Weaving Together Mobility, Sociality and Technology', *Journal of Pragmatics* 41: 1924–37.

Ling, R. (2004) *The Mobile Connection: The Cell Phone's Impact on Society*, San Francisco, CA: Morgan Kaufmann.

Luff, P. and Heath, C. (1998) 'Mobility in Collaboration', in *Proceedings of CSCW '98*, New York: ACM Press.

Luff, P., Hindmarsh, J. and Heath, C. (eds) (2000) *Workplace Studies: Recovering Work Practice and Informing System Design*, Cambridge: Cambridge University Press.

Meehan, A.J. (1989) 'Assessing the Police-Worthiness of Citizen's Complaints to the Police', in D.T. Helm, W.T. Anderson, A.J. Meehan and A.W. Rawls (eds) *The Interactional Order*, New York: Irvington, pp. 116–40.

Mondada, L. (2004) 'Ways of "Doing Being Plurilingual" in International Work Meetings', in R. Gardner and J. Wagner (eds) *Second Language Conversations*, London: Continuum, pp. 27–60.

—— (2007) 'Multimodal Resources for Turn-taking: Pointing and the Emergence of Possible Next Speakers', *Discourse Studies* 9(2): 195–226.

—— (2008a) 'Doing Video for a Sequential and Multimodal Analysis of Social Interaction: Videotaping Institutional Telephone Calls', *FQS (Forum: Qualitative Sozialforschung/ Forum: Qualitative Social Research)* (www.qualitative-research.net) 9(3).

—— (2008b) 'Production du savoir et interactions multimodales. Une étude de la modélisation spatiale comme activité pratique située et incarné', *Revue d'Anthropologie des Connaissnces* 2(2): 267–89. Online: www.cairn.info/revue-anthropologie-des-connaissances-2008-2-page-219.htm.

—— (2008c) 'Documenter l'articulation des ressources multimodales dans le temps: la transcription d'enregistrements vidéos d'interactions', in M. Bilger (ed.) *Donnees orales, les enjeux de la transcription*, Perpignan: Presses Universitaires de Perpignan, pp. 127–55.

—— (in press) 'The Management of Knowledge Discrepancies and of Epistemic Changes in Institutional Interactions', in T. Stivers, L. Mondada and J. Steensig (eds) *Morality of Knowledge in Interaction*, Cambridge: Cambridge University Press.

Pollner, M. (1987) *Mundane Reason: Reality in Everyday and Sociological Discourse*, Cambridge: Cambridge University Press.

Pomerantz, A. (1984) 'Agreeing and Disagreeing with Assessments: Some Features of Preferred/Dispreferred Turn Shapes', in J.M. Atkinson and J. Heritage (eds) *Structures of Social Action*, Cambridge: Cambridge University Press, pp. 57–101.

Psathas, G. (1986) 'Some Sequential Structures in Direction-Giving', *Human Studies* 9: 231–46.

Relieu, M. (2002) 'Ouvrir la boîte noire. Identification et localisation dans les conversations mobiles', *Réseaux* 20(112–113): 19–48.

Sacks, H. (1972) 'An Initial Investigation of the Usability of Conversational Materials for Doing Sociology', in D. Sudnow (ed.) *Studies in Social Interaction*, New York: Free Press, pp. 31–74.

Sacks, H., Schegloff, E.A. and Jefferson, G. (1974) 'A Simplest Systematics for the Organization of Turn-taking for Conversation', *Language* 50: 696–735.

Schegloff, E.A. (1972a) 'Notes on a Conversational Practice: Formulating Place', in D. Sudnow (ed.) *Studies in Social Interaction*, New York: Free Press, pp. 75–119.

—— (1972b) 'Sequencing in Conversational Openings', in J.J. Gumperz and D. Hymes (eds) *Directions in Sociolinguistics: The Ethnography of Communication*, New York: Holt, Rinehart and Winston, pp. 346–80.

—— (1991) 'Reflections on Talk and Social Structure', in D. Boden and D.H. Zimmerman (eds) *Talk & Social Structure*, Berkeley: University of California Press, pp. 44–70.

—— (2007) *Sequence Organization in Interaction*, vol. 1, Cambridge: Cambridge University Press.

Schutz, A. (1962) *Collected Papers, Volume 1: The Problem of Social Reality*, The Hague: Nijhoff.

Sharrock, W.W. (1974) 'On Owning Knowledge', in R. Turner (ed.) *Ethnomethodology*, Harmondsworth: Penguin, pp. 45–53.

Suchman, L. (1996) 'Constituting Shared Workspaces', in D. Middleton and Y. Engeström (eds) *Cognition and Communication at Work*, Cambridge: Cambridge University Press, pp. 35–60.

Urry, J. (2007) *Mobilities*, Cambridge: Polity.

Whalen, J. (1995) 'Expert Systems versus Systems for Experts: Computer-aided Dispatch as a Support System in Real-world Environments', in P. Thomas (ed.) *The Social and Interactional Dimensions of Human–Computer Interfaces*, Cambridge: Cambridge University Press, pp. 161–83.

Whalen, J., Zimmerman, D.H. and Whalen, M.R. (1988) 'When Words Fail: A Single Case Analysis', *Social Problems* 35(4): 335–62.

Zimmerman, D. (1992) 'Achieving Context: Openings in Emergency Calls', in G. Watson and R.M. Seiler (eds) *Text in Context: Contributions to Ethnomethodology*, Newbury Park, CA: Sage, pp. 35–51.

10 Studying mobile video telephony

Julien Morel and Christian Licoppe

Since the development of third-generation (3G) mobile networks, service providers have made mobile videophony services available. This marks a 'mobility turn' in videophony, which was initially developed with the 'Picturephone' for home and office (Lipartito 2003) where video communication relies on fixed cameras (orientable to the speakers) rather than handheld devices which can easily be oriented any time and in any direction with one hand. In contrast to traditional 'fixed' videophony, this 'mobility turn' requires 'mobile methods' of inquiry (Büscher and Urry 2009). This chapter aims to fill a gap in mobility studies by describing methods that can be used to record and analyse actual mobile video calls.

Mobile video calls appear as a new and emergent practice that allows participants a greater sense of virtual mobility, virtual co-presence or 'being there' when communicating with others (Gaver 1992). Figures show that in most European countries about 3 per cent of mobile-phone users make mobile video calls. But this situation might change, as mobile video telephony has become part of a significant push from the industry to develop the use of mobile multimedia services. Apart from marketing studies or studies oriented towards the interest of mobile video calls for particular types of user, such as those with impaired hearing (Cavender *et al.* 2006; Richter 2007), there has been little research on the uses of private mobile video calls. An exception is a recent study based on interviews and diaries which showed that 50 per cent of calls were for 'small talk' (i.e. social and emotional calls), 28 per cent to show something and talk about it and 22 per cent to achieve a particular goal such as coordination or practical arrangements (O'Hara *et al.* 2006).

Mobile video calls are also a particularly interesting mode of interaction in which the continuous production of images by both participants is woven into the fabric of the interaction: since it is straightforward to orient the camera in any direction, frames are produced and inspected for their potential communicative intent, leading to particular problems in the management of visual contexts on the move (Licoppe and Morel 2009). Understanding this requires the development of new methods to capture the audio and screen activity of the mobile phones, and gain some degree of access to the overall context of mobile users. We discuss here two complementary ways of doing that, with mobile video-glasses (which give access to part of the visual context but do not always allow a good visual access to the mobile phone screen) and direct audio and video capture (which gives very good access to mobile-phone screens but leaves out the context of the user on the move). The ability to record naturally occurring encounters has proved extremely fruitful to the study of mediated interactions. The possibility of repeatedly watching video recordings and transcribing them affords access to the sequential organization of complex multimodal coordination, and to the way participants' verbal and non-verbal behaviours are made accountable as a continuous practical accomplishment (Goodwin 1981; Heath and Luff 1992). We show here how to do such audio and video recordings with mobile users. Beyond the study of mobile video telephony, our methods of observations can be used in fine-grained ethnographic studies of any kind of mobile multimedia services.

Recording mobile video calls with video-glasses

One way to record mobile behaviour is to provide users with video-glasses, that is, special glasses with a small camera affixed in the middle. There are two types of video-glasses. They can be wired to a DV recorder that the user carries in a pocket in a special jacket. In this set-up the microphone of the DV recorder is used for the sound capture. Recently, wireless models have been commercialized, in which the image is sent by radio frequency through an emitter to a portable DV recorder. This eliminates the need for a special jacket or backpack and makes the whole device less cumbersome. Such an apparatus can also be used for video ethnographies of the uses of mobile services in transit, such as Internet use on the move (Voilmy *et al.* 2008).

(a)   (b)

Figure 10.1 The wireless video-glasses recording system: (a) a subject wearing the video-glasses; (b) the video-glasses are linked to a high-frequency emitter, which is connected to a portable DV recorder, together with a separate wearable microphone. Although wireless video-glasses are less cumbersome than standard models, the image quality is not quite as good, for the wireless transmission is more sensitive to interference.

We recruited two users who wore video-glasses and recorded about 15 mobile video calls with this system. They usually stopped wearing the glasses after a few days because of their conspicuousness. In the following section we see that participants are very aware of their appearance in mobile video calls when wearing mobile video-glasses.

A user-centred view

The video-glasses apparatus provides a perspective roughly similar to a 'subjective view' (see Figure 10.2) with two important constraints. First, the video recording matches only the overall orientation of the user's head, but does not account for eye movements within a given orientation of the head. Second, there is often a slight vertical angular discrepancy between the orientation of the head and the recorded image. Unless the user wears the video-glasses at the very tip of her/his nose, the recorded image documents an orientation slightly higher than that of the user. One advantage of this is that apart from a view of the mobile phone and its screen, part of the user's proximal environment is captured. Such recordings may therefore help to distinguish between two types of activities: looking at the screen and attending to the proximal environment at the periphery of one's attention field, versus looking away from the screen and focusing attention on something in the proximal environment.

The width of the video-glasses' visual field is interesting when one wants to understand the user's involvement with her/his mobile screen and with what goes on around her/him, or to explore the kinds of activities preceding or following a mobile video call and the transition from one to the other. Before recording, the researcher has to choose between using a wide angle (which allows for a wider view of the proximal environment but makes it more difficult to see the mobile screen properly) and a narrow focus (which will make the mobile screen legible but will limit access to the proximal field).

The following transcript of a videophone interaction provides an example of shifting orientations during a mobile video call where an unexpected noise interrupts.

Figure 10.2 A typical video-glasses capture of the uses of the mobile phone.

Excerpt 1 (Transcription conventions are explained on p. 181)

20 A : pourtant il a un téléphone trois g::: (0.8) et j'y arrive pas.
         but he has a three g phone (0.8) and I can't reach him
21   A 😐
22   (0.1)
23 B : et est ce qu'il est en trois g
         and is he in three g
24   (0.2)
25   [ ]
26   XXXXXXXXXXXXXXXXXXXXXXXXXXXXXXXXXXXXXXXXXXXXX
27   [   ]
28 A :   attend: deux s'condes (.) y a la sonnerie là
         wait a sec' (.) there's a ring there
29   😑 a---------------------------m-------------
30   XXXXXXXXXXXXXXXXXX
31   A 😑 --------------
32   (1.0)
33   A 😑 ---r---
34 A : j'suis bientôt arrivé d'façon donc °euh: bon°
         I'll soon be there anyway so °er: well°
35   A 😐
36   (0.7)
37 B : (inaudible)
38 A : bah voilà:
         er well

After A and B have started a mobile video call (with A sitting in a tram), a shrill noise occurs, announcing the closing of the tram doors (line 26). The noise and its duration are figured by the 'xxxxx' in the transcript. At the start of the noise, the video-glasses image, as shown in Figure 10.2, displays an orientation of A towards his mobile phone screen (from which one might assume that his main involvement is with the mobile video call, with only a peripheral monitoring of the proximal environment, facilitated by the fact that he is seated). Shortly after the occurrence of the noise, A refers to it: he requests a pause in the conversation as long as the noise lasts (line 28). This shows that the noise is loud enough to affect the conversation with B, and that A anticipates it will stop soon. Almost exactly as he begins this turn he starts to raise his head (this is marked by the 'smiley' icon in line 29). His head movement reaches a maximum at the m index in the same line, and Figure 10.3 shows the recorded image at this moment.

He is then looking away from the phone, and seems to be looking in the direction of the door. His change in gaze orientation is visible to B, although B cannot infer where he might be looking, for A continues to hold the mobile phone's camera to show a headshot. A then lowers his head, which returns to its initial position roughly one second after the end of the turn (line 33). This shows how

Figure 10.3 Video image at the apex of the head rising.

the orientation of one participant's visual field may move away from the mobile screen (and therefore the mobile interaction frame), because of a noise loud enough to be heard by both parties. This occasions the collaborative conversational accomplishment of an 'internal bracketing' (Goffman 1974) of the mobile video conversation for the duration of the noise. The negotiated suspension of the conversational activity stream is accomplished in a way which posits the noise as an 'external' source of interference and cause for interruption.

We see here how the video-glasses are a useful resource, allowing remote participants (as well as analysts) to identify the interleaving between visual orientations, sequential conversational organization and a noticeable sound 'event' which reflects the unfolding change in A's involvement. More generally, although this method does not always allow a close reading of the fine details of the remote participant's actions on the mobile screens, it makes observable the practical methods by which mobile users manage perturbations and interruptions. This is significant for understanding the competency involved in fluidly negotiating the accomplishment of ongoing activities faced with various sources of perturbation. Such a competency plays an increasingly important role in a mobile and connected world, where, for instance, any kind of social situation is vulnerable to the ringing of a phone. A better understanding of these competencies may provide insights for industrial designers as well as social science.

Interactional treatment of video-glasses

While the glasses appear ordinary enough to remain usually unnoticed in public places, they give their wearers an unusual appearance that familiar parties frequently notice and remark upon in video calls, particularly in their openings. This is particularly pronounced not least because callers usually frame themselves as headshots to interact during such videophony calls (see the 'talking heads' interaction mode discussed below), and the care participants show with respect to the way they will appear in these headshots, by adjusting their appearance to produce a proper videophone interaction frame (De Fornel 1994). The following excerpt shows a mobile video call captured with our video-glasses-based recording apparatus. It shows some features that are characteristic of mobile video calls. It is also significant in the way the change of the caller's appearance (due to his wearing the video-glasses) is topicalized early in the call.

Preparing the connection takes about ten seconds. Before it is established, participants can also look at their control image for a few seconds (typically two to three seconds). This is usually exploited by users to accomplish several actions. First, they adjust the frame so that their head is in the middle of the screen. This prepares their involvement in the distant interaction, for when the connection occurs participants will find themselves in a 'talking heads' format, which is the closest way mobile video calls may approximate the ecological 'eye-to-eye huddle' (Goffman 1963) of co-present interaction. Second, they accomplish some non-verbal actions displaying a degree of concern with the presentation of self. This is often the case for the caller, for whom the waiting time is longer, to adjust her/his hair or/and clothes and to reorient her-/himself to get a better light, etc. These are all actions aimed at improving the way her/his face will be displayed in the video link about to be established. Third, during or immediately after these adjustments, participants very often look fixedly towards the screen/the camera, in a way that makes the establishment of a mutual gaze possible as soon as the video link is switched on. Such an orientation is important with respect to the organization of mobile video call openings, for it makes different types of recognition and organization possible. These depend on the availability of cues and testify to the ability of the technical system to provide participants with one another's images, supporting visual recognition, informing participants about the potential availability of recipients, etc. The various adjustments which we have described, for example, the positioning of the upper portion of the body on the screen and the pre-orientation of the gaze, seek to ease focused interaction, accomplished in a way that approximates co-present face-to-face interaction. With this comparison it is not our aim to liken the standard interactional framing for mobile video calls ('talking heads' within head-shots) to that of face-to-face interaction than to highlight the participants' normative orientation to establishing, in the very first frames, a mutual visibility organization that is interpretable and accountable on the basis of the everyday experience of face-to-face interactions.

Excerpt 2 provides an example of what may happen after connection (caller wears video-glasses).

Excerpt 2

```
1        ring
2  B :   ☺ -----
3  A :   coucou !
         hey!
4              [  ]
5  B :   😁 ------
6              [  ]
```

7 A : oh: rigole pas
oh: don't laugh
8 (0.5)
9 A : j'ai pas l'style avec mes lunettes (0.2)
I'm not very hip with my glasses (0.2)
10 mais bon. (.) on fait avec
but well (.) one has to keep on going
11 (0.5)
12 B : ☹ --
13 A : bon. (.) qu'est ce que j'voulais dire [...]
well (.) what was I going to say [...]

After the connection is established (line 2) we see how the recipient:

- has framed herself in a headshot of almost the whole of her face;
- is looking in front of her (one may assume she is prepared to look at the caller's face);
- is already smiling, prior to her visual recognition of the caller (which was identifiable through his phone number).

As soon as the first images are made mutually available, she is able to frame herself in a proper headshot. Through the stability and orientation of her gaze she provides a cue regarding her identification of the caller, her orientation towards his visual recognition and her availability for the call (i.e. through her smile). These visual components allow the caller to provide a familiar greeting ('coucou', line 3) that is usually used between well-acquainted persons when they happen to find themselves suddenly in a situation of mutual accessibility, or as a move to make their mutual visibility relevant. During and after this initial greeting, B's initial smile widens and turns into a small laugh (line 5 and Figure 10.4b). A will display his interpretation of this laugh as marking her assessment of his appearance as unusual and funny because of the video-glasses. He first asks her to stop laughing (line 7). The request is expressed in a joking tone of voice (of the 'stop kidding I can't help it' type), and is not granted by the caller who goes on laughing. He then goes on by providing an assessment of the non-

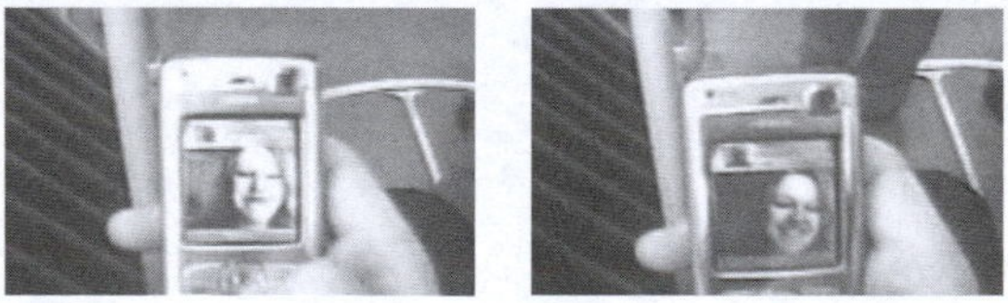

(a) (b)

Figure 10.4 (a) B's face at connection (line 2); (b) A growing smile that climaxes at line 5 and is treated as marking her recognition of A's strange appearance.

hipness of his appearance (line 9), which he follows by a topicalization (line 10) of his helplessness to do anything about it.

The altered face that he presents to her in the mobile video call because he is wearing video-glasses, and the fact that it occasions a 'reparative' (Goffman 1973) account in the form of a 'negative self-assessment', might be considered as experimental bias. However, it is also interesting to look at the way it constitutes a practical resource in the accomplishment of mobile video call openings that also testify to a reflexive orientation towards the presentation of self in such video-mediated interactional settings. Glasses may affect their wearer's presentation of self, but participants in mobile video call openings remain involved in the accomplishment of an accountable, focused interaction, and are mutually responsible for it proceeding recognizably. The assessment of the other participant's face as it is displayed is embedded in the participants' practical concerns regarding the achievement of a proper opening for their mobile video calls. The widening of the recipient's smile in Excerpt 2, up to its turning into a laugh, also provides a resource to confirm that the visual connection has been established (leaving it up to verbal turns to confirm that the audio channel is working). It acts as a cue that indexes her availability and contributes more generally to the joint construction of an interactional frame. It is a general feature of videophone conversations that their openings offer a privileged place for the treatment of the participants' appearance (De Fornel 1994).

Almost all the users we interviewed expressed a concern with the way they appeared in mobile video calls: 'when I am about to make a mobile video call, for instance I tidy up my desk or I adjust my hair, it looks trivial, but we routinely take into account the fact that we will be seen'. Rather than treating the altered appearance – due to the video-glasses – and its topicalization in mobile video calls as unwanted disruptions of openings, it is more relevant to analyse them as they appear and are managed in the interaction, with respect to the way they contribute to opening sequences. Departures from normal appearances make particularly salient some normative expectations (such as the mutual concern for the propriety of the presentations of self that will be displayed) that might have remained unnoticeable in standard openings. More generally, we deem it important not to neglect the analytical resource which is provided by the way participants notice and refer to 'mobile methods' used by the researchers.

The 'direct' capture of mobile video calls

An apparatus for the video capture of mobile screens

Video-glasses record the mobile action field of their wearer. Such data is well-suited to an analysis focusing on their activity and the way they orient towards varied multimodal resources in their environment. The direct capture of the mobile video call is focused on the ongoing mobile video interaction and disregards events in the wider context (what goes on outside the mobile phone's camera frame), unless they are mentioned and treated by the participants in their videophonic interaction (for example, the noise interference in Excerpt 1). The direct capture of a mobile video call provides a video equivalent of the tape recordings of audio telephone calls.

A few mobile phones currently provide an audio and video plug that allows one to record mobile screen activity plus outgoing audio flux. This is so with the Nokia N93 and N95 phones used in this study. Initially designed on TV sets to allow screen captures, and then transposed onto mobile phones, such output does not enable the recording of ingoing audio flux, which is essential to all voice-based communicative behaviour. This method provides a more precise image of mobile phone screens than that obtained with video-glasses. We first connected such phones to DV recorders, and connected the recorder to an additional microphone to record the incoming talk (the users are asked to place the microphone not far from their cell phones and to refrain from using earplugs). We then gave users the full apparatus, as shown in Figure 10.5, which also meant that they had to use a phone other than their own for the duration of the observation.

We have been able to recruit eight pairs of users and to record about 80 mobile video calls (we are still in the process of recruitment so as to obtain a larger corpus). The image quality is good enough to transcribe a large proportion of the user's non-verbal behaviour (visible in the smaller control image) and *a fortiori* that of her/his correspondent (visible in the main image). It can also

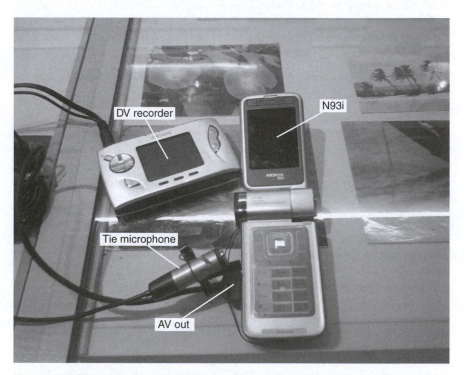

Figure 10.5 The recording apparatus. In this configuration, the synchronization of outgoing and incoming audio is made within the DV recorder.

record all kinds of mobile screen activity beyond mobile video calls. A good example of the kind of data this recording apparatus provides and the way it may be used is the visualization of the pre-connection sequence that precedes a mobile video call in the following example. Callers often use their control image in the few seconds before the recipient's image appears to adjust their position to produce a portrait frame with their full face (Figure 10.6a and b).

The adjustment of the caller's position shows that the caller orients towards the production of a 'proper' camera shot at connection: a headshot with the whole of the head visible on the screen (in portrait mode). This frames the participant in the mobile video call as a 'talking head'. This mode of performing mobile video calls in a mutual 'talking heads' format is dominant in our corpus. Even when one participant wants a reframing, for instance to show something, the ensuing change of the interaction frame is accomplished within a normative orientation towards the 'talking heads' format as the default format for mobile video calls. We see two reasons for this. First, it seems to be a general feature of videophony that, whether fixed or mobile, the participants orient towards the rule that the person who speaks must be featured on the screen and looking (roughly) in the direction of the camera on her/his site. This is also a way to reconstruct in video-link settings the kind of 'eye-to-eye ecological huddle' that characterizes interpersonal co-present interaction (Goffman 1963: 18). In the case of person-to-person fixed video calls this often leads to intermediate shots, which feature the face, the torso and part of the table or sitting arrangement. The 'talking

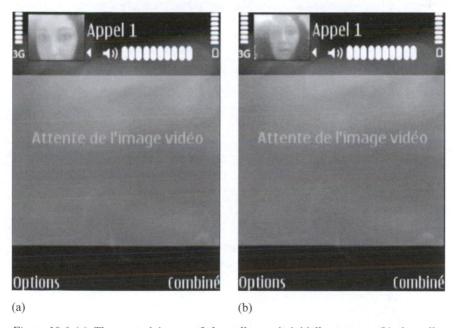

(a)   (b)

Figure 10.6 (a) The control image of the caller as it initially appears; (b) the caller rapidly adjusts her head position before the recipient's image appears.

heads' mode in mobile video calls appears as a particular trade-off that takes into account that rule, technical features (such as the camera aperture) and embodied constraints: when it is handheld, it is more comfortable to carry the mobile phone with a flexed arm. At that distance, and with usual apertures, headshots are the best way to satisfy the rule that the person who talks appears on the screen and is oriented in a way that makes it seem that she/he is talking through the screen. Even though this has not always been the case, current media such as TV have made that shot a familiar feature of the media rendition of intimate face-to-face conversations. It is, moreover, interesting to note that in a corpus of TV ads on mobile video calls, participants were always featured in this mode of interaction (unless one participant wanted to use the camera to show something to the other).

Using the recording as a conversational resource

Although this recording apparatus is now mostly invisible for the other party, both parties remain aware of it. Participants retain an orientation to the fact that they are being recorded, and they may mention that mutual awareness and use it as a conversational resource. Rather than treating this as a problem hindering the analysis, we identify the interpretive and procedural groundings from which participants topicalize the fact of the recording itself as a meaningful resource for the talk-in interaction. The following transcript, recorded with that apparatus, shows how it is able to provide data on videophonic interaction that allows for a fine-grained step-by-step analysis of the way participants display their awareness of the images they make, see and record.

Excerpt 3
```
1       (1.1) ((mutual image, mutual look = 0.8s))
2  A :  ah oui (.) deux minutes
        ah yes (.) just a minute
3       (0.3)
4  A :  ça va ?
        you ok ?
5  B :  (1.2) ouais:: et toi:
        (1.2) yeah:: and you:
6  A :  (0.1) bah euh t/ (0.6) t'as une tête (.) bizarre/ UH
        (0.1) well er t/ (0.6) you got a face (.) strange/ UH
7                                [  ]
8  B :                          bah écoute (.) j'suis
                                well listen (.) I'm
9       élégan::te !
        elega::nt!
10      (0.6)
11 A :  h.h.h.h.h.h.h >ah ah ah ah< hhh t'es trop belle (.) >ah ah ah ah ah ah
        h.h.h.h.h.h.h >ah ah ah ah< hhh you're too beautiful (.) >ah ah ah
```

12   ah< euh hh
13   (0.2)
14 B : BEH QUOI (.) J'ETAIS EN TRAIN D'me laver les ch'veux (.)
        SO WHAT (.) I WAS JUST washing my hair (.)
15   TU M'APPELL:ES
        AND YOU CALL ME
16   (0.2)
17 A : uh uh uh uh hhhh c'est trop/ hhhh c'est trop bon ça hhh bon:. (.) et::
        uh uh uh uh hhhh it's too / hhhh it's too good that hhh well:. (.) and:
18   c'est d'accord pour l'ciné ce soir: ?
        it's okay for the movies tonight ?

The opening here is slightly peculiar because the caller is still on another phone
as the mutual images become available. She terminates that conversation in line
2, in a way that is visible and audible to the call recipient. She then displays her
orientation and availability with respect to the mobile video call with a greeting
(line 4) that is answered and returned (line 5). The completion of the greeting
sequence offers a slot to the caller to produce the reason for the call, but she
chooses instead to produce an assessment of the call recipient's unusual appearance. This launches a sequence discussing and accounting for the call recipient's
look (lines 4–17) that appears as a prototypical pre-expansion sequence (Schegloff 2007), for just after its completion the caller will produce a turn referring
to the reason for the call, by re-discussing a joint plan to go to the movies that
evening (line 18).

Figure 10.7 The caller's mobile screen when she first comments on the call recipient's appearance (line 6).

This pre-expansion sequence starts with a first assessment in which the caller describes the recipient's face as unusual. This may refer either to the towel she is wearing as a turban, or to the fact that her image is cut so that the lower part of her face does not show (see Figure 10.7), or both. The call recipient responds with a second assessment that stresses elegance rather than strangeness (for a turban-like headdress evokes fashion), with an affirmative rising tone that posits it as a counter-assessment (lines 8–9). The caller then laughs, which marks the ongoing discussion as joking banter between friends and prefaces reformulation of the initial assessment into a kind of 'extreme case' formulation (Pomerantz 1986) that legitimizes her noticing in the first place, in the 'you're too beautiful' (line 11). This elicits a justification from the call recipient. It starts with a 'so what' preface which signals that what is to come is a potential challenge. She then explains her appearance: she was washing her hair, and that is when the caller called (lines 14–15). This shifts part of the responsibility for her appearance onto the caller herself, and her timing of the call. This delicate and playful banter reveals fascinating aspects of lived intimacy and friendship.

As discussed by Goffman, body washing is an activity that is not meant to be public and is supposed to be accomplished backstage. This is partly to veil the kind of work required to present an 'idealized face' for a public performance, which is meant to be effortless, sincere and authentic (Goffman 1973). Both participants orient towards the fact that the call recipient would avoid wearing a towel in public. Their banter can be read in two ways. First, it marks the video call as a kind of public performance (which makes the fact of B presenting herself on-screen with a towel on her head unusual and noteworthy). This interpretation is based on the idea that the sudden connection of the video link may open a public window onto a personal and private scene; it may be even stronger for media users who are familiar with the 'Big Brother' format and interpretation of camera shots in TV reality shows. The second kind of reading is as a personal mediated conversation between friends who are entitled to laugh such an interpretation away, which reaffirms their intimacy and closeness. Their joking dialogue makes this tension a salient feature of the ongoing conversation. It ends with an assessment by the caller, which relaxes the tension a little by shifting from comments on the call recipient's appearance to comments on the whole situation as funny (note the switch from the second-person pronoun in line 11 to a neutral third-person pronoun in line 17). The caller eventually follows up on this more general assessment by providing a reason for the call (lines 17–18).

The two participants carry on discussing their evening arrangements for some time, but revert to the issue of their appearance in the mobile video call in the closing section of the video conversation.

Excerpt 4

```
1  A :  béh ouais:: si i rentrent ce soir ça craint (0.3)
          well yeah:: if they come back tonight it sucks (0.3)
2         >bon beh écoute< (0.2) te
          >well er listen<(0.2) ye
```

3　　　te tu tu (.) m'tiens au courant alors (0.1) d'accord: ?
　　　　ye you you (.) you keep me posted then (.) okay?

4　B :　(0.5) mais tu t'es faite toute be::lle !
　　　　(0.5) but you've made yourself all pretty!
5　　　(0.3)
6　A :　c'est vrai ? (0.2) c'est vrai ch'uis bien ?
　　　　really? (0.2) it's true I look good?

7　B :　(0.5) bah ouais: (.) chais pas (.)
　　　　(0.5) well yeah : (.) dunno (.)
8　　　t'as l'air tou::te jolie là comme ça:::=
　　　　you look all pretty like this.:=:
9　A :　=ah:: c'est gentil=
　　　　=ah:: that's kind=
10　B :　=moi j'suis toute moche avec ma serviette sur la tête uh uh
　　　　=I'm ugly with my towel on my head uh uh
11　　　　　　　　　　　　　[　　　]
12　A :　　　　　　　　　　　ah ah ah ah hhhhh hhh
13　B :　ET EN PLUS T'AS ENREGISTRE CA (.)
　　　　AND BESIDES YOU'VE RECORDED THIS (.)
14　　　T'ES DEGUEULLASSE (.)
　　　　YOU'RE A BITCH

15 B: TU SAIS COMMENT J'(VAIS) VIVRE=
         YOU KNOW HOW I'LL LIVE=
16 A : =ah ah ah ah hhhh uh uh
17 B : T'ETEINS CET ENREGISTREMENT TOUT D'SUITE
         STOP THAT RECORDING RIGHT NOW
18 A : bon (.) j'arrête alors >ah ah ah ah< ah (0.3)
         okay (.) then I'll stop >ah ah ah ah< ah (0.3)
19   bon (0.2) eh bin j'te rappelle
         (0.2) so, I'll call you
20   tout à l'heure (.) >ou non< tu m'rappelles pour savoir
         back later (.) >or no< you call me to let me know
21   si tu viens ou pas
         if you're coming or not
22   (0.2) d'accord ?
         (0.2) okay?
23 B : (1.1) oui:: j'te rappelle
         (1.1) yes I'll call you back

After finalizing their arrangements, which usually orient conversation towards 'opening-up closings' (Schegloff and Sacks 1973), the caller initiates a possible closing sequence with her 'okay' in line 3. Instead of providing the expected second pair part or elaborating their future arrangements, the call recipient uses that slot to compliment the caller on how 'pretty she has made herself look' (line 4), with a possible orientation towards how she plans to look later, particularly in the evening.

The caller responds by readjusting her face on the screen so as to have her face (and only her face) fully framed, along with a rather self-indulgent question. Both actions contribute to her receiving a compliment and inviting some further elaboration from the recipient of the call (line 8). The latter reformulates her appreciation of the caller's good looks in a way that compares her own looks unfavourably (line 10). This reformulation of the assessment appears as a response to the caller's reframing herself within the camera shot, as if to display herself for an assessment. B's second assessment elicits a response of thanks from the caller (line 9), but it also returns to B's own towelled-up appearance. She takes the next turn and immediately goes on to produce a self-deprecatory assessment of how she herself is looking (line 10). With this alternation of assessments (between the caller and herself, between positive and negative, etc.), she compares the way they look, and ranks them both in a hierarchy of good looks, with herself at the bottom.

This is precisely the moment the call recipient chooses to topicalize and make relevant the fact that this mobile video call between friends is not as ordinary as it might seem, because it is being recorded on the caller's side. The empirical research becomes an occasion to pursue the playful discussion of their looks and to fuel the competitive assessment of those looks, for it introduces the possibility that the call as a document might be viewed by unknown others (which indeed it is), and in that sense entails a form of mutual public exposure. As they are on record, this is a sort of public encounter with respect to the public order to which the aesthetic asymmetry of their appearances might be consequential and have to be accounted for (it puts B at a social disadvantage as would be the case in co-present social gatherings). The fact that the conversation was recorded as part of a research protocol therefore appears as a resource to play on the rights and obligations of each party with respect to the way the sudden video connection in mobile video calls creates a situation of visual exposure and access to both parties' appearance, without providing them with time for more than minor prior adjustments.

The call recipient marks her sensitivity to this by increasing the pitch of her voice, thus signalling that what is being said marks a change in the status of the ongoing interaction, which is reinforced at the start of the turn with the expression 'et en plus' ('and moreover'). The call recipient follows with a joking negative assessment of the caller's behaviour. This is marked to be treated as a joke (the call recipient is smiling when she says this). If the recording was a real problem she could have ignored the incoming call. The joke is well taken with an intensification of their initial banter, and also shown by the caller's laugh in response to the negative assessment made of her behaviour (line 14) and by the following demand to stop recording (line 17), playfully escalating the joke further. This mock order tacitly acknowledges that her appearance is already on record even if the caller cut the call immediately, and B does not ask for the destruction of this recording which would be the only way to ensure the privacy of her current looks. It is treated as a mock order by the caller who laughs, and then uses this pre-closing banter to proceed the conversation, moving on to their final arrangements and closings (line 19).

It is an inherent feature of all methods documenting the unfolding of natural encounters that, unless they are taken without the participants' knowledge (which would of course raise 'hard' ethical issues), they modify somehow the very experience of the encounter itself: what transpires in the social occasion, however intimate or personal, is also potentially public. Analysts too often tend to erase from the data they use in communications and papers those in which such an orientation of participants towards the fact that such interactions are 'public' (in the sense of the recordings being made available to strangers) is displayed in an overt manner. Some even argue that after a time, participants 'forget' that they are being recorded, and get on with their business as usual. This kind of exchange shows that this is not completely the case. Participants are aware that they are recorded, and this awareness is a part of the ongoing interaction. It may become relevant or not, depending on the kind of recording and analysis performed with the data, and on the details of the phenomena under study. These issues may be even more salient in mobile video calls (rather than, say, audio phone calls) because (a) the 'recording' apparatus is more visible to the participants, and (b) not only the participants, but also other co-present parties on both sides may have, may be given or may gain visual access to the mobile screen, which includes their visual appearances and part of their immediate environments, depending on how the shot is framed. This does not make such mobile methods of recording useless for they are invaluable in giving analysts access to fleeting aspects of mundane interaction (and especially so in situations of physical or virtual mobility) which they would not be able to examine otherwise. But analysts should exert some caution before claiming that the recording apparatus is precisely that and only that, and to use such claims to bracket it outside of the analysis itself.

Conclusion

We have described two methods to record data of naturally occurring video communications. In the first one a user wears video-glasses affording partial access to the mobile screen and the wearer's wider visual field and head orientation. This method is very useful to get some insight into the user's context and to analyse the way users manage their mobility and mobile screen activity. The first example we analysed exemplifies this: it shows a user in a public-transport setting in which sudden noise interference occurs, and who reorients his head and gaze orientation in response to this. The video-glasses make visible and analysable some features of the joint management of mobility and screen-based activity.

The second method we have described provides precise audio and video capture of what goes on with the mobile-phone screen. This method involves a direct recording on mobile phones that have a video output, and the addition of a wireless microphone connected to the recording device. To exemplify its potential, we have shown the kind of self-presentation work that is often accomplished by participants in the few seconds before the start of the call. This requires precise video capture, both because it involves the use of the control image (a smaller screen within a small screen), and because these are transient postural readjustments that users mostly accomplish without thinking and without realizing. Such an interesting phenomenon, which shows the care with which video-phony users treat their self-presentation in mobile video calls, even with intimate co-participants, would be lost in traditional interviews and surveys (because the users have little if anything to say about it) and with video-glasses (because they would not provide a clear enough image).

Technologies for video-recording ongoing interactions on the move are getting smaller and more mobile, but they do not blend smoothly enough in their wearer's clothing or body to go completely unnoticed. Recorded persons are transformed into a kind of cyborg. This also makes available the research (which rests on the acquisition of such audiovisual data) as a resource and a topic for the current interaction. We think that under these conditions, where research subjects carry or wear (and may control) the recording equipment, it might be more difficult to sustain the belief that after a time subjects forget the recording apparatus, so that the analyst may presume it becomes irrelevant to the way they go about their business. It may be the case that with 'mobile methods' we have to consider mobile-capture technologies not just as a recording apparatus, but as part of the phenomena we want to study.

General conventions for transcripts

(1.3)	silence expressed in seconds
(.)	micro-pause (less than 0.1 seconds)
>fast<	marks a faster enunciation of the speech within the brackets
<slow>	marks a slower enunciation of the speech within the brackets
=	latched turns
°softly°	segment pronounced very softly (doubled if segment virtually imperceptible)
interrupt/	slash indicates an interruption
lo:::ng	speech drawn out
<u>loud</u>	the part of the speech which is underlined is spoken louder
<u>LOUD</u>	the part of the speech in capitals and underlined is spoken very loudly
?	interrogative intonation
downward.	dot marks a descending intonation
[ ]	brackets mark the beginning and the end of a turn that overlaps with the preceding turn
(unsure)	brackets indicate uncertain transcription of poorly audible talk
xxxxxx	repeated x signs mark a noise, their number its duration, their size its relative loudness
☺☹☻	smileys (KiconEdit) constitute a convenient way to represent some relevant features of non-verbal behaviour (orientation of gaze or of head, some facial expressions, etc.).

Bibliography

Büscher, M. and Urry, J. (2009) 'Mobile Methods and the Empirical', *European Journal of Social Theory* 12(1): 99–116.

Cavender, A., Ladner, R. and Riskin, E. (2006) 'MobileASL: Intelligibility of Sign Language Video as Constrained by Mobile Phone Technology', in *ASSETS '06*, Portland, OR, 22–25 October, pp. 71–8.

De Fornel, M. (1994) 'Le cadre interactionnel de l'échange visiophonique', *Réseaux* 64: 107–32.

Gaver, W. (1992) 'The Affordances of Media Spaces for Collaboration', in *Proceedings of CSCW '92*, Toronto, 1–4 November 1992, pp. 17–24.

Goffman, E. (1963) *Behaviour in Public Places: Notes on the Social Organization of Gatherings*, New York: Free Press.

—— (1973) *La mise en scène de la vie quotidienne: Les relations en public*, Paris: Les Editions de Minuit.

—— (1974) *Les rites d'interaction*, Paris: Les Editions de Minuit.

Goodwin, C. (1981) *Conversational Organization: Interaction between Speakers and Hearers*, New York: Academic Press.

Heath, C. and Luff, P. (1992) 'Media Space and Communicative Asymmetries. Preliminary Observations of Video Mediated Interactions', *Human–Computer Interaction* 7: 315–46.

Licoppe, C. and Morel, J. (2009) 'The Collaborative Work of Producing Meaningful

Shots in Mobile Video Telephony', in *Proceedings of the 11th International Conference on Human–Computer Interaction with Mobile Devices and Services*, ACM Press.

Lipartito, K (2003) 'Picturephone and the Information Age: The Social Meaning of Failure', *Technology and Culture* 44(1): 50–81.

O'Hara, K., Black, A. and Lipson, M. (2006) 'Everyday Practices with Mobile Video Telephony', in *Proceedings of CHI 2006*, ACM Press, pp. 871–80.

Pomerantz, A. (1986) 'Extreme Case Formulations: A Way of Legitimizing Claims', *Human Studies* 9: 219–29.

Richter, A. (2007) 'Mobile Videotelephony: Test of 3G Telephones', *Hjälpmedelsinstitutet (SHI)*, 17–24.

Schegloff, E. (2007) *Sequence Organization in Interaction: A Primer in Conversation Analysis*, Cambridge, Cambridge University Press.

Schegloff, E.A. and Sacks, H. (1973) 'Opening up Closings', *Semiotica* 8: 289–327.

Voilmy, D., Smoreda, Z. and Ziemlicki, C. (2008) 'Geolocation and Video Ethnography: Capturing Mobile Internet Used by a Commuter', *Mobilities* 3(2): 201–22.

11 Mobile positioning

Rein Ahas

Information and communication technology plays an important role in the development of contemporary mobilities. Innovation has been rapid, expanding communication networks and increasing overall communication patterns, closely connected to the widespread availability of mobile phones since the last decade of the twentieth century.

Nowadays, mobile phones accompany most of us every day and everywhere we go, and they have opened up new possibilities for the investigation of human behaviour. For example, mobile phones and mobile-based electronic questionnaires have become important resources for survey research. The linking of a survey or questions with the location of a telephone is one of the next technological developments in the area, which will make it possible to investigate fundamental questions of human behaviour more precisely and provide focus to applied research. Geographical research performed on the basis of telephone location data can, however, also open up new avenues in the investigation of spatial mobility, and new possibilities will arise thanks to the increasing pervasiveness of mobile phones and the simplicity of information-gathering using this technology.

This chapter describes mobile positioning-based research methods. Mobile positioning or the determining of a mobile phone's location is possible in most mobile networks all over the world. It was originally introduced for the development of Location Based Services (LBS) for mobile-phone users, with the most successful service among them being emergency call positioning, called 'E911' in the US or 'E112' in Europe. Positioning data can, however, also be used to track the spatial mobility of a person or groups of people (Mountain and Raper 2001; Spinney 2003; Ahas and Mark 2005). This is a very rapidly developing field in geographical and urban studies, and many research institutions and information technology companies are now involved in data-gathering and experiments based on mobile tracking. But there are downsides involved with the introduction of every new technology. Telephones have become such intimate companions for us that the mere knowledge that it is possible for them to be monitored disturbs people. The discovery of a person's precise location is one of a number of new factors that violate privacy and security (although see Büscher *et al.*, Chapter 8).

In this chapter we will examine the main facts that should be known when initiating and organising research based on mobile positioning, and we provide an overview of existing research known to us. One very important topic is the experience of developing cooperative relations with mobile operators and research subjects. The chapter is based mainly on our experiences in Estonia, as the Department of Geography of the University of Tartu, Positium LBS and Urban Mark Architects have been developing mobile positioning methods since 2001. Estonian mobile networks belong to the GSM – Groupe Spécial Mobile or Global System for Mobile communications, one of the dominant standards for mobile communications – and 3G standard, as does all of Europe. Since our study partner EMT (www.emt.ee), which is the biggest mobile operator in Estonia, uses the GPRS/EDGE&WCDMA/3G network software and the MPS 9.0 positioning platform by Ericsson, the examples in this chapter are based on these technologies but the information provided is applicable to most networks. Rules and technical indicators may differ in different countries, cultures and mobile networks.

Mobile positioning

Technical aspects of mobile positioning

Although the technical parameters and terminology used by mobile operators using different hardware and software may vary, most mobile communications and networks have a common logic and architecture. Mobile positioning determines the geographical coordinates of the location of a mobile phone by radio waves. The geographical coordinates are determined in the same manner as for all geographical objects: x for longitude, y for latitude, z for altitude. In addition, each coordination determination is automatically accompanied by the positioning time, t. The simplest method for mobile positioning is to establish a network cell where the mobile phone is located. This method is called Cell Global Identity (CGI) (Zhao 2002).

Mobile positioning is performed based on network, GPS or handset. In the case of network-based positioning, the location of the phone is determined in relation to the mobile network antennae. Usually the direction and distance of the phone from the antenna or antennae are measured (triangulated). One of the most common methods in the GSM network is CGI + Time Advance (CGI + TA), which means that the CGI proceeding from the antenna as well as the distance of the phone from the antenna are determined using radio waves. As the determination of the distance in the Ericsson network, for example, is performed by 550m sectors (Swedberg 1999), the result of the positioning is also a sector or a 'banana' in which the phone is very likely to be located (Figure 11.1). In addition to that, the positioning of a phone by triangulation between several antennae is also common. The regular systems for network-based positioning are usually not very accurate; however, when additional hardware and software are used, mobile phones can be found quite accurately.

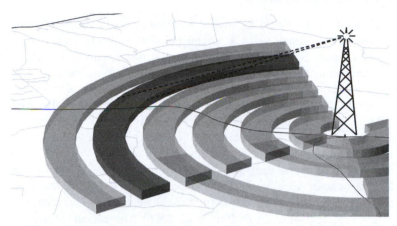

Figure 11.1 Positioning of a mobile phone using CGI + TA method in the network using Ericsson MPS 9.0 mobile positioning platform hardware.

Location determination based on GPS is similar to network-based systems, but in order to find (triangulate) a phone, a signal from GPS satellites is used. First-generation mobile phones with GPS receivers lack integrated solutions and only use the signal of the GPS receiver. More modern systems are Network Assisted GPS (A-GPS) systems with an integrated mobile network and satellite-based location determination. A-GPS location determination is more accurate than GPS, as it also positions the phone in the case of limited visibility of satellites. The EU has begun the development of the Galileo navigation system (http://ec.europa.eu/transport/galileo) which enables civilian users to obtain better location information.

For research purposes, handset-based location determination is initiated in the phone (by the phone owner) to send location data directly to the research organisation; it is independent from the mobile operator. The phone finds its location in relation to the antennae, GPS satellites or other sensors and shows (sends) the information to other phones or a server. This kind of location positioning is inexpensive and is independent of the operator's legal and other demands. The most common system is Google Mobile, but there is also, for example, the *Nutimap* system, in Estonia (www.nutiteq.ee).

The new positioning solutions also employ 'soft' approaches in location tracing. Handsets, for example, can recognise the 'names' of the antennae, using their own memory such as in Google Mobile. Handsets designed for travel-behaviour research also have sensors attached, e.g. a barometer to detect the use of an elevator, or aural sensors to provide information about the environment (Ohmori *et al.* 2006).

Active and passive mobile positioning

Active mobile positioning is used for mobile tracking in which the location of the mobile phone is requested using a special radio wave query (Ahas *et al.* 2007). In order to track certain phones for research projects, permission in the form of a written contract with the phone holder is required. In addition, a questionnaire about travel behaviour is sent to respondents, in order to obtain more information about their travel behaviour. Active mobile positioning is also used for most LBS applications such as emergency calls and 'friend finder' types of applications and handset-based positioning solutions, such as parents able to pinpoint their children's location in some networks.

Passive mobile positioning uses a mobile operator's memory files, i.e. the location data that is automatically stored in memory or log files: billing memory, hand-overs between network cells, Erlang (power consumption) of antenna, etc. (Ahas *et al.* 2008; Reades *et al.* 2007; Ratti *et al.* 2006). The easiest method for passive mobile positioning is a 'billing log' that is recorded for call activities. Call activity is any active use of a mobile phone: call and SMS messages in and out, Internet, services, etc.

The geography of mobile networks

The cellular network is based on a set of base stations, which usually have one tower and several directed transmission antennae. The radio coverage of a single antenna forms a network cell; several antennae form a cellular network. Every network cell in a mobile-phone network has a unique ID and geographical coordinates, and the location of a phone in the cell can be easily determined for every call activity (Figure 11.2). The size of a network cell and all cellular networks is not fixed; the phone normally switches to the closest antenna or the one with the strongest radio coverage or best visibility. If the network is crowded or visibility is hindered, the phones can be switched to other antennae. The maximum distance from a handset to an antenna in the GSM network is normally limited to 35 km. There are amplified antennae used in GSM networks in less inhabited or coastal areas that cover greater distances.

Research history

Studies of human spatial behaviour have been performed throughout history, and many scientists as well as powers that seek to control society (dictators, secret services) have dreamed of precise monitoring methods. To date, most studies have been performed using travel diaries and questionnaires, but today GPS-based experiments have become common.

The connections between government, science and everyday life are complex and often expose significant tensions and deep contradictions. For example, inspired not least by people's fears of being monitored, fantasies of a monitored 'Orwellian' society have been expressed in spy films, where the monitoring

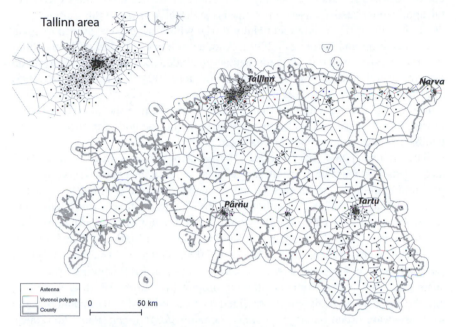

Figure 11.2 Network cells in the EMT GSM/3G network for Estonia and Tallinn metropolitan area represented with Voronoi Tessellation polygons.

methods used in such films often posit utopian precision rarely found in real life.
These fictional accounts often gloss over interdependencies between (national,
personal, commercial) security and personal privacy, as the sketch profile of
current geographical research below shows.

In geography, travel-behaviour research and mobile positioning began to
emerge with the LBS boom at the end of the 1990s. The US Wireless Communications and Public Safety Act of 1999 gave a significant boost to this area, spark-
ing a debate on the applications of the technology and issues of privacy
(Froomkin 2000). Privacy sits in awkward tension with increasing demands for
security at this juncture, as security needs have been one of the major driving
forces behind the development of LBS. In addition to emergency assistance, the
tracking of children and expensive vehicles are also increasingly popular services for mobile operators, independent service providers and software developers. The idea of using positioning data in geographical studies was proposed by
several geographers at the beginning of the new millennium. Mountain and
Raper (2001) proposed geographical approaches for developing the use of positioning data in modelling spatio-temporal movement of individuals; Asakura and
Hato (2001) carried out the first travel-behaviour survey using mobile phones;
this was soon followed by the first tracking experiments in Estonia, in 2002
(Ahas and Mark 2005). Spinney (2003) opened a broader discussion about the

use of positioning data in geography. A number of studies involving experimental applications also focused on traffic issues (Bolla *et al.* 2000; Saitoh *et al.* 2001; Lovell 2001; Asakura and Hato 2004), which have always been of great interest (Nurmi and Koolwaaij 2006). Another subject explored using positioning in geography was related to tourism and included location-based information systems, travel guides, monitoring systems (Kracht 2004; Ten Hagen *et al.* 2005) and cartography, as there was a need to address new types of maps. Specialists with GIS and cartography experience were mostly behind the first studies with positioning data, since they were familiar with the methods for such analysis, and had a better understanding of its potential.

The second phase of positioning-based geographical studies in 2004–7 already involved active research and extensive research experiments. Specific positioning projects were carried out in Graz, Austria (Ratti 2005), Tartu, Estonia (Ahas *et al.* 2007), Portugal and Holland (Vodafone Group 2004) and Japan (Asakura and Hato 2004). Mobile positioning has been used in urban media projects (Ratti 2005), planning studies (Ahas and Mark 2005) and tourism studies (Asakura and Iryo 2007; Ahas *et al.* 2008; Shoval and Isaacson 2007). At the tenth Venice Biennale of Architecture in 2006, an MIT working group presented its extensive real-time positioning project Live Rome (Ratti *et al.* 2006), and the Estonian working group presented its mobile-based tourism analyses and location-aware urban poetry map under the name *Joint Space* (Pae *et al.* 2006). In recent years mobile positioning-based behavioural studies have reached new levels, with mobility analyses concerning the management of public space and epidemiological threats in contemporary society (Gonzalez *et al.* 2008).

In terms of specialised terminology, we should highlight terms such as Virtual Air (Mannings and Pearson 2003), which visualises possibilities for mobile positioning, and the Social Positioning Method (Ahas *et al.* 2004), which has been emphasised as a means to release mobile positioning from GIS domination and develop it in accordance with the needs of human geographers and planners. The MIT working group has introduced the term Cellular Census for passive data-collection (Reades *et al.* 2007), which is an ingenious term. The *Journal of Location Based Services*, with Jonathan Raper as Editor-in-Chief, has been published by the Taylor and Francis Group since 2007.

Work with network operators

Technical platform of mobile operator

In the case of passive tracking experiments based on the positioning activities of mobile network operators, the most important problem lies in finding a suitable operator and reaching agreement. In order to find a suitable operator, one should consider the following circumstances. First, the operator's radio coverage should cover the study area. In smaller countries, for example Estonia, operators cover almost 99.9 per cent of the country's territory. In bigger countries, operators' radio coverage is often limited, especially in sparsely populated areas. In the

Figure 11.3 The 'friend finder' service interface of Estonian operator EMT, available to all phone users. The respondent must confirm tracking with an SMS message (www.emt.ee).

case of detailed studies, the shadow effect of relief forms such as mountains can also become a problem. This problem is common in tracking and navigating projects concerning hiking and ski routes.

Second, one should consider the technical readiness of the mobile network operator. To a certain extent the location of a phone can be determined by all operators, and this is prescribed by the positioning requirement in the case of emergency calls, which is already in operation in most Western countries. More accurate positioning tools or solutions based on a special positioning server are available only with some operators. The availability of such services can be established from the operator's service menu; one should look for 'friend finder', 'find closest' and other similar services (Figure 11.3). If there are no such services in the operator's menu, one should ask the operator.

Involvement of operators and their customers

The involvement of the operator is an essential part of mobile positioning experiments. Generally, most mobile operators equipped with positioning platforms have invested significant resources to develop those systems, and are willing to sell services for research purposes in order to make the systems earn return. Usually, the prices of the operators' menus available for positioning such as 'friend finder' service are high and this is a major problem if researchers envisage extensive tracking experiments. In the case of large positioning experiments, discounts may be available. The producer price can be significantly cheaper, and bigger experiments can also be economically attractive for mobile operators as research will yield huge quantities of locations.

Sometimes operators are interested in the public attention that is generated by such experiments. There is intense competition in the mobile-communications market and cooperation with scientists can help convey the operator's innovative approach as well as the high quality of the network; in addition, involvement in public research and cultural projects publicises the operator's social awareness.

The most sensitive issue for operators is the fear concerning privacy and surveillance. There is a great danger of provoking public criticism and losing customers for fear of secret surveillance or the leaking of data, which is why properly addressing the fear of observation can be considered one of the key activities in the development of positioning-based services. The long-term cooperation between Estonia's biggest mobile operator EMT, the Chair of Human Geography of the University of Tartu and the spin-off company Positium LBS has been developed step by step in the process of testing positioning-based products and communicating with the public via newspaper articles and TV news. Through this experience, it can be stated that the key word for the involvement of operators and respondents is transparency which can be achieved with information exchange and dialogue with the public.

Use of active mobile positioning in mobility studies

The so-called 'digital track' recorded by mobile phone or GPS can be used for various studies and experiments. Most active mobile positioning-based studies – that is, live tracking with the permission of the tracked person – also require an additional questionnaire survey or interview with the respondent to describe the purpose of the activities, the means of transportation and personal details. Tracking studies based only on quantitative location data (digital track) generally do not provide sufficient information about human behaviour and thus have little to add to contemporary studies of human geography and mobility. This is one of the main criticisms of such experiments that has been expressed by social scientists and planners.

Network-based tracking

Network-based tracking is the most common positioning method used today. Technically, there are three ways to conduct network-based tracking:

• Researchers can use a standard positioning service from the operator's menu, for example 'friend finder', and conduct positioning with visual observation on the Internet and fill observation tables with this data manually. This means that no permission from the operator is needed. Respondents can permit positioning by researchers individually using the same tools as 'friend finder'. The problems here are high price and the bias caused by manual work in filling observation manuals.

- The second option is to reach an agreement with the operator so that they can position respondents who have given their consent for this. Positioning can be initiated at a certain frequency by the operator within their system. The operator then passes on the data to researchers. This makes it possible to automate queries and diminish errors caused by manual work. The only problem is the difficulty of involving operators.

- The most professional option is to reach an agreement with the operator in order to initiate queries from the server of the conductor of the experiment. For this purpose it is necessary for the operator to trust researchers and their systems, as the operator will enable them to access their system's positioning server and create a mechanism authorising the respondents' permission to be included, for example via text messages.

Handset-based tracking

Handset-based tracking is becoming popular because it is independent from mobile operators and cost-effective. With mobile phones, one can conduct very simple and inexpensive movement studies by saving or observing the CGI information displayed on the screen. CGI shows a person's location with good accuracy and it is free of charge and there is no need for special software. More complicated handset-based positioning requires that one downloads special software onto the phone. In the simplest solutions, this can be done using a text message. However, some phones already have location-determination software, for example some Nokia phones. Earlier handset-based inquiries were conducted by issuing a respondent specially adjusted phones or Personal Digital Assistant. Today, it is more comfortable and cheaper to download special software onto the handset that sends location data to the server at certain intervals. With this method, costs are quite low; the difficulty is the recruitment of respondents willing to download such software to their phones. Again, openness and transparency are key here – by explaining the purposes and processes of research to potential participants, engagement can often be secured.

Sampling and involvement of respondents

The most important aspect in mobile positioning studies is sampling, because the penetration, use and representativeness of phones is dependent on many factors. One needs to consider the market share of operators, and how the penetration of phones is different in geographical areas and social groups. Interestingly, the penetration and usage of mobile phones has much smaller social differences or 'digital divides' than computer use.

But even in Estonia, where we have only three mobile operators and mobile phones are widespread, it can be difficult to sample a representative spread of people within the customer base of a selected operator, and reach an agreement with those people. This is why the recruitment of respondents takes much more time and effort than a normal survey. In order to obtain permission for positioning, one must introduce the terms of contract and data use, and the respondent must sign a positioning contract. Later, operators like to send the respondent a text message in order to verify the agreement to be 'positioned' and to make sure that the real user of the phone is aware of the positioning. In Estonia, for example, we have sent the following message to respondents every morning:

Thank you for agreeing to participate in the mobility study performed by Positium LBS. You will be positioned 56 times per day up to March 3rd; all gathered data is anonymous when used. If you no longer wish to participate in the study, please send the message OFF to 1723. Additional information from Positium at 1723.

Example 1: Study of commuters in the new suburbs of Tallinn using active mobile positioning

In 2006, we conducted a study of spatial mobility in the new suburban residential areas of Tallinn. In connection with improvements in the standard of living, rapid suburbanisation is taking place throughout Eastern Europe. Urban sprawl is one cause behind the rapidly growing number of cars in those regions. The aim of the study was to examine the connections between the new residential areas in the suburbs of Tallinn and the city centre. Within the study, a descriptive inventory of dwellings was conducted and a random sample of 600 households was compiled. All households were thoroughly interviewed (60 minutes) as to their home, family and modes of transport. A travel diary concerning 'a typical work day' was filled out. Mobile positioning took place among customers of the two larger mobile operators in Estonia – EMT and Elisa. Of 600 respondents, 220 agreed to participate in the positioning study. In addition, 57 people were recruited by snowball method from the same dwellings and thus 277 respondents were positioned in total. The positioning was conducted from the server of Positium LBS, where inquiries carried out by the positioning servers of the operators were initiated. During daytime, from 6 a.m. until 12 p.m., the positioning interval was 30 minutes, and during the night it was two hours; the experiment lasted for eight consecutive days.

Analysis revealed several interesting aspects of everyday activities:

•   The homes and workplaces of respondents measured with mobile positioning differ significantly from the official records obtained from the citizens' register.
•   Workplaces of women living in new residential areas and children's schools are most closely related to the centre of Tallinn.

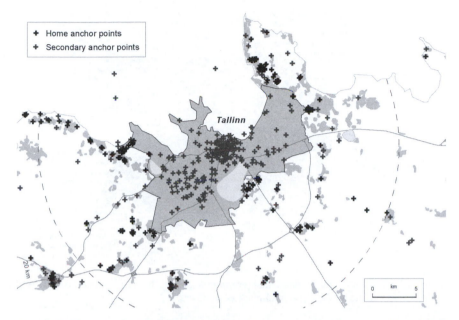

Figure 11.4 Locations of residents of new residential areas in the period 18:00–20:30 outside homes and workplaces.

- Men's workplaces were more evenly distributed over the entire urban region and often were not confined to one location in the city.
- The majority of services are consumed in the city centre. This was shown by the city-centre locations of the free-time anchor points outside home and workplaces (Figure 11.4).
- Residents of the new dwelling districts mainly use personal cars, and make an average of 1.6 home–work–home trips during a day.
- Housewives are very mobile and often move throughout the whole urban region.

Results of this study showed that new suburban communities living outside Tallinn are connected and committed to urban life and lifestyle and not with enjoying classical 'suburban' values. As offers for new houses are rare in the inner city and prices are higher, people often choose to live in new suburbs near the city, while continuing to participate in city life (Tammaru *et al*. 2009). This has generated issues of spatial mismatch in amenities and rising transportation demand.

Example 2: Location-Aware poetry at Venice Biennale

The interactive capability of the mobile phone can be used for recording respondents' opinions in certain locations. Combining voice calls or text

Figure 11.5 Location-aware poetry map composed during the tenth Venice Biennale of Architecture (www.urbanmark.ee/venezia).

messages with active mobile positioning can significantly enrich studies. The mobile positioning-based interactive urban map that represented Estonia at the tenth Architecture Biennale in Venice in 2006 is a good example (www.urbanmark.ee/venezia) (Pae *et al*. 2006). The initiator for creating the system was the Estonian bureau of Urban Mark Architects with the Chair of Human Geography of the University of Tartu and Positium LBS. The project was supported by EMT and Ericsson. An interactive 'location-aware poetry' map *Joint Space* was composed, where Estonian poets were able to move around and create poems related to places and mood. In sending poetry from the place of creation by mobile-phone SMS messages, a live poetry map was compiled. The map included messages from different poets and presented the poems at the locations at which they were created. This is one way of interpreting the urban space and spirit of a place, and also a way of learning and understanding mobile lifestyles (Figure 11.5). The project was about sensing and analysing space in a humanistic manner. Location-aware tagging can also be used as a location-aware questionnaire or tool for participatory research projects.

Use of passive mobile positioning in mobility studies

Passive mobile positioning does not trace the location of the phone actively but uses the location data of phones from the already existing memory files of the mobile operator. Our experience here in Estonia is mainly related to information regarding the location of calls or the so-called Home Location Register in the Ericsson system (Ahas *et al*. 2008).

In using passive mobile positioning data, the involvement of the operator is critical. If the operator is not interested in and does not profit from the study, access to the data for this method of study may not be possible. Moreover, the operators' requirements for using the information and the protection of their customers' privacy are very strict. One must take into consideration laws, international agreements and also issues concerning business confidentiality. In our practice, special analyses and seminars have been conducted in cooperation with the Data Protection Inspectorate and lawyers.

The other range of problems includes the quantitative character of the related data, as they show the movement of human beings in time and space, but few other characteristics can be derived from the data. In addition, the large amount of data makes data processing and analysis complicated. Passive mobile positioning studies of space–time movement of individuals or human flows have been used for tourism studies or traffic analyses because of better spatio-temporal accuracy than traditional statistics.

Data processing

Using passive positioning data, extensive preparation work is needed in order to check the data for gaps, errors and bias which are usual in automatically collected databases. The main difficulty of finding and correcting such errors lies in the large amount of data. It is not possible to find and correct errors manually if there are thousands or millions of records in a database. We developed a special procedure and software to find errors and to fill gaps in GSM and GPS data (www.positium.ee).

The spatial layout and interpolation of the data also requires special geographical processing. The data presented by antennae (point) or cells (area) or positioning sectors should be presented according to the method and aims of the analysis. The important problem of geographical processing arises from the fact that spatial fixity (size, borders) of the network cell is affected by many factors. The mobile network itself is also continuously changing: antennae are added and taken down; the capacity and direction of the existing ones are adjusted. That is why, in order to obtain comparable data layers for certain areas or time periods, a great deal of data processing is necessary.

Sampling issues

As in active mobile positioning, sampling is an important issue. Phone penetration and phone use is a major factor influencing study results. But passive positioning has several further peculiarities. For example, when we use the hand-over data regarding movement between network cells, the non-movers are less represented in the data. When the data regarding the location of calls is used, the people who use mobile phones less often are less represented. When the Erlang data of antennae are used, the measured strength of Erlang can be much higher for multimedia (pictures, video call) transfer than normal calls and SMS messages, and it is necessary to evaluate signals in the antenna. All of these sampling factors need special treatment regarding the particular perspective of the study.

Furthermore, the lack of contextual data in passive mobile positioning data creates a need to use quantitative indicators. For example, one can calculate personal anchor points for individuals or for places that are visited on a regular basis: workplaces, homes, places for leisure, etc. (Ahas *et al.* 2009).

Example 3: Mapping commuting and catchment areas with passive mobile positioning

The most common type of spatial mobility is everyday commuting between home and work. On the basis of commuting, the catchment areas of cities and urban regions are measured and monitored. This information is important input for the planning and management of infrastructure and transportation networks in urban regions. We developed a methodology for mapping such catchment areas of cities on the basis of daily, weekly or seasonal commuting patterns. Linking actual home and workplace locations can help to visualise and measure the catchment areas of certain cities. It is possible to distinguish between catchment areas of business and holidays; summer and winter; or day and night times. Figure 11.6 shows the range of the daily commuting area of Tallinn according to data from 2008. Similar data and methods make it possible to map human flows

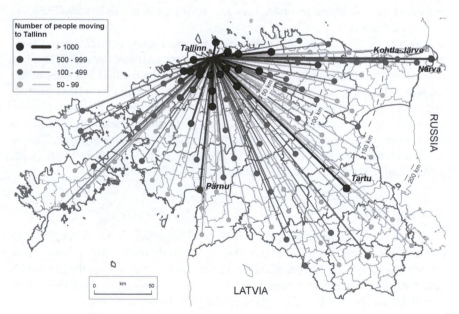

Figure 11.6 The commuting area of Tallinn, mapped with daily commuting patterns between home and work anchor points, using passive mobile positioning data from 12 months in 2008.

visiting certain areas at certain times. Thus, this analysis can also be related to mapping the catchment of tourism events (fairs, festivals) or other activities, providing a gauge of money spent in a region or environmental impacts of events.

Conclusions

Mobile-phone positioning, along with other tracking tools and new digital media, has become a very popular data source for geography and mobility studies. What makes positioning data special is the widespread use of mobile phones, real-time capability and phone-based digital questionnaire survey opportunities. New methods of data-gathering and the great number of potential respondents make it possible to obtain valuable information about people's everyday spatial behaviour and everyday life. There are many ongoing research projects and experiments with mobile positioning, location-aware questionnaires and digital travel diaries in phones.

There are also problems involved with the introduction of new methods and sources of data. These include: how to connect existing knowledge with new sources of data, sampling and data processing. Often the tracking experiments are in the infant stage of 'playing with moving dots'. Since positioning experiments have mainly been developed by GIS specialists, they often remain visual animations that fail to address deeper issues, integrating and expanding social science insights. From the point of view of research strategy, it is important to keep in mind that mobile positioning is not an objective in itself. Positioning data offer an opportunity to obtain more temporally and spatially precise data to answer research questions. For that reason, in the case of such new approaches, it is important to gather together larger, interdisciplinary research teams that include both experienced researchers and those who are able to solve the technical issues involved with new methods. Without the theoretical and methodological input of social scientists and human geographers, these experiments will remain quite primitive.

The other problem with mobile positioning studies is the concern with surveillance and privacy and the difficulty in engaging mobile-network operators to cooperate with researchers. However, the potential of the new method is so promising that it makes it possible to overcome the related fears and difficulties. Mobile positioning has great potential in integrating 'location-aware technologies' with traditional research methods and tools, through, for example, digital travel diaries and questionnaires, ethnographic studies and participatory methods. In humanistic approaches, the mobile positioning may introduce new digital layers of information to landscape research and semantics of place. Especially interesting developments are in the field of developing real-time applications for research and planning purposes. New qualities in this field will arise from the huge quantity of mobile-phone holders as respondents and the precision of digital data.

Acknowledgements

The author wishes to thank EMT Ltd, Positium LBS, Urban Mark Architects, Hendrikson & Co, Anto Aasa and Siiri Silm for their help. The project was funded by Target Funding Project No. SF0180052s07 of the Ministry of Education and Science and Grant of Estonian Science Foundation No. ETF7562.

Bibliography

Ahas, R. and Mark, Ü. (2005) 'Location Based Services: New Challenges for Planning and Public Administration?', *Futures* 37(6): 547–61.

Ahas, R., Aasa, A., Roose, A., Mark, Ü. and Silm, S. (2008) 'Evaluating Passive Mobile Positioning Data for Tourism Surveys: An Estonian Case Study', *Tourism Management* 29: 469–86.

Ahas, R., Aasa, A., Silm, S., Aunap, R., Kalle, H. and Mark, Ü. (2007) 'Mobile Positioning in Space–Time Behaviour Studies: Social Positioning Method Experiments in Estonia', *Cartography and Geographic Information Science* 34: 259–73.

Ahas, R., Mark, Ü. and Kalle, H. (2004) 'Sotsiaalne positsioneerimine', *Akadeemia* 16: 508–29.

Ahas, R., Silm, S., Järv, O., Saluveer, E. and Tiru, M. (2009) 'Using Mobile Positioning Data to Model Locations Meaningful to Users of Mobile Phones', *Journal of Urban Technology* 17(1): 3–27.

Asakura, Y. and Hato, E. (2001) 'Behavioral Monitoring of Public Transport Users through a Mobile Communication System', *Journal of Advanced Transportation* 35: 289–304.

—— (2004) 'Tracking Survey for Individual Travel Behaviour Using Mobile Communication Instruments', *Transportation Research Part C* 12: 273–91.

Asakura, Y. and Iryo, T. (2007) 'Analysis of Tourist Behaviour Based on the Tracking Data Collected Using a Mobile Communication Instrument', *Transportation Research A* 41: 684–90.

Bolla, R., Davoli, F. and Giordano, F. (2000) 'Estimating Road Traffic Parameters from Mobile Communications', *7th World Congress on ITS*, Turin, pp. 534–8.

Froomkin, A.M. (2000) 'The Death of Privacy?', *Stanford Law Review* 52: 1461–543.

Gonzalez, M.C., Hidalgo, C.A. and Barabasi, A.-L. (2008) 'Understanding Individual Human Mobility Patterns', *Nature* 453: 779–82.

Kracht, M. (2004) 'Tracking and Interviewing Individuals with GPS and GSM Technology on Mobile Electronic Devices', *7th International Conference on Travel Survey Methods*, Costa Rica, 1–6 August 2004.

Lovell, D.J. (2001) 'Accuracy of Speed Measurements from Cellular Phone Vehicle Location Systems', *ITS Journal* 6: 303–25.

Mannings, R. and Pearson, I. (2003) 'Virtual Air: A Novel Way to Consider and Exploit Location-Based Services with Augmented Reality', *Journal of the Communications Network* 2: 29–33.

Mountain, D. and Raper, J. (2001) 'Modelling Human Spatio-temporal Behaviour: A Challenge for Location-Based Services', *Proceedings of the 6th International Conference on GeoComputation*, Brisbane, 24–26 September 2001. Online: www.geocomputation.org/2001/papers/mountain.pdf.

Nurmi, P. and Koolwaaij, J. (2006) 'Identifying Meaningful Locations', paper presented at the Third Annual International Conference on Mobile and Ubiquitous Systems: Networks and Services (MobiQuitous), San Jose, CA, IEEE Computer Society.

Ohmori, N., Nakazato, M., Sasaki, K., Nishii, K. and Harata, N. (2006) 'Activity Diary Surveys Using GPS Mobile Phones and PDA', *Transportation Research Board 85th Annual Meeting*, Washington, DC.

Pae, K., Ahas, R. and Mark, Ü. (2006) *Joint Space: Open Source on Mobile Positioning and Urban Studies*, Tallinn: Positium.

Ratti, C. (2005) 'Mobile Landscape: Graz in Real Time', *Proceedings of 3rd Symposium on LBS & TeleCartography*, Vienna, Vienna University of Technology. Online: http://senseable.mit.edu/graz.htm.

Ratti, C., Frenchman, D., Pulselli, R.M. and Williams, S. (2006) 'Mobile Landscapes: Using Location Data from Cell Phones for Urban Analysis', *Environment and Planning B: Planning & Design* 33: 727–48.

Reades, J., Calabrese, F., Sevtsuk, A. and Ratti, C. (2007) 'Cellular Census: Explorations in Urban Data Collection', *IEEE Pervasive Computing* 6: 30–8.

Saitoh, K., Hidaka, H., Shinagawa, N. and Kobayashi, T. (2001) 'Vehicle Motion in Large and Small Cities and Teletraffic Characterization in Cellular Communication Systems', *IEICE Transactions on Communications* E84B: 805–13.

Shoval, N. and Isaacson, M. (2007) 'Mapping Tourists on Digital Age', *Annals of Tourism Research* 34: 141–59.

Spinney, J.E. (2003) 'Mobile Positioning and LBS Applications', *Geography* 88: 256–65.

Swedberg, G. (1999) 'Ericsson's Mobile Location Solution', *Ericsson Review* 4. Online: www.ericsson.com/ericsson/corpinfo/publications/review/1999_04/93.shtml.

Tammaru, T., Leetmaa, K., Silm, S. and Ahas, R. (2009) 'New Residential Areas in the Tallinn Metropolitan Area', *European Planning Studies* 17: 423–39.

Ten Hagen, K. Modsching, M. and Kramer, R. (2005) 'A Location Aware Mobile Tourist Guide Selecting and Interpreting Sights and Services by Context Matching', *2nd Annual International Conference on Mobile and Ubiquitous Systems: Networking and Services*, San Diego, CA, July.

Vodafone Group (2004) 'Vodafone Group – Features: Case Study: Relieving Traffic Congestion in Portugal and the Netherlands'. Online: www.vodafone.com.

Zhao, Y. (2002) 'Standardization of Mobile Phone Positioning for 3G Systems', *IEEE – Communications Magazine* 40: 108–16.

Index